Gulchekhra-Begim Makhmudova

FLASK
OF THE CRYSTAL
HOOKAH – IV

THE SECRET OF THE
KHORASAN TREASURE

London 2025

HERTFORDSHIRE PRESS

Published by Hertfordshire Press Ltd © 2025
e-mail: publisher@hertfordshirepress.com
www.hertfordshirepress.com

FLASK OF CRYSTAL HOOKAH-IV
or THE SECRET OF THE KHORASAN TREASURE

by Gulchekhra–Begim Makhmudova ©

English

Translated by Yelden Sarybay
Edited by Timur Akhmedjanov
Design by Alexandra Rey

British Library Catalogue in Publication Data
A catalogue record for this book is available from the British Library
Library of Congress in Publication Data
A catalogue record for this book has been requested

ISBN: 978-1-913356-95-8

Dedicated to my parents - Matluba and SaidJalol
who have taught us – their children, grandchildrens
and great-grandchildrens in their lifetime
to show Love and Kindness…

The Flask of the Crystal Hookah IV: The Secret of the Khorasan Treasure" is an adventure-detective drama where the theft of a priceless Abbasid artifact triggers a sweeping mystery that spans from Iraq to Uzbekistan. As two thieves spark a chain of unexpected events, an elderly man holds on to a cryptic silk belt and Saltanat Azamatova, descendant of Feruz-begim, uncover secrets buried since the Caliphate. Blending crime, history, and the echoes of empire, this gripping tale explores the enduring power of memory and the treasures hidden within us all.

The novel is intended for a wide audience.

Tashkent – 2024

1

Baghdad, Iraq, the Abbasid Palace, 2023

"Everything all right, Haidar?" asked Basil—director of the Palace and, at the same time, head of the tour guides—turning to the guard.

"Yes, Master Basil!" Haidar answered brightly and respectfully, bowing slightly to his boss. "Everything's calm as usual. We're guarding this charity house without fail! Sorry if that sounds odd—but this place really did start off as a Muslim madrasa. And I understood correctly that you've hired a few more guides for the summer?"

"Yes," Basil nodded. "It's peak visitor season right now. Have you seen how many people have been coming lately?"

The half-sleepy guard wanted to yawn but held back and simply nodded. Then he asked:

"Master, sorry to bring this up, but… won't hiring more people affect the Palace's security?"

"What?" Basil asked, not immediately following. "You mean the large number of visitors?"

"No, I mean the new tour guides," Haidar clarified. "I'm just wondering… can we trust them all? Everything's calm so far, sure, but... have you done thorough police checks on each of them? Taken down all their passport details?"

"Well... to be honest, I haven't gotten around to everyone yet," the director admitted, frowning slightly at being lectured by a subordinate. "But don't worry, I know the procedure very well. I'll get it done in the next few days. Though I doubt professional historians and guides would steal valuable exhibits. Everyone in Baghdad respects this Palace!"

"Maybe they wouldn't do it themselves. But who knows?" Haidar persisted. "Maybe, for the right price, they might tip off a thief."

"All right, I'll keep that in mind," Basil agreed. "But enough talk—let's get to work! You've made me uneasy with all this. I'm going to quickly check all the areas where tours are given, just in case. As for you, hand over your shift and head home. Actually, wait—you'll leave once I'm back from my rounds."

Only a few minutes later, Haidar and the other on-duty guards heard the director's frantic shout and the wail of an alarm. Immediately, they all dashed upstairs to the second floor, where the museum's deep niches and pointed arches were located—the source of the signal.

"What happened, Master?" Haidar asked his boss, bewildered.

"Weren't you just saying everything's calm?" Basil snapped, echoing him sarcastically.

"Well, yes... it seemed that way..." Haidar faltered, alarmed. "Did something happen?"

"No, nothing! Except that right here, from inside this display case in the niche, under glass, they've stolen a precious ninth-century ceramic bowl!"

"But the glass isn't even broken!" Haidar pointed out. "How did they manage that?"

"And there's no sign they used a laser to cut it," noted another guard, Muhammad. "If they'd brought a laser into the museum, security would've stopped them at the entrance. And the lock on the glass display is still there—intact."

"I believe you were right, Haidar, about a tour guide tipping them off," Basil surmised. "Someone who knew the display-case lock code that I'd given and passed it on to the thieves. Then, under cover of night, they slipped in, unnoticed by you, guard, walked right up to the case, entered the correct code on the electronic panel, opened it, and took the bowl! I don't hide these codes from my staff because the antiques need daily wiping with a special solution and careful storage under proper temperature conditions."

"Master Basil, what kind of bowl was it?" Muhammad asked.

"I'll explain," Basil said, barely containing his anger. "A ceramic bowl from the Abbasid era, made in Basra. It was handcrafted from extremely fine ceramic, with bird and flower motifs. It also had a Kufic calligraphic inscription that read, 'What was done is worth it.' That's an early style of Arabic calligraphy—the same style used throughout the Abbasid Caliphate."

"Wow!" Muhammad whistled. "Must've been pretty valuable!"

"No—it was absolutely priceless!" Basil corrected him indignantly. "And you call yourselves guards?! Now how in the world are we going to track it down—and, more importantly, find whoever stole it?"

"I'll call the police right now," Haidar offered.

"No, don't!" Basil stopped him. "If the police get involved, journalists will jump on the story. And our attraction's reputation will suffer. Let's at least try to handle this ourselves first!"

The guards agreed with their boss and promised to do whatever it took to catch the thief—or thieves—or at least try.

"They likely got in during the night," Haidar suggested.

"Yeah, right when someone was sleeping on the job," Muhammad teased.

"I never sleep on the job!" Haidar protested. "Though… come to think of it, I did feel oddly drowsy last night. No idea why—after that tea."

"Maybe someone among the Palace's nighttime visitors slipped you a sleeping draught," Basil mused. "When you were distracted or stepped away."

"Or while he was making his rounds," Muhammad added. "They probably came in with the last tour group yesterday evening, when the place was full, got the code from the traitorous guide, waited until night, and pulled off the theft."

"Yeah, that's possible," Haidar admitted. "But I'll hunt down those brazen thieves!"

"Agreed, my friends," Basil said. "Though I suspect it won't be easy. It seems we're up against professionals who planned this thoroughly. But we have to try! Finding them is a matter of honour for us all."

* * *

Tashkent, Uzbekistan, later the same day

"Boss will be pleased with us," Sanya remarked as he and his friend waited for their ordered taxi at the airport. "We carried out his assignment perfectly!"

"Are you sure, Sanyok, that we didn't leave any trace in that Arab Palace?" Vanya fretted, gnawing on his nails with the hand not holding a bag. "What if the entire Iraqi police force is already on our tail—or even Interpol…?"

"We worked in gloves and wore dark masks," Sanya replied calmly. "There's no way the cameras could've caught our faces. And the lighting there at night was really dim—you saw it yourself. We were lucky with that."

"Yeah. Because of all the ancient artifacts there, the staff try to maintain temperature control for conservation purposes," Vanya added.

"You shouldn't have rushed me," Sanya grumbled. "We could've grabbed something else, too! You said yourself there were all sorts of antiques. I even saw some ancient gold coins at the Palace. I wonder how much they'd fetch on the black markct?"

"No way!" Vanya cut him off sharply. "You want the boss to wring our necks for taking extra risks? We can't set him up like that. He was there himself, planned it all, and gave us clear instructions: take only that unique ceramic bowl—and that's it."

"I wonder what makes it so special—other than it being old and pretty?" Sanya mused. "Maybe some Baghdad thief once held it in his hands?"

"Not a thief—more likely one of the Arab Caliphs!" Vanya corrected him. "And also… who knows? Maybe there's some hidden mark on it besides the inscription?"

"Could be," Sanya agreed. "Did you hear what the tour guide said about that Palace?"

"Which part?" Vanya asked, grumbling under his breath.

"He said there's a folk legend that, in olden times, its courtyard had a tree made of gold and silver, hung with diamonds!" Sanya reminded him. "It's how Iraqis express their belief in the prosperity of the Arab state during the reign of the powerful Abbasids!"

"Great, how marvellous," Vanya scoffed. "Hey, Sanyok, did we really need to fly here, to the capital? Why couldn't we just head straight to the boss? I'd really like to get paid faster!"

"Of course not!" Sanya shook his head. "Don't you remember? The boss told us to stay put with that bowl at your aunt's dacha and keep a low profile. Once he confirms through whatever channels that everything's fine, he'll come for the antique himself. Then—assuming he keeps his promise—he'll pay us."

"Fine," Vanya agreed reluctantly. "Oh, here's our taxi!"

2

Samarkand, Uzbekistan, the same year

"Hello, Grandpa," said Marat, arriving at the construction site he was supervising on his boss's behalf. "You're here again? Why haven't you left? We asked you to leave just yesterday!"

"I have nowhere to go, sonny," the old man replied.

"Please understand, we need to clear everything for the foundation pit of the new building—including this annex," Marat explained. "We're supposed to start digging now. The client's waiting."

"I can't, sonny, I'm sorry," the old man insisted. "This was my grandson's house. I want to wait for him right here. What if he comes back?"

"That won't work." Marat shook his head. "My boss won't allow it."

"Could I at least speak with him myself?" the old man asked. "Will you take me to him? Maybe he'll understand."

"All right," the young man said reluctantly.

* * *

"Marat, why did you bring this old man to me?" the head of the construction firm asked his young assistant in surprise. "You say he's living at the construction site?"

"Yes, Kudrat-aka," answered Marat Nigmatov, while the old man waited in the firm's corridor. "We've cleared out almost all the rubble, but we've run into a snag: the old man doesn't want to leave. He's as poor as a wandering dervish—basically homeless, but he doesn't look it. He's clean, well-kept. We asked him to leave, but he won't budge. He says it was his grandson's house. Except there's no house there anymore—we tore it down, and the remains of the walls have nearly all been hauled away. Only one small annex is still standing."

"And the grandson's name? It's not, by any chance, Daniyar Salimov—the one I bought that house from?"

"That's exactly it, Boss!" the assistant nodded. "You sure are sharp!"

"I don't need your flattery," Kudrat said curtly. "But that Daniyar sold me the house and left with his wife and father to settle abroad somewhere. He never mentioned having an old grandpa here in the city—let alone a homeless one! Couldn't you manage to kick him out? Doesn't the old man have an apartment somewhere?"

"Not in Samarkand," Nigmatov said, shaking his head. "His only place was his grandson's house. The old man himself is from the regions. From Bulungur."

"Bulungur? Ah! That used to be the famous Vedar, right?" Kudrat said thoughtfully.

"Yes, I think so," the assistant replied. "Sorry, Boss, I'm no geography whiz."

"That's more a question of history," the better-educated businessman corrected him. "Vedar was a small city that disappeared from the face of the earth. It was located in what is now Bulungur District of Samarkand Province. It was founded in the early Middle Ages and became famous for its fabrics. Mostly Arabs lived there, and they produced cotton textiles that became quite well known. By the way, Hawqal gave them high praise."

"Who's that?" Marat asked, puzzled. "You're the one who used to be a historian and archaeologist, but I…"

"And you're an ignoramus," Valiev noted. "Abu'l Qasim Muhammad ibn Hawqal was a tenth-century Arab geographer and traveller. He was originally from Baghdad, but he spent over thirty years journeying across various lands. His book *Roads and Kingdoms* includes a wealth of information about the history of the Arab Caliphate and neighbouring regions. It even details routes of the Great Silk Road! Hawqal also wrote about Khorasan…"

"Khorasan? Never heard of it. What's Khorasan?" Marat interrupted.

"Khorasan was a historical region that encompassed what is now Pakistan, Iran, Afghanistan, and Central Asia," Kudrat continued. "Some of ancient Persia's main cities were located there: Nishapur, now in Iran; Merv and Sanjan, now in Turkmenistan; Herat, now in Afghanistan. Khorasan also included our own Tashkent, Bukhara, Samarkand, and Khorezm. Of course, back then, some of these cities had different names. Anyway, according to Hawqal: 'There was no emir, vizier, qadi, rich man, commoner, or soldier in all Khorasan who did not wear Vedar's textiles over their winter garments. For them, it was a sign of refinement and elegance… These Merv fabrics were dense yet delicate. The price of a piece ranged from two dinars to twenty. They ordered them shipped from Babylonia, took them there, and boasted of wearing them!' Babylonia is modern-day Iraq. As for ancient Vedar, it was apparently destroyed during the Mongol invasion. That area is now Bulungur."

"Boss, speaking of fabrics—that's exactly what I wanted to tell you!" Marat suddenly interjected, excited.

"Oh? And what might that be?" the businessman asked without much enthusiasm.

"Well, the reason I brought this old man—this *aksakal*—to you is that he's got a very old *belbak* he never parts with," Nigmatov began, using a tone more suited to a storyteller or tour guide.

"A *belbak*?" Kudrat repeated, curious. "So what?"

"Yes!" Marat exclaimed. "A *belbak* is a square of fine fabric used in the East as a sash for a robe—or sometimes to stash coins."

"I know that! Are you here to give me lessons?" Valiev snapped irritably. "That's not what I'm asking. Why would we care about his old, ragged *belbak*?"

"It's not ragged at all—just ancient," the young assistant clarified. "I have a hunch, Boss, that some kind of old map is embroidered into its pattern. And I know how you love anything antique and historical—those bits of old treasure and curios."

"Those are called *artifacts*," the former archaeologist said, suddenly perking up. Marat noticed a familiar glint in his boss's eyes—that look of someone anticipating a profitable find. "An ancient map, you say? Right on the *belbak*? Remarkable… Could be a treasure map, for all we know. Though… that's none of your concern. You know what?"

"What is it, Kudrat-aka?"

"Bring that old man in to see me! I want to talk to him."

"Yes, Boss! As you say!" Marat nodded.

* * *

"Hello! My name is Kudrat Valiev," the office owner introduced himself to the old man.

"Very good," the visitor replied pleasantly. "And a good day to you."

"And may I ask your name, esteemed elder?" Valiev inquired politely, sliding over a comfortable chair for the man and doing his best to appear the very picture of courtesy and warmth.

"My name?" the old man repeated, his jaw working slowly. "I'm Abbas Salim. I'm an Arab. My son and grandson go by 'Salimov' in the Uzbek style. I remember that much clearly. But I forget a lot of things these days—getting very old. I'm over ninety now."

"How wonderful!" Valiev replied with a deliberately bright smile, though he couldn't quite hide his surprise at how well the old man was holding up. He asked his secretary to bring tea and sweets for both of them.

"Please, help yourself, Abbas-aka," Valiev offered. Then, feigning concern, he asked, "Why didn't your son and grandson tell you they were leaving the country? Could it be you just missed them somehow?"

"They did call," the old man mumbled toothlessly. "I suppose they said something about it. Maybe I just didn't understand… I wanted to see them at least once more before they left for good. But I guess I was too late."

"So they never visited you in your village?" Marat interjected.

Valiev shot his young assistant an angry, disapproving glare—an unspoken order to stay quiet.

"No, they didn't come," the old man said quietly. "I don't think they've come to see me in a long time. Many years. But they left me an address," he added, brightening at the memory of his last meeting with his son and grandson. "Here, I've got the note right here in my pocket. I barely managed to make it to Samarkand… But good people helped me along the way, giving me rides little by little."

"I see—you were hitchhiking, and kind souls gave you lifts," Valiev deduced. "Probably for free. You likely don't have much money, right? You can set your *belbak* on the table! Why are you holding it so tightly, like it's glued to you?"

"I use it as a pillow at night," the old Arab said guilelessly, placing the precious item on the table. "And by day, I tie my *chapan* with it. But it's quite warm in here, so I took it off. You have good heating, yes?"

"Yes, we keep it well heated in winter," Valiev chuckled. "But it's summertime now—just hot everywhere. May I see your *belbak*? Is it made of old silk?"

"Possibly…" said the old man. "My father gave it to me for safekeeping ages ago, when I was young. And his father or grandfather passed it on to him."

"How has such an ancient fabric stayed in such good condition?" Valiev asked curiously.

"I believe it's magic silk," Salim answered with a mysterious smile. "Or perhaps it's been enchanted. It brings good fortune and wealth to its owner—and it never wears out. Tell me that's not amazing?"

"I believe you're right, *aksakal*," Valiev said, not arguing.

With the old man's permission, he picked up the *belbak*… and was transfixed with amazement.

Embroidered on the fabric of the man's belt—cut from what

was clearly a much larger piece—was a… part of an ancient map. Among the stitched depictions of geographical features were strange symbols that might have indicated the path to some hidden treasure.

Right away, Kudrat realized that—assuming he wasn't jumping to conclusions—the map had only one flaw: it wasn't complete. He was about to question the old man on this point but decided to wait so as not to tip him off.

Still, as a businessman who liked to move quickly and decisively, Valiev got straight to the point:

"How much do you want for this *belbak*, dear *aksakal* Salim?" he asked.

"What? I'm sorry, I don't understand," the old man stammered.

"Well, in this world, everything can be bought or sold," the businessman declared, revealing his personal worldview. "Every item has its price. So please, name your price for your *belbak*—or at least for this part of it."

"Young man," the elder said hesitantly, to Valiev's surprise, "it's true that this *belbak* is mine. Even though it's not whole, you can see it's still large, soft, and comfortable. So it's not for sale. I rest my head on it when I sleep. And use it to wrap my *chapan*. It's more comfortable for my back, thanks to the warmth of the silk."

"What if I give you a nice, warm cushion as a gift?" Valiev offered, putting on a look of sincere concern. "And I could buy you… let's say a dozen high-quality *belbaks* made from the finest Arab silk or Uzbek *khan-atlas*! How about that?"

"Oh, but why? I have no need for a pillow!" the old man said, shaking his head and gripping his heirloom. "I already have my *belbak*. It came from my father, and before that, from his father or grandfather."

"I remember, you've said all that," Kudrat said impatiently, his irritation beginning to show.

Alarmed by the sudden edge in Valiev's voice, the old man got to his feet.

"Well, I'd better be going now, if you don't mind," he murmured. "I need to find a place to stay the night, since the builders asked me to leave my grandson's house."

"Oh, but wait—how about this," Valiev said, latching onto a fresh idea. "You let me have your ancient *belbak*—just for a while— and I'll rent you a decent apartment here in Samarkand for a whole month. Deal? Eh? Come on now—just hand it over!"

"All right, well…" The old man stroked his beard, still clutching the memento of his ancestors. "I'll get going, all right? I've already taken too much of your time. You seem very busy, and I don't want to be a burden."

"So I'll rent that apartment for you," the increasingly desperate businessman pressed on. "In exchange for the *belbak*! Would you like it on Registan Square? Or near the canal, if you prefer?"

"No, thank you," Abbas said, shaking his head. "It wouldn't be right for you to spend your money on me. Besides, I always need my *belbak*. I sleep with my head on it."

At that moment, Valiev barely stopped himself from shouting at what he saw as the stubbornness of an old fool. But then a brilliant scheme popped into his mind—only a simple, cunning trick would do the job.

"You see, *aksakal*," he said in a plaintive voice meant to inspire sympathy, "you're so lucky. You have something to rest your head on at night—a soft, warm *belbak*. But I… ah…"

"You don't have one of your own?" the elderly man asked, falling right into Valiev's trap. From what Kudrat could see, the old man had no sense of deceit and wouldn't even know how to defend himself if he did.

"No, I don't have such a wonderful *belbak*!" Kudrat cried, nearly in tears. "So my nights are cold and uncomfortable."

"Well then, here, have mine!" the kind-hearted old man said, parting with his beloved possession as if tearing off a piece of his own heart. "But please, don't offer me money or apartments. That would offend me. Take it as a gift."

"Thank you!" Valiev beamed. "Thank you so much, dear *aksakal*! I'll be delighted to accept your generous present."

"May it serve you well, sonny," the elder said, his eyes watering. He felt genuine pity for the "poor" young businessman who apparently had no old *belbak* of his own.

Seeing his guest to the door, the businessman added:

"Abbas-aka, I just… have one more question, if I may?"

"Of course, dear," Abbas replied. "Ask me anything."

"Do you only have this single *belbak*? Are there any others like it? Perhaps another piece of it somewhere? Or one like it? Say, another part of it. Where could it be?"

Valiev didn't dare say the words "the other half of this ancient treasure map" out loud.

"I don't know," Salim answered honestly. "I've always just had this one."

To keep the old man from launching into his well-worn story about how he got it from his father and so on, Kudrat glanced at his watch, pretending to be busy and rushed.

Finally, the old man left.

Valiev's assistant, Marat Nigmatov—who had been quietly watching the one-man show his boss had put on—was now gazing at him with unconcealed admiration.

"Wow, boss!" Marat exclaimed. "You really are a master—tricking that old simpleton so smoothly! That takes some skill, getting exactly what you needed for free!"

"Learn from me while I'm still around," the businessman said with a smile, thoroughly pleased with himself.

"Should I at least see him out?" Marat asked. "I feel sorry for the old fellow. He might get lost in a big city. Would you allow me?"

"And why would you need to do that?" Kudrat snapped, his expression hardening. "Don't you have enough to do already? Didn't you promise to clear and prep the Salimov property for the foundation pit by tomorrow? The buyer's waiting—and already paid an advance!"

"Yes, of course, boss," Marat conceded quickly. In truth, he didn't much relish dealing with the rambling old man—he simply felt a bit sorry for him.

Bowing obsequiously to his employer, he left to get back to work.

* * *

The old man made his way slowly down the stairs—he was afraid of elevators—and stepped outside.

He felt a twinge of regret at parting with the object so dear to his heart, but also a surge of happiness for having done a good deed, convinced he had helped someone truly in need.

After walking a few hundred meters down the street, not knowing where to go or what to do, the exhausted old man spotted a bench, trudged over, and sat down.

He looked forlorn and disoriented.

And then, a miracle happened.

"Please stop the car," said a young Uzbek woman to the driver, who happened to be passing by just as the old man—sitting there all alone—came into view.

Something in her heart stirred with unexplainable compassion.

The woman got out and approached the *aksakal*.

"Hello, Grandfather," she greeted him warmly. "Is everything all right?"

"Hello, my daughter," said Abbas Salim with a tired smile, touched by her kindness. "I'm not sure. I think… not really. My heart aches a bit."

"Maybe it's just fatigue," she suggested.

"Probably," he admitted. "I'm awfully tired."

"I'm Saltanat Azamatova," the young woman said. "I'm a translator from Tashkent—our capital. I came to Samarkand on business for my company, and now I'm heading home. Are you here all by yourself?"

"Me?" The old man looked confused. "Yes. I came to this city looking for my son and grandson, but it turns out they left the country for good. I had no idea…"

"So, you've got nowhere to go right now, is that right?" she asked gently.

"That's right, daughter," he nodded.

"Well, would you like me to drive you home?" Saltanat offered. "If it isn't too far. Where did you live before coming to Samarkand? In a province?"

"Yes, in the Bulungur district," the old man shared. "But to be honest… it's lonely there. My wife passed away long ago. And my sister and nieces and nephews live in Tashkent."

"Then why don't you come with me to Tashkent?" she invited him with heartfelt warmth. "You can stay as a guest with our family, and maybe visit your sister and her children too. What do you say?"

"Would that really be all right?" he asked, worried. "I wouldn't want to trouble you."

"It's not just all right—it's exactly what needs to happen," Saltanat said with a smile.

A radiant joy lit up the old man's face. And for her part, Saltanat—the daughter of Tamilla Mahkamova and great-granddaughter of Feruz-begim—perceived the purity and kindness in his soul, and drove him to Tashkent without a second thought, to the welcoming arms of her close-knit family.

3

Marakanda, the Hazrat Khizr Mosque,
the residence of the ruler appointed
by the Arab Caliphate to govern Khorasan, 808 CE

"O my lord and sovereign, mighty and merciful ruler of the world and the great Caliphate, allow me to approach by the grace of the Almighty!" Thus began the formal, traditionally florid greeting of Tahir ibn Husayn, a member of Khorasan's powerful landowning class and the son of the hereditary governor of Pushang and Herat.

The Caliph Harun al-Rashid gave a gracious wave, inviting him to sit.

"Thank you humbly for ordering my release!" Tahir continued. Long accustomed to such extravagant praise, the astute Arab

Caliph remained outwardly calm, almost indifferent. He sensed that something was weighing on ibn Husayn's mind—that his speech had not yet reached its true point.

"I simply find it unjust, Tahir, to keep my best, most loyal subjects locked in prisons," the ruler commented.

"And the entire world knows of your great sense of justice, most honoured Caliph!" responded the nobleman of Khorasan, offering yet another lavish compliment. "That is precisely why I have come—to speak on a matter of justice, if you will allow it, of course."

"I'm listening closely, Tahir," said the Caliph, who happened, due to recent political events, to be in bustling Marakanda rather than at home.

"If it pleases you to hear my opinion, I think you should spare Rafi's life—even though he's a rebel!" Tahir blurted out boldly.

The Khorasani was well aware that he was taking a risk; speaking so frankly could easily anger the ruler. Yet he was driven by the hope of improving the Caliphate's stance on those who had risen against Mahan, the governor of Khorasan.

"Could you substantiate that?" the Caliph said mildly, in an unusually good mood and inclined to hear his guest out.

"My lord, Governor Ali ibn Isa ibn Mahan is a cruel, unprincipled tyrant," Tahir began, his voice shaking slightly. "Both you and I know he's off waging battle right now. But this is his home, so I hope his servants aren't eavesdropping on us. Naturally, no one would dare touch you, but as for me... I may be taking a risk. Yet I can't remain silent, because the people's patience has reached its limit! The governor of Khorasan himself and his men commit all manner of lawless acts."

"Really?" Harun asked, surprised. "I wasn't aware, though I

make every effort to understand my subjects' affairs and lives. Well then, continue, Tahir, son of Husayn."

"Your Majesty, even noble families are persecuted under Mahan's rule. You know my own family has not been spared these hardships! I myself was unjustly accused and sent to prison, where I was treated terribly. I, your loyal servant, barely survived."

"You have my sympathies, Tahir. My sympathies to your entire family," the Caliph replied, serene as ever. "I have great respect for your lineage. I'm aware you are the son of Husayn, our governor in Pushang and Herat, and he is the son of the former governor Mus'ab. And rumours have it your great-grandfather, Ruzaiq, was descended from the legendary hero Rustam, husband of the Saka queen Tomyris. I hold the memory of such ancestors in high regard. And you, Tahir—you're a brave warrior in your own right. In defending the ideals of the Caliphate, you lost an eye in battle. Everyone knows and respects that. And some fools, unafraid of our wrath, dare to mock you, calling you al-A'war—'the one-eyed.' But don't worry; if we learn their identities, we will punish them."

"I am grateful, Your Highness," Tahir said, bowing.

"As for the rebellion," Harun went on, "you see, Tahir, any group of people is, to some extent, a headstrong mob—a force of nature that needs to be ruled wisely and, sometimes, forcefully. That requires the use of power and strength. Do I need to spell this out? Haven't you studied statecraft and the art of war?"

Tahir had no rebuttal, so he kept silent while Harun continued:

"Furthermore, our governor in Khorasan, Mahan, is loyal to the Caliphate and to me personally. And this Khorasani noble, Rafi ibn al-Layth—he may also be an Arab, but from what I've been told, and from my own impression, he is a dangerous threat to the entire Caliphate. One cannot simply rise up in revolt against a power ordained by the Almighty! That is not the right of mere mortals—or perhaps of any man, including the Caliph. Besides, when people are given too much freedom, they might even, for all we know, rob me. And trust me, I have plenty worth stealing. By the way, you've never visited my palace in ar-Raqqah, have you? Come and see it for yourself sometime! I invite you."

"I thank you most humbly, my lord," Tahir replied with a smile. "I've heard rumours of your unparalleled wealth, and of the exquisite taste of your wife, Umm Ja'far Zubaidah! They say your private chambers are adorned with gold filigree, set with large rubies and pearls…"

"That's true," the Caliph said, smiling contentedly. "What else do they say?"

"Well, I hear that your turban is set with precious gems, and, incredibly, a massive pearl the size of an egg or a lemon," Tahir continued. "And your wife Zubaidah is famous not just for her building projects, but for the splendour surrounding her: gold, silver, silks, brocade, jewels. Supposedly, just one of her ceremonial gowns costs fifty thousand dinars. It's said she's always coming up with new types of adornment, and she's introduced dresses embroidered with precious stones."

"I suppose all of that is true," the Caliph confirmed. "We both do like precious objects. And what else?"

"Of course, my lord! Apparently, Zubaidah herself designed a canopy held up at the corners by twisted gilt columns. The top is trimmed with sable furs and colourful silks, while the underside is ebony-black, accenting the delicate patterns in the silver inlays, which themselves are set with Nishapur turquoise, Ceylon sapphires, pearls from Qatar, Egyptian emeralds, Yemeni rubies, and African coral… Why, it's practically a treasure hoard in its own right, my lord! If someone ever had to hide it away, they'd need an artist or a geographer to map out its location."

Harun al-Rashid laughed, assuming Tahir's remark was an awkward joke.

"Tahir, I like how you think. You may call me 'you,' informally, from now on," the Caliph said. "And know that I keep all my wealth right at hand, in my palace."

"I understand, and thank you, my lord. But aren't you worried that the greatest thieves might actually be found in your immediate circle?" ventured ibn Husayn. "Take your wife's father, your vizier Ja'far! I've heard damning verses about him from a court poet. Please, O Majesty, be cautious with Ja'far! He might rob you or even poison you—all for wealth."

"Very well, I'll keep that in mind," the Caliph replied, first smiling, then frowning slightly. "Perhaps someday I'll have him executed. Though… it's not your place to meddle. Is it, sonny? Right. Now, as for Governor Mahan of Khorasan… perhaps you may counsel me—should I remove him from office? And maybe I should make you governor instead?"

Tahir's cheeks burned, and he grew visibly anxious. Seeing his reaction, Harun laughed.

"I'm joking. It's too soon. You're not ready for it. Still young and too hot-headed. Maybe someday. But there's a time for everything. In fact, I've already sent my general against that troublemaker Rafi. And our governor Mahan is meek as a lamb now! So even if I do remove ibn Mahan, I'm afraid I still wouldn't replace him with you… And letting Rafi off the hook? Sorry—I can't do that either."

* * *

When Tahir returned home, he asked his wife Benu, more in confusion than anger, "What was a man doing here?"

"Oh, my dear husband!" she exclaimed. "He's a tailor. I asked him to come take my measurements for new fabric. I want it made into a lovely abaya for my birthday. I've told you—I want a wonderful outfit for my birthday…"

"Ah, yes, that's right! Very well, my moon, my dear," Tahir nodded. "So… is the tailor any good?"

"Maruf? Yes, he's quite skilled and knows his craft," Benu replied. "And he's not greedy. His village is well known for its master weavers and tailors. He showed me some samples—they're absolutely gorgeous! He can make women's abayas, men's tunics, chitons, togas, warm jubbahs, even belbaks—the sashes."

"Belbaks? That's splendid! And what's the name of this village?"

"It's called Vedar, my lord. Three or four parasangs northeast of Maracanda. A lot of Arabs live there, and nearly all of them are weavers and tailors."

"Well, I'm happy for you, Benu," said Tahir, the noble Khorasani. "Feel free to hire him again for anything else you might need. And one more thing… let this Maruf of Vedar know that I, your husband, might have need of his services one day. Perhaps I'll order a belbak from him."

"All right, I will," she promised with a smile, assuming her husband was joking.

"I wonder," Tahir mused, ending his conversation with Benu, "when Caliph Harun eventually leaves this world, which of his children will inherit that magnificent pearl in his turban? Imagine what that might be worth! Surely a fortune... Ah, what a shame that his heir is—not I! Then again..."

4

Baghdad, Iraq, the Abbasid Palace, 2023

Taking advantage of a scheduled maintenance day at the Palace, Basil—the director and chief tour guide—summoned all his staff to a meeting.

"All right, colleagues," he began, barely hiding his displeasure, "it's been a few days now, and we still haven't found the thieves who stole the Abbasid-era ceramic bowl."

"We tried looking for them—subtly asking our regular visitors—but..." The guard Muhammad shook his head in frustration. "It's as though the thieves vanished without a trace."

"We don't even know their names or have any solid description," Haidar added with a sigh.

"But, Master Basil, we can at least punish their accomplice," one of the newly hired tour guides, Gharib, suddenly declared in a loud voice.

All the employees at the Palace turned to him in surprise.

"Oh?" Basil asked. "Gharib, do you mean to say you know who it is?"

"Yes, Master, I do," the museum exhibit specialist replied without hesitation, pointing straight at a middle-aged man sitting nearby. "It's him—Ikram!"

"*Ikram?*" Haidar blurted out in disbelief. "But he's been with us for ages, and we've never seen him do anything like that. Just look at him, Master—does he seem like a scout for thieves? I'd say he's the last person here who cares about making a quick buck."

"You all don't believe me, do you?" Gharib snapped, startling everyone with his sudden anger. "Then go search his locker. Right now—before this scoundrel hides the evidence! I've seen it myself."

Neither Basil nor the others wanted to believe that Ikram—kind, helpful Ikram—could be the one to betray Baghdad's most important cultural and historical site.

But when Ikram, at Basil's request, opened his personal locker, two silver coins clattered to the floor.

"These are seventh-century dirhams," Basil explained to those who weren't familiar with them. "Old silver coins of the Arab Caliphate. They were introduced during the reign of Caliph al-Muqtadir bi'Llah of the Abbasid dynasty, who ruled from Baghdad… How could you do this, Ikram?!"

"I never expected this from you, Master Ikram!" Haidar said indignantly.

"Yes, everyone here respected you," Gharib added with a mocking sneer. "I can understand a historian's passion for artifacts, but stealing them? How shameful!"

"I—I didn't take them…" Ikram stammered, thoroughly confused. "I don't even know how they ended up in my locker. Someone must have planted them—"

"Oh, right!" Gharib interrupted gleefully. "Maybe it was the Palace ghosts playing a prank? Or the spirit of the house's owner, Caliph Bi'Llah himself? He's the one who took them, huh? And then snuck them into your stuff? Is that what you're saying?"

"I don't know how," Ikram began again, trying to defend himself. But he could see it was no use; no one would believe a word. He fell silent.

"You're fired, dear Ikram," the director of the Palace said coldly, delivering his colleague a grim verdict. "I used to address you with respect, but honestly, now you've lost it. I'll return these coins to their display, where they belong—under electronic lock and key. You—collect your things and leave. And don't ever come back to this Palace, not even as a visitor."

Ikram, glancing sadly at the now ex-coworkers who had come to condemn him, gathered his few and inexpensive possessions and left.

"And still… this is so very odd," Muhammad remarked after him. "Ikram—a thief?!"

* * *

Outskirts of Tashkent, that same day

"Vanyok, did you get that tour guide Gharib's contact info?" Sanya asked.

"Yeah, I jotted it down somewhere," Vanya replied, lounging contentedly at his aunt's dacha, both of them munching on a vegetable salad. "Why?"

"He's a good guy to have around," Sanya said. "If he didn't rat us out and kept himself off the radar, we could do more business with him. It was so smooth working together! He gave us the code to the display case in no time! Plus, he spiked the guards' tea with sleeping meds. Then we slipped in at night, quietly punched in the code, took the bowl, closed the case, and snuck back out of the

Palace without a hitch. Genius! That guy was a real catch, huh? What do you think?"

"Sure. But going on another thef—uh, *job* with him?" Vanya hesitated. "I'm not so sure, Sanya. That's only if the boss is okay with it. We have no idea what those folks in Baghdad are really like. Who knows… it's a risk to trust them again."

"Maybe you're right," Sanya acknowledged with a nod. "But there were plenty more valuables in that palace—I was practically drooling over those jugs, bowls, coins—so many priceless items."

"Oh, definitely." Vanya's eyes lit up at the memory. "They had some truly gorgeous, ancient pieces… real antiques! We could've made a fortune."

"We'd be millionaires by now!" Sanya sighed dreamily.

"Still, San," Vanya said, reeling in his friend's imagination, "you must always remember: if we do anything behind the boss's back, he'll snap our necks like a pair of chickens."

"Yeah, yeah, I know," Sanya groaned. "Can't a guy dream?"

"Of course you can," Vanya laughed. "Just stick to your knitting, that's all I'm saying! By the way, did you send the boss a photo of the bowl?"

"Sure did," Sanya nodded.

"What'd he say? We didn't screw it up and take the wrong thing, did we?"

"Nope, we're all good on that front. I just wish he'd call already," Sanya grumbled. "I want to get paid what we're owed!"

"We should be getting more than just peanuts," Vanya reminded him, "provided the boss doesn't scam us and actually pays the agreed amount."

"I think if he wants to keep getting these kinds of treasures on the cheap, he'll treat us fairly," Sanya reasoned. "He won't risk shortchanging a pair of skilled thieves who know their stuff!"

"True enough," Vanya said with a shrug. "Guess we'll see."

"Wait," Sanya whispered, raising his hand for silence. "He's calling. I'll put him on speaker. Hello, boss?"

"Sany, is everything good with my souvenir? Are you keeping it at the right temperature, like I asked?" The voice on the other end of the line was stern.

"Yeah, boss, of course everything's all right! Don't worry about it. Everything's quiet in Iraq? No fuss?… Great. When are you coming? Tomorrow? Got it—we'll be waiting. See you then!"

5

Doha, State of Qatar, Al Bidda Park, the same year

A young man named Sharaf bought his girlfriend some ice cream and suggested they stroll through the park's paths. Yet he noticed that her eyes lacked any real joy.

"Are you not happy that we're together right now?" he asked, hoping for a pleasing response.

"I like this park," replied Jahiza. "It's beautiful, and the air here is refreshing—though it's a bit hot during the day. But that's not really what matters. What's more important is that you could have taken me to a fancy restaurant at least once! Doha has so many of them."

"I'm sorry, Jahiza," Sharaf said, blushing. "You know I can't afford that just yet. My parents aren't wealthy, and I'm just starting out on my path to a successful life. But in the future…"

"Then what exactly do you want from me right now?!" she demanded, her voice annoyed and even indignant. "Why are you wasting my time?"

"No, it's nothing like that!" Sharaf protested, clearly flustered. "I love you! You must know that. I've told you before, and you can see it in my eyes…"

"Words, eyes," she mimicked. "All of that is empty, romantic fluff for losers, Sharaf. I'm used to a life of comfort and privilege. Can you give me that? Will you guarantee it?"

"Why would you need that?" he asked, genuinely puzzled. "Your father's already wealthy—he gives you everything you want. Besides… is that really the most important thing in life?"

"No," Jahiza conceded. "But I can't be dependent on my father forever. I want to get married."

"And I'm ready! Please, marry me!" Sharaf blurted out, practically proposing on the spot.

"Why don't you get down on one knee?" she shot back sarcastically. "You know, I might actually say yes—if you give me a gold ring with a diamond of at least two carats. Better yet, a D-color diamond cut in the shape of a heart… That would prove your heartfelt devotion. What's wrong—why'd you drop your head like that? Huh? Can't manage it? Then there's no point in fantasizing about a future together, or anything serious between us. Sharaf, don't you see? I do like you, even appreciate you. I'm grateful that you let me use your notes during our seminars and exams, helping me get good grades. Actually… if you want, I could pay you for that service, the same way people pay private tutors."

"Why are you talking like this?" Sharaf murmured, hurt. "I've always helped you from the heart! And I love you with all my heart."

"All right, sorry," she said, softening. "But you must understand me as well: you're asking me for something impossible. That's it, I'm tired. Can you please drive me home now in your Rolls-Royce? Oh! Silly me—how could I forget that you don't have one? Well, then I'll just call my personal driver!"

"But… why did you agree to meet me today at all?" Sharaf asked, dejected.

"I only came to see whether you were ready to stop being a loser and become someone of social standing—or not. And, Sharaf, I've concluded that all you have are naïve romantic notions, daydreams, and illusions. In the twenty-first century, that's nowhere near enough to build a happy life—let alone a family."

* * *

Doha, the Jaber Family Home, later that same day

"Sharaf, my dear boy," said Karima with a warm smile as she prepared lunch for the family, "will you tell your father and me when you're finally going to marry your girlfriend, this Jahiza? We need to get ready—buy whatever we need, rent a banquet hall, invite the guests!"

"Mama, there isn't going to be any wedding," Sharaf answered gloomily. "I've realized that, for now at least, she doesn't love me. An entire year of courtship, and she's never once returned my feelings. And I do have my pride—I'm a man, after all! This is hard for me. Plus, her parents…"

"What about her parents?" interjected his stepfather, Nazih

Jaber, eyebrows knitted. "Sure, they know we're not some important sheikhs. So what, they want a son-in-law from a truly distinguished family? They named their daughter 'Jahiza'—'she-wolf'—and they're practically wolves themselves. They'll devour anyone outside their own pack who isn't their equal. Now, if our boy suddenly became incredibly rich, then maybe…"

"How can you say such things, dear husband?" Karima objected. "Is that really how it is?"

"Sadly, Mama, yes, Father is right," Sharaf said, echoing his stepfather's thoughts with a sigh. "At the Law University where we study, we're all 'equal' in theory. Except that some of our classmates wear high-end designer clothes we can't afford. They laugh at our cheap rags from the market. And outside the classroom, the social gap grows even bigger…"

"I was always sure, my son, that this girl liked you, that she respected you," Karima said, her eyes filling with tears. "Your father and I want nothing more than your happiness."

"Thank you, Mama," Sharaf said. "But how can I get rich—and quickly? That's impossible. We don't pump oil or own hotels like her father, Ustadi Sarwan, and her mother, Ustadkhati Fatima. Nor do I even run a firm that harvests pearls from the Gulf… I'm just a regular law student who'll be a lawyer someday. But I'd do anything—not for a luxury lifestyle, but so that Jahiza would be with me! To earn both her love and her family's respect. If only I could… find a treasure or something!"

"A treasure, you say?" Karima suddenly perked up. "Hold on just a moment."

She dropped everything she was doing and rushed out of the kitchen, returning a few minutes later. While she was gone, Sharaf and Nazih exchanged puzzled looks, unsure of what she was up to.

When Sharaf's mother came back, she was holding a very old scrap of fabric, worn thin with age—something like a piece of a headscarf.

"Mama, why are you bringing us this cloth?" Sharaf asked, perplexed.

"Son, take a look for yourself," Karima answered with a smile. "A long time ago, my cousin gave it to me to keep. He was very ill and passed away shortly after. I've been holding onto it ever since. The amazing thing is, despite being so old, it never seems to wear out—even with time and dust. And there's more: look closely, and you'll see a pattern sewn into it that forms an ancient map. Actually, just part of a map. And it's no ordinary map, Sharaf."

"Really?" the young man asked, intrigued. "What's so special about it, Mama?"

"It's a map showing the way to the ancient treasures of Khorasan!" Karima explained. "You may not have heard of it, but Khorasan was a region that came under the Arab Caliphate as early as the third century. It was extremely wealthy… But you understand, of course, you'll need to find the map's other half too."

"Where on earth would I find that?" Sharaf sighed in discouragement. It sounded like a tall order.

"You must go to what was once Khorasan—primarily modern-day Uzbekistan," Karima advised him. "Summer's here, and you're on break. Go there and see where luck takes you—you'll have plenty of time to search."

"What, I'm supposed to go by myself?" Sharaf asked, alarmed. "Off to a foreign place so far from home? Where would I stay? Some hotel? Would you come with me? That's expensive, but—"

"Don't worry. There's a good option," Karima reassured him. "First of all, you need to do this on your own, without us. You'll grow stronger from the experience, gain wisdom, and learn to stand on your own two feet—just like your father, Nazih. Second, listen to what I'm about to tell you—something my husband Nazih already knows. Long ago, before I met Nazih, I got to know an Uzbek doctor named Said Mumtazov. He was a pupil of the world-famous Professor Fedorov, and he came to Qatar and the Emirates in the late eighties for an ophthalmology conference. Later on, he kept returning here to perform eye surgeries and consult with our medical teams. Around the early 2000s, I was working as a paramedic at Doha's central hospital.

"That's where your mother met this Doctor Said," Nazih interjected.

"Yes, exactly," Karima nodded. "Back in 2001, during one of his visits, Doctor Said saw me checking a patient's blood pressure and giving injections. He came over to me himself to say he admired my conscientious work and my caring attitude toward the patients. I was impressed by his calm seriousness, his skill—everyone had heard about his brilliant eye surgeries—and at the same time by his kind, open, and clear way of looking at the world. We ran into each other occasionally. One day, he invited me to a café. We had a wonderful time chatting, and soon became friends. Then… we fell in love with each other."

Hearing this, Sharaf's eyes widened. He was beginning to sense where his mother's story was headed, but decided to hear her out without interrupting.

"Unfortunately," Karima continued, "Said couldn't stay with me in Qatar—or in my homeland, Lebanon—though I asked him to. And I couldn't bring myself to leave my parents here to move with him to Uzbekistan's capital. So, in the end… we had to part ways. A couple of weeks later, I learned that I was pregnant. But

I chose not to reach out to Said. I was hurt that our relationship hadn't turned out the way I'd dreamed, so I decided not to tell this man—whom I truly loved at the time—that I was expecting his child. I believed I could raise the baby on my own. And as you've guessed, my son… that child was you."

"Yes, Mama, I get it," Sharaf said quietly.

"You were born, and two years later I met Nazih—a wonderful man, a native Qatari. We fell in love, and Nazih proposed. At first, I refused because I worried he wouldn't love you as his own child. But thankfully, I was wrong. Isn't that right, habibi?"

"That's right, my Karima," Nazih confirmed. "I love both of you more than anything in the world, Sharaf. You're dearer to me than if you were my own flesh and blood. I've known about Doctor Mumtazov for a long time—your mother and I keep no secrets from each other. Now, it's time for you to know. And here's my advice: go to Uzbekistan and meet your biological father. I have no objection."

"All right," Sharaf agreed. "Mama, do you have any way to get in touch with him?"

"No, I don't have his personal contact information anymore," Karima admitted. "But I did find the website of his private eye clinic. Here's the link… Talk to him, son! Try to find out if he's married, if he has other children. Maybe you'll even become friends with them. Just… please promise you won't stay there forever. After your search—whatever happens—come back to your home country. And don't forget about me and Nazih. At least call or write to us every now and then, all right?"

"Of course I will, dear Mama and Father," Sharaf said, smiling warmly. "That's exactly what I'll do."

6

Madinat as-Salam (Baghdad), Mesopotamia, Abbasid Caliphate, March 809 CE

"Habibi, could you explain why we rushed here so quickly?" asked Lubana bint Ali ibn al-Mahdi of her husband, the heir apparent of the Arab Caliphate, Abu Abdullah Muhammad ibn Harun al-Amin.

"Do you like this palace, Lubana?" Amin replied with a question of his own.

"Yes, it's beautiful," his wife said with a smile. "Are we going to live here now? Why not in Raqqa? That's where your parents—the Caliph and his wife—are currently staying!"

"That's because my father, Caliph Harun, dislikes Baghdad—he finds it unbearably hot," Amin explained. "Besides, when my great-grandfather, Caliph al-Mansur, founded the Abbasid Caliphate, he designated Baghdad as its capital! And as such, everything necessary for our royal life is already right here."

"Your father Caliph Harun is gravely ill—he could die at any moment," Lubana reminded him. "I assumed you, as his loving son, would be at his side in Raqqa at such a time."

"I thought you were more perceptive than that," Amin chided her. "I have to secure the throne here before any of my brothers can even think of laying claim to it."

"But... who would dare?" the prince's wife asked in surprise.

"You're the eldest son of Caliph Harun and his recognized heir! Besides, you yourself told me that seven years ago your father made all his sons swear to abide by his decision on the succession, promising to respect the line of inheritance he set."

"Yes, I know," the prince said. "My father himself appointed me to succeed him—with my brothers as witnesses. But let me tell you: they're like a pack of jackals, just waiting to pounce on any prey within reach! And that throne, and the Caliphate's riches, are their greatest obsession. And in any case, why should I sit by my father's bedside in mourning, guarding a body that is practically on its way to the grave? If you must know, Lubana, my father Harun does not deserve too much respect. He became a military leader thanks to his mother, a former Yemeni slave named al-Khayzuran. The Caliph freed her, then married her. You're aware that the Caliph's wives are always scheming against one another, each trying to promote her own children. My father's mother, Khayzuran, was the same—she persuaded Caliph Muhammad ibn Mansur to grant young Harun command of the army."

"She must have thought it would help your father Harun's career," Lubana ventured.

"Exactly!" Prince Amin replied. "And that's precisely what happened: Harun turned out to be a competent commander, successfully waging war against Byzantium and building a fleet to raid the islands. He was a patron of the arts… but his character!"

"Yes," Lubana agreed softly, "I've observed a bit of that myself. He never gave alms to the poor—in fact, to support the luxury of his court, he was ruthless in collecting taxes. And he was often harsh toward non-Muslims, imposing restrictions on them."

"Correct," Prince Amin concurred. "Some of my father's impulsive decisions throughout the Abbasid territories have unsettled the empire. They call Caliph Harun's reign a 'golden age' of the Abbasid Caliphate, but personally, I believe it was the Arab merchants who spread his fame as a wise and just ruler. Trade blossomed under him, and merchants expanded their business from China to East Africa."

"They certainly told the whole world about their Caliph and his fabulous wealth," Lubana added.

"And that wealth is precisely what we should be thinking about first," the prince reminded his wife. "I have to leave something substantial for our son's inheritance!"

"You're a wonderful father, my Caliph!" Lubana exclaimed flatteringly.

"I'm not Caliph just yet," her husband said with obvious pride, "but soon I will be. Any day now—once my father Harun departs to the better world above—family members and relatives will start arriving here at the palace. I'll be seated on the throne, and before everyone present and those who come, our servants will endlessly proclaim: 'Long live Caliph Amin!'"

***

In the same place, a few days later

"Long live Caliph al-Amin!" Zubaidah shouted as she entered the throne hall of the palace. "Are you well, my son?"

Until just recently, he had been Prince Amin; now, he was the Abbasid Caliph. He winced at the tone of offense, outrage, and sarcasm in her voice.

"Greetings, Mother," he stammered awkwardly, then quickly collected himself. For the first time in his life, upon seeing her, he did not rise to his feet. "Forgive me for not standing. I am the

Caliph now, and that means everyone else—even you, Mother—is my subject. Is that not so?"

"Certainly, my boy, of course," Zubaidah agreed sourly, barely restraining her anger. "But perhaps you could at least invite your mother to sit next to you on that lovely divan? Your wife could scoot over—or stand up, yes?"

With a motion of his hand, Caliph Amin signaled his wife to move aside, then gestured for his mother to sit not far from him.

Lubana obeyed hesitantly, relinquishing her seat near the throne to her husband's mother.

"You must not have heard: your father has died," Zubaidah informed Amin.

"No, Mother, I already know," he replied, restraining his displeasure at her tactless behavior. Then he drew out his next words deliberately: "I am the Caliph of this state. I learn of everything that happens among my servants and slaves before anyone else."

"I see," she nodded, having to swallow what was nearly an outright insult from her own son. "But you acted shamefully. You didn't even say your farewells to your parent, leaving all the ceremonies to me, your feeble mother!"

"Weren't your other beloved sons, Princes Ma'mun and Mu'tasim, there with you?" Amin asked, feigning surprise. "I have many affairs of state to attend to. What are they busy with, I wonder? Couldn't they step up and behave like real men—take care of everything?"

This time, she said nothing, lacking an immediate retort.

"And one more thing, Mother," the new Caliph said icily. "You may keep your canopy in Raqqa—the one with gilded columns, silks, and all those gems. I allow it. Consider that my filial token of gratitude. But as for my late father's turban—may his soul rest in peace!—set with precious stones and that lemon-sized pearl, I order you to bring it to me here as soon as possible."

Zubaidah raised her eyes to her son, staring as though she hardly recognized him. But seeing that he was no longer the kind, pliant, soft-hearted prince, but rather an angry, fearsome, and imposing ruler of the Arab Caliphate, she stood, bowed, and said in all seriousness—without a trace of irony:

"I hear and obey, my lord! Your command shall be carried out!"

* * *

Marakanda, Khorasan, Abbasid Caliphate, 810 CE

"What do you think, dear—has Amin had his fill of playing Caliph yet?" Benu asked Tahir.

Tahir laughed at his wife's ironic question, stroked his beard, and answered:

"Of course, one shouldn't speak ill of the ruler of a vast empire, but between us: our Caliph Amin behaves extremely frivolously, irresponsibly, and recklessly! He often forgets about his rival brothers, even though they're always looking for a chance to usurp his throne! Which means they're just waiting for a convenient and suitable moment to exploit his mistakes and wrest control of the Caliphate from their older brother. Meanwhile, Amin has been neglecting state affairs, indulging in pleasures and all sorts of depravity. The people resent it, and he's becoming quite unpopular."

"What about his vizier, Fadl ibn Rabi'?" Benu asked. "Isn't he able to talk some sense into the young ruler?"

"He has some influence on policy," Tahir replied, "but things have deteriorated so badly that I doubt the Caliph can hold on much longer. He recently quarreled with his brother, Prince Ma'mun, after noticing his wife paying Ma'mun some attention at a reception. Amin got jealous and angry. It would have been wiser for him to keep quiet and bury the grievance, but instead he confronted Ma'mun outright! And Ma'mun—who already doesn't take kindly to his elder brother, to say the least—is by far the biggest threat to him."

"Yes, Ma'mun has always been ambitious," Benu observed. "No doubt he's convinced that he alone among Harun's sons truly deserves to rule the Caliphate!"

"I believe you're right, my habibti," Tahir agreed. "In fact, I received a letter from Ma'mun just yesterday—he wants me to come to Baghdad for a private discussion. I have a good idea what that might be about."

"He's likely hoping for your political support," Benu guessed. "After all, you're the son of a governor and a noble, influential figure in the Caliphate."

"Yes, but there's more to it," Tahir confided. "I'll share this with you, but please, wife, don't worry too much... You know I have some military experience, and it's obvious to me that a civil war is brewing between Caliph Amin and Prince Ma'mun. Add to that the various popular uprisings stirring up chaos! All of this hinders Ma'mun's plan to secure the throne. He wants to inherit a stable realm, not a mess, from his reckless elder brother. So I suspect he may first ask me to crush the rebellion of Rafi ibn Layth. Then, in any subsequent war, he might give me command of part of his forces."

"I absolutely don't want you going to war, risking your life, habibi Tahir!" Benu cried, distressed.

"Sadly, I must—it's my duty," Tahir said, striving to remain calm. "You know how I've long dreamed of being appointed governor of our Khorasan! I have to do whatever Ma'mun requires. Unlike the weak-willed, irresponsible Amin, Ma'mun considers me a friend. He might trust me with that prestigious governorship!"

"I understand," Benu said, tears welling up in her eyes. "May the Almighty protect you, my dear."

7

Outskirts of Tashkent, 2023

The moment Kudrat Valiev stepped into the dacha and laid eyes on the antique ceramic bowl, he strode right over to it. Picking it up, he carefully cradled it in his hands, studying every detail with delight.

"Yes, this is the one—from the ninth century, Abbasid dynasty!" he confirmed, unable to contain his excitement. He was, after all, a former archaeologist and an expert on such things. "Until now, I've only ever seen it in photographs or behind glass in the Abbasid Palace display. But here it is, as if resurrected from the dust of centuries… And now it's mine! It was worth traveling from Samarkand to Baghdad first, then over here. Good work, boys. Well done."

"Excuse me, boss—about our payment, like you promised?" Sanya piped up immediately, money being the only thing in life that truly interested him.

Without taking his enraptured gaze from the bowl, still holding it tenderly in his left hand, Kudrat reached into his pocket with his right, pulled out a thick wad of bills, and tossed it onto the table with the dismissive air of someone throwing a bone to obedient dogs.

Both Sanya and Vanya lunged for their reward at once. Yet Vanya, knowing that his friend wouldn't dare swindle him in front of the boss, let Sanya count the money. Once Sanya was done, he split the sum evenly and handed Vanya his share.

Their faces lit up upon receiving the crisp reward for their "valiant" efforts.

"Boss, do you still need us?" Vanya ventured, eager for more adventures.

"Yes," Kudrat nodded. "In fact, that's what I wanted to talk to you about now. Here, have a look at this image with these unusual patterns."

He pulled a large printed photograph out of his pocket—it showed designs from a very old map.

"Use one of your phones to photograph this ancient map and do an online image search," Kudrat instructed, giving them a new assignment.

"There are some strange names written here in unfamiliar letters," Sanya noted. "Are those place names? Something ancient? Or do they still exist somewhere?"

"That's none of your concern," Kudrat replied firmly. "All I care about is any matches you find. Download everything that's even remotely similar. Include any precise data on other maps like this. Check with museums, libraries, or cities where they might be kept. Then pass all that info on to me. Once I've gone through and studied the results, I might send you out in search of the original map."

"Understood, boss!" Sanya shouted enthusiastically.

"Don't worry—we'll take care of it!" Vanya chimed in with equal optimism.

"Then get started on it right away," the boss commanded.

***

Tashkent, the same day

"Good morning, miss! Sorry, can I see Doc Mumtazov?" asked Sharaf in halting English at the reception desk of the eye clinic.

"Good morning, sir! Excuse me, can I help you?" the young receptionist replied politely in English, answering his question with another. "Would you like to see a doctor?"

"Yes, I do, thanks," the young man said. "I would like to see Doctor Mumtazov."

"Okay, just a minute, sir," the girl said.

She dialled the internal number for the chief physician and said:

"Said-aka, there's a visitor here from another country. No, I don't know where from yet, but he specifically wants to see you."

"All right, Olya. Let him in, please."

Said Mumtazov spoke English fluently. He invited his guest to sit in a comfortable chair and asked his secretary to bring them some tea.

"I'm listening, young man," Said said with a friendly smile.

"Doctor, I'm not even sure where to start," his visitor admitted, somewhat embarrassed—an unexpected feeling in front of the clinic's director. "You see… My name is Sharaf Jaber, but that's not my real last name—it's my stepfather's. I came here from Qatar, and…"

"Pleased to meet you," Said smiled. "It's a wonderful country! I've been there several times, though it was a long while back."

"Yes, I know you were there…" Sharaf responded, choosing his words carefully. "I guess you haven't visited in many years, have you? Otherwise, maybe you would have met… Actually… My mother told me that… that you're my father!"

Having finally voiced the crux of the matter, Sharaf let out a sigh of relief—but was quickly seized by the same fear he'd felt off and on all day. He wondered how this man would react. Would he accept him kindly, or refuse even to hear him out? Or simply not believe him?

Caught off guard by such a revelation, Said stared at the young man in undisguised astonishment, teetering on indignation.

"Forgive me, sir… are you joking?" he managed after nearly a minute, his voice strained. "How can this be? Is this some kind of cruel prank? Or a provocation?"

"No, *ustadi*," Sharaf said, embarrassed, using the respectful form of address. He felt awkward in light of the doctor's reaction. "My mother's name is Karima—she's a nurse, a Lebanese woman from Doha. That's in Qatar… You travelled there many times for work, Dr. Said… you met her!"

Taking an old printed photograph of his young mother from his small shoulder bag, Sharaf held it out to Said.

To Sharaf's relief, the moment Said glanced at the picture of the woman, he recognized her immediately and was overwhelmed by a rush of memories so strong that tears sprang to his eyes.

"Karima…" he whispered, his voice trembling. "Yes, of course… I remember. Back then… I loved her… How is she now?

Is everything all right with her?"

"She's fine, thank you. She's in good health. She sends her regards."

Sharaf felt uneasy repeating to Said that he was the man's son and needed his help here in Uzbekistan. A shy, well-mannered young man, he stayed silent, waiting for the older man—this "complete stranger," yet his biological father—to speak next.

"Well…" Said fumbled for words, his shock momentarily scattering his thoughts. "Are you sure… that is, are you sure? That you're my…? Sorry. How old are you, Sharaf?"

"Twenty-one," the young man said timidly. "I was born in 2002. I'm a law student in Doha. Please don't think, *ustadi*, that I've come to ask for anything. My life is fine—I just wanted to meet you."

"All right, let's do this," Said suggested. "I'm swamped with work right now. Why don't you wait here until lunchtime, okay? I'm sure you have your luggage with you. No need to check into a hotel yet—you can store your suitcase here in my office, in that cabinet over there. Good, yes, that's perfect. Feel free to look around the clinic and wait for me. Or take a walk around the area—there's a walkway nearby. Then come back around lunch. We'll go to a café and talk. Sound good?"

"Yes, *ustadi* Said," Sharaf nodded. "I'll do whatever you say."

Over lunch, Sharaf told him everything he could about himself and his family. He omitted only one major reason he had come to Tashkent—the search for treasure guided by the fabric map.

While Sharaf spoke, Said listened, his thoughts whirling: how would he bring the young man home, and how might his wife react? And what if his daughter Malika showed up? She often visited her parents. What if her husband, Bahadir Fattakhov, dropped by? Or any one of the large extended family descended from Feruz-begim stopped in? Fate sometimes arranged the most awkward coincidences.

And what would he tell them all?

"Look, everyone, I have an adult son from outside my marriage! He lives in Qatar; his mother is Lebanese…" He could only imagine the reaction of all his relatives! God knows what they might think. They had always respected him, seen him as a model of integrity and morality. Yes, he could explain to Sitora—his wife—and everyone else that his relationship with Karima, the young man's mother, was years ago, well before he met his wife, and certainly before Malika was born. And up until today, he hadn't known a thing about Sharaf's existence! Would they believe him? Although… Sharaf could confirm it all. But Sharaf didn't speak Uzbek, and not all of Said's family members spoke English—or Arabic, for that matter. Still, that was a minor issue. They'd understand somehow! Someone like Saltanat could translate, if she visited.

When they finished eating and talking, they got up from the table—and a middle-aged man suddenly approached Said. It was Abdullah Fattakhov, his daughter's father-in-law.

They greeted each other warmly:

"Hello, Said! How are you? Everything all right?"

"Hello, Abdullah-aka! What brings you to these parts? Maybe you'd like to stop by my office? We could check your eyesight—you haven't been in for a while."

"Oh no, thanks, Saidjon—maybe another time," Abdullah said, smiling. "I just happened to be in the area on some business. Then I got hungry and came into this café since it's lunchtime. They do serve decent food here!"

"Yes, it's not bad," Said agreed. "Too bad we just finished eating, or we could've sat together. Maybe next time!"

"Is that your nephew?" the older man asked curiously, glancing at Sharaf. "I've never seen him before. I can see the blood relation—he looks a lot like you!"

After exchanging polite farewells, Abdullah went on his way, while Said and Sharaf returned to the clinic. But Abdullah's words left Said reeling.

What was it he said? "A nephew"?! He looks "a lot like you!" Indeed… He was just glad Abdullah hadn't come right out and asked, "Well, Said, is this young man your son by any chance?"

Still… he couldn't just cast Sharaf aside because of these fears—fears of being unfairly disgraced, judged, and misunderstood.

"Sharaf, listen…" Said said, doing his best to hide his tension. "I've made a decision: we'll go back to the clinic, pick up your things, and head straight to my house. Don't be shy, don't feel awkward, alright? We're family, you and I. Come on, son—no need to be afraid. Everything will be fine."

8

Outskirts of Tashkent, two days later

Businessman Kudrat Valiev—who was also a historian and archaeologist—burst through the unlocked door of someone else's dacha without knocking or showing any courtesy. Skipping any greeting, he impatiently demanded.

"Why did you call me at this hour? What—did you really find something resembling my map? Show me! Where?!"

Feeling proud of himself, Sanya—the one who'd first discovered an online photo resembling the old map—hoped he might earn a little extra for his efforts. He shouted,

"Here, boss, take a look! This article is about an old library in Baghdad—"

"What? Baghdad again?!" Kudrat interrupted, startled.

"Well, yeah… We found a photo by sheer luck," Sanya continued. "Because, as you know, nobody uploads pictures of entire library collections onto the internet. I doubt we'd even find a catalogue! Libraries usually don't share that info publicly."

"And certainly not a list of all their maps," Vanya added. "We just got lucky."

"Exactly!" Sanya nodded. "See, the picture here is low-quality, not very clear, but we can still make something out."

"Hold on, boys," Kudrat snapped. "Your map is old, sure, but it clearly isn't on cloth! How did you search for it? You're both amateurs. Go find something better!"

"Boss, I think it's actually a faithful copy of the second half of the piece you have," Sanya assured him. "It's probably on fabric too. We need to get hold of it and check. You don't really care that it's on fabric—only that it shows the route to the ancient treasure, right? The cities, rivers, and so on! Correct?"

"Fair enough," Kudrat grumbled, capitulating.

"And it looks exactly like the design on your *belbak*—the photo of which you gave us," Vanya chimed in. "We checked not just the Russian-speaking internet, but everywhere online, in different languages."

"Of course, we don't speak those languages," Sanya explained, "but we did exactly what you asked—ran searches for images similar to the one you gave us. I was the first to find something interesting in an Arabic article, with a side note in English saying 'Baghdad.' It also mentioned a library called 'al-Qadiriya.' I'm pretty sure this is it—jackpot! So, boss, since I'm the first to find the map you wanted, will I… get a bonus?"

Kudrat nodded. He looked closely at the photo the pair had printed. Sure enough, the map was strikingly similar to the embroidered one on the old man's *belbak* from Bulungur.

Delving into his pocket, the boss pulled out five hundred dollars. He handed two hundred to Vanya and three hundred to Sanya.

"Thanks," Vanya mumbled, clearly not thrilled.

"Oh wow, boss, thanks a million!!" Sanya shouted happily. "Always ready to—"

"Don't talk too much," Kudrat cut him off. "Here's some more money for plane tickets to Baghdad. Buy your tickets and get on the next available flight. Find that library. Go there during the day first—figure out where they keep their old maps and so forth. Then… well, probably best like this: you'll sneak in at night and steal the original. We can't make out any names on that blurry photo, so I need the actual map. Got it?"

"Yes, boss!" Sanya and Vanya answered in unison.

"And listen," Kudrat warned them sharply. "Stay away from the Abbasid Palace for now. It isn't safe. Someone could've spotted you there last time. If you don't want to get nabbed by the Iraqi police, keep a low profile. Understood? If I find out you went back to the Palace, or—worse—stole anything else from there without my say-so, I'll deal with you both. Harshly!"

"Got it, boss," Sanya said quickly to calm him. "Everything'll be fine."

"We'll handle it perfectly," Vanya added.

"You might just take this money for your tickets and disappear for good," Kudrat remarked, "but first off, I'd find you no matter where you hide. Second, you'd be giving up a much bigger payday. I'm willing to pay well for the original of that second map—more precisely, the second half of my map. Choose wisely."

"Don't worry, boss, we won't let you down!" Sanya promised.

"All right," Kudrat said with a distrustful nod. "I'm flying back to Samarkand. My construction business demands my attention. But starting two days from now—by which time you should be done—I'll be waiting for your call."

* * *

Baghdad, Iraq, the Abbasid Palace, the following morning

Haidar, the guard, knocked on the director's office door.

"May I come in, Master Basil?" he asked, peeking in.

"Yes, Haidar, come in," Basil said. "Anything happen?"

"Thankfully not yet, ustadi Basil," the guard answered, setting his boss at ease. "I wanted to ask: did you manage to run all the tour guide's background checks with the police? Did they find anything suspicious about any of them?"

"Haidar, I did just what you recommended," the Palace director admitted. "Honestly, if we hadn't lost that ninth-century ceramic bowl, I might never have followed through. But we ran checks on every new employee, and none of them had so much as a minor record. The police database turned up nothing. I'm at a loss as to how we'll catch this inside accomplice."

"Exactly," Haidar sighed. "He helped the thieves make off with that bowl, so who's to say he isn't in league with them to clear out the entire Palace?"

"What do you suggest we do?" the director asked, sounding discouraged.

"I've got one idea, Master," Haidar answered, allowing himself a faint smile. "I've noticed that one of our new guides, Gharib, has been jumpy and irritable recently. He's always dropping his things, snapping at other guides for no reason, always glancing over his shoulder like he's worried someone's watching him."

"Really?" Basil said, surprised. "Gharib? I never noticed anything odd about him. Then again… maybe you're right, Haidar… Still, remember how he was the one who accused Ikram of helping the thieves? He called him out and shamed him in front of everyone."

"I do remember, Master Basil," Haidar replied with a frown. "But you know there are people like that: complete cynics and hypocrites, who rant about others to divert any suspicion from themselves! Also, I forgot to mention—yesterday Gharib showed up for work wearing a brand-new Italian designer suit. Where'd he get the money for that? Might be that me telling you about him is just a coincidence, but still…"

"Yes, I see your point. I don't believe in coincidences like that, either!" Basil agreed. "But you know what they say: innocent until proven guilty. How do we catch him—assuming he's our culprit?"

"It will take time and effort," Haidar said, beginning to lay out his plan. "But here's what I propose: we can test not only Gharib, but all the guides! We'll need to bring back that programmer who set up the electronic locks. So, ustadi Basil, here's my idea…"

* * *

Baghdad, the Al-Qadiriya Library of Ancient Manuscripts, two days later

"We're not scholars or 'bookworms' to be rummaging through these old books and papers!" Sanya grumbled, shining his flashlight around the basement of the library's archives. Even in the daytime, it was fairly dim, and at night no one ever bothered turning on the lights. "When I agreed to come back to Baghdad and poke around in this archive, it never occurred to me how hard it'd be to find that old map!"

"I don't see how we'll ever find it," Vanya muttered, fully agreeing with his friend. "Not only can we barely see anything; I just don't think I'm smart enough to hunt down a 'needle' in a haystack this big. Feels like the only thing that could help us is a miracle… Hey, Sanyok, look—this says '9th century.' Could be the right area, right? The map should be here, in one of these books!"

"Yeah, Van, I'm looking…" Sanya said. "No sign of it! My eyes are killing me from searching in the dark. This is pointless, I swear. It's not here. Maybe we should just go? We don't want the guard wandering in, raising an alarm, or worse—getting grabbed by the cops! You do remember we were taking a massive risk coming back to Baghdad at all?"

"Yeah, don't I know it," Vanya whispered.

"Wait, Vanya, I think… Wow! I've found it!! Yes!! I'm a genius! Always the first to find stuff!"

"Shut up!" Vanya hissed. "Don't be an idiot! Someone might hear. Let me see. Is this it? Sure does look similar. Hold on—

compare it to the photos on your phone: the boss's piece looks… well, a bit different. But this one, from the book on this shelf, does match the photo from that article we found online. Nice going, Sanyok! How'd you manage that?"

"No clue. I said only a miracle could help us. And so it did," Sanya replied happily. "And hey, if it means living the good life, there's nothing I won't do. The boss is going to pay us a fortune! We can each snag ourselves a fiancée and the four of us will sail off on some cruise liner!"

"Keep dreaming," Vanya whispered. "Grab the map and let's get out of here! Hide it properly. Let's go."

* * *

Baghdad, a hotel, that same night

Once Sanya and Vanya got back to the room they were sharing—trying to save money—the first thing each of them wanted was a shower to wash away the library dust. But Vanya was clearly on edge.

"What's the matter? Want another look at the map?" Sanya asked.

"Yeah, let's give it a good once-over," Vanya said with a sudden burst of energy, as if his partner had read his mind. "I've got this feeling… never mind. Let's see it."

Sanya pulled the stolen map from his bag, then took out his smartphone. The two friends carefully compared the original to the images: the one they'd found online and the one Kudrat Valiev had given them.

"Sanya, I think we got the wrong map," Vanya said in alarm,

voicing his suspicion.

"What?!" Sanya protested. He didn't want to accept the dangerous turn of events. "Look—this one totally matches that photo from the article!"

"Okay, it matches, but that's not the point," Vanya insisted, shaking his head. "You can see perfectly well yourself: the embroidered map on the boss's belbak is completely different. Yeah, this piece is also incomplete, but… it's not the one! What do we do now?"

"Boss is going to kill us," Sanya stated flatly. "So… to avoid returning empty-handed and getting ourselves knocked off, let's just nab something else from that Palace, yeah? And pick up a little something for ourselves! I've had my eye on those gold coins from the Arab Caliphs. We can sell them somewhere, and then we won't just go on a one-week cruise—we'll do a world tour! Imagine how awesome it'd be, man! We'll buy whatever we want, live like kings. C'mon, Vanya, whaddya say?"

"No way!" Vanya waved his hands. "The boss specifically told us to stay away from that place. And it will be truly dangerous. How do you not get it? We could get recognized. Besides, where would you even sell a bunch of antique coins? You got some fancy auction connections? Didn't think so!"

"We can find amateur coin collectors," retorted Sanya. "I'm sure there are those kinds of people in Russia or Uzbekistan. Trust me, they'd jump at the chance to buy this gold! We can just call up that guide at the Palace—Gharib—and work it out! He'll give us the code to the case with the gold coins!"

"Oh, I'm sure nobody else is after them!" Vanya sighed sarcastically. "And by the way, last time the boss gave us money to bribe that guide. Now, do we have that kind of money? Gharib's no fool—he's greedy. It's all too dangerous. We've talked about this already. Robbing stuff at home is one thing, but here it's a different story."

"It's not dangerous if we're careful and smart!" Sanya insisted. "We might not be well-educated, but we're no pushovers. We can pull this off! Quiet—I'm calling him now... Hello, Mister Gharib? Hello! It's those foreign friends of yours—Alex and Johnny. Yes, yes, the ones with the terrible English. Sorry, that's just how it is. The important thing is you understand us, right? You remember us? Great. Everything okay on your end? No trouble? Great... Mind meeting tomorrow? We've got a proposition. Okay!"

Sanya hung up. Vanya could see the excitement and lust for money burning in his partner's eyes.

"He said he'll meet us near the Palace at a café during his lunch break," Sanya told Vanya.

"I'm not sure we're doing the right thing," Vanya repeated, uncertain.

"I am sure," Sanya said, cheerfully slapping him on the shoulder. "We're practically there. Half the work's done. You'll see, buddy, we'll be set for life. Think of those coins as already in our pockets! Soon we'll be rolling in it—rich and powerful! We'll be the ones hiring guys like us. Or even like our boss! Ha-ha!"

"Unless we get caught. Or Kudrat punishes us for going rogue," Vanya pointed out.

"He won't," Sanya said confidently. "He wants to own the world, after all. And we're helping him do it—he'll end up thanking us... Man, I can't wait for tomorrow!"

9

Tashkent, the same days

Said was driving Sharaf to his home.

"Son, have you called your mother yet, since you arrived?" he asked.

"Yes, yes, I did," Sharaf nodded, smiling—he appreciated the attention from his newly discovered father. "Everything's fine with Mom. She and my father both send their warm regards."

"Thank you. Next time you call them, please send my regards too… Sharaf, I think on the way we should stop by the grocery store."

"Excellent! And if it's all right with you, I'll buy something to go with the tea," the young man added.

"That's not necessary," Said protested. "It's better if you don't spend money right now—you might need it here. I'll take care of the shopping."

Having filled their bags with food, the two men continued on. Said switched on the radio. Unexpectedly, there was a brief interview with a child psychologist discussing children abandoned by their parents. The subject made Said anxious, and at a crosswalk, he nearly drove through a red light. By the time he moved on again, a speeding driver in a brand-new Toyota was already barrelling straight toward them, well above the speed limit.

Sharaf panicked when he saw it.

The oncoming driver rammed into Said's Chevrolet, leaving a large dent in the front before speeding away from the crash site without slowing down.

The Chevrolet came to a stop in the middle of the road. Said was seriously injured—shards of the shattered windshield had struck him in the head.

Sharaf was so rattled he didn't even think to call an ambulance. On top of that, not knowing Uzbek or Russian made it harder for him to think clearly or ask for help.

But in this dramatic situation, fortunately, several passing drivers pulled over. Three of them immediately called Tashkent's Emergency Services and the Traffic Police (UBDD).

The medical team examined Said and took him to the nearest hospital.

Sharaf went along with him. In the ambulance, realizing the accompanying passenger was a foreigner who spoke neither Uzbek nor Russian, the doctor found Said's smartphone—miraculously intact—dialled the number listed under "Wife," and informed Sitora of what had happened.

By the time a worried Sitora Mumtazova arrived at the hospital with her daughter Malika, Said was already undergoing surgery. Both women went to see the department head to find out just how badly their loved one was hurt. He told them the injury was quite severe—that the patient was still unconscious and likely wouldn't regain consciousness anytime soon. This news left them both in shock. Sitora and Malika grew quiet, tense, and withdrawn.

They approached the door of the intensive care unit, where no outsiders were allowed. At first, they paid no attention to the unfamiliar young man standing in front of the doors, assuming that some other relative of his was in one of the operating theatres or

ICU rooms. But when he greeted them politely in English, giving only his name, they were taken aback.

"Excuse me, who do you have in there?" Malika ventured to ask, trying not to seem impolite. Both she and her mother studied him carefully. Meanwhile, Sharaf—who understood that the young lady in front of him was, in fact, his half-sister—observed her refined beauty with restrained admiration.

"I… I ride in one car with Dr. Mumtazov," Sharaf explained.

"What?!" the women said, even more startled—especially Sitora. She, like her daughter, was fully fluent in English. "Why on earth would you be riding in my husband's car? Is he your personal chauffeur now?!"

"Mama, calm down," Malika tried to soothe Sitora, who was close to losing her composure. "We don't know the circumstances… Maybe Dad had some reason for it?"

"What reason could there possibly be?!" Sitora snapped. "You, young man—did you need something that caused Dr. Mumtazov to end up in this terrible accident, lying on the brink of life and death?! You're the reason he's in intensive care right now, unconscious, right? Because of you, they're pulling shards of broken glass out of him and trying to stitch up his punctured organs?!"

"No, please," Sharaf answered softly, tears welling up, unable to help feeling guilty. "I… we only met Dr. Mumtazov today. He invited me over to your house…"

"Oh, really?! Perhaps you're some eminent figure in world medicine—since my husband decided to bring you to our place without telling me a thing! Even drove you there himself!!" Sitora was growing angrier. "And yet here you are, not a scratch on you— how convenient!"

Sharaf kept silent this time, realizing that at the moment, it was no use trying to justify himself in front of a woman in a state of shock. He only looked at both of his interlocutors again with sincere sympathy, knowing full well that he couldn't just blurt out, *"By the way, I'm actually Said's son!"*

"If you'll allow me, I'll go now," Sharaf said quietly, once they had all stood there in silence for quite a while. He decided he would wait for news of Said's condition somewhere else—perhaps outside the hospital—where no one could lash out at him.

"Not yet. Stay where you are, young man," said a hefty, stern-faced man who suddenly appeared beside them. He showed his ID and introduced himself. "Investigator, Major Zakir Bahromov. I need all of you to identify yourselves, please."

Realizing that a foreign national who spoke neither Uzbek nor Russian was present—and noticing that Malika spoke to the young man fluently in English—the major asked her to translate.

At that point, Malika felt torn. On one hand, she had no emotional energy left for formalities, questions, or interrogations. On the other hand, she and her mother had spent the past three hours doing nothing but waiting—anxiously and endlessly—for the surgery that meant everything to them. They were terrified for Said, while this unfamiliar young man stood right beside them, literally in their line of sight, fuelling their pain and frustration. Plus, curiosity gnawed at them—why had the head of their household been with this stranger?…

"Did you see the person who hit you, Mr. Sharaf Jaber?" asked Major Bahromov.

"No, sir," Sharaf said, shaking his head. "I didn't have time to figure anything out—I was just so scared. It happened in an instant."

"I understand," Zakir replied. "All right, I'm going to need to take you with me for a simple procedure—I'll need your signed statement declaring that you won't leave the country. That's standard protocol. Later, if necessary, we'll involve your consulate or Interpol."

"Interpol? Why?" Sharaf asked in surprise. "I'm not a criminal. I haven't done anything wrong. I'm so sorry about Dr. Mumtazov! And I'm sorry that we… that we—"

"Speak up!" Bahromov ordered impatiently.

"No, sir, that's… personal," Sharaf mumbled, opting not to continue. "I had nothing to do with it. I was just sitting in the passenger seat—and somehow I got out without any major injuries. Really, it's just my left shoulder that hurts. The paramedic checked it—it's badly bruised."

"Right, I understand," Zakir nodded. "But we'll still need your signed statement."

"Are you serious, Major?!" Malika broke in, switching to Uzbek to speak to the investigator. "What is this about a signed statement or even Interpol? What has this guy done? All he did was ride in our dad's car! Shouldn't you be focusing on the criminal who hit my father? Where is he? Who is he?"

"No, miss, we haven't found him yet," Zakir answered, keeping his composure, though he disliked her tone. "Our team is reviewing camera footage from near the crash site and from directly across from where the two cars collided. I've been told that it was a young man behind the wheel."

"A young man again!" Sitora exclaimed. "It's always these irresponsible young men causing trouble!"

She gave Sharaf a resentful look. He couldn't understand exactly what she was saying, but he picked up on the hostile tone and guessed the general meaning. Despite everything, he was glad

Malika—his half-sister—had, in a way, spoken up for him.

"Mama, calm down," Malika tried once more. "I'm sure the police will find the jerk who hit Dad, and he'll get what's coming to him."

The investigator and Sharaf left together. The two women had no idea that about two hours later, after a visit to the police station, Sharaf returned to the hospital and sat quietly in the courtyard, not daring to go up to the ICU again. Meanwhile, Sitora and Malika finally met with the surgeon and critical care physician who had operated on Said in the intensive care ward.

"Hello," he said wearily but kindly. "I'm Erkin Davlatovich, a neurosurgeon. And you're Dr. Mumtazov's family, correct? Don't be surprised—I know him. We're colleagues, after all. I think everyone in Uzbekistan knows him. Right, so I performed the first operation on Said-aka. It went well. We removed all the glass from his head. Meanwhile, my colleagues stitched up his liver and spleen. We'll monitor his condition going forward—he'll need time to recover. Then he may need more operations. For now, his condition is stable but serious."

"May we see him now?" Sitora asked through tears, desperately hopeful.

"No, he's still asleep and hasn't come around from the anaesthesia," the doctor replied. "And I wouldn't recommend disturbing him. It's already late. I suggest you both go home and get some rest. You'll need your strength to care for him. Come back in the morning—I'll likely allow a short visit then."

"Thank you, Doctor," said Sitora, still unable to stop crying.

"Thank you so much, Dr. Erkin Davlatovich," Malika added. "Do we need to bring any medication for my father?"

"Not for now, no. But I expect we will later. I'll give you a list.

Tomorrow morning, if you have no health restrictions, you could donate blood for Said-aka. He lost over a litre in the accident, so blood is crucial. The blood bank is in the same clinic, just in a different building. The nurse can show you the way."

Once the two women had left, Sharaf went upstairs, found the surgeon, and asked—this time in English—about Dr. Mumtazov's condition. Speaking broken English he hadn't used in years, Dr. Erkin Davlatovich managed to convey the essential information, having first confirmed that the young man was indeed related to Said. Though Sharaf had very little money, he offered to bring anything that might be needed for "Doc Mumtazoff." The surgeon replied, "Not for now. I'll let you know if anything comes up."

10

Sharjah, United Arab Emirates, Archaeological Museum, a few days earlier

A small group of officials—colleagues of archaeologist Nazih Abu Jalil, all specialists in Emirati archaeology—welcomed him to the museum with great honour. Among them were the Head of the State's Department of Tourism and Antiquities, Saud ibn Mahshud; an archaeologist from Abu Dhabi's Department of Culture and Tourism, Abdullah Khalfan Al-Qaabi; and the young head of the Sharjah Archaeology Museum collections, Bob

Downey—an American who had come to the Emirates a few years earlier for an internship and ended up staying permanently.

"Welcome back to your home city of Sharjah!" Mahshud exclaimed warmly.

"Thank you, sir, Head of the Department of Tourism and Antiquities," Nazih replied politely, though without his usual enthusiasm on such occasions.

Everyone present noticed that something was clearly bothering Nazih—he kept glancing around anxiously, as if someone were chasing him.

"Is something wrong, dear Nazih?" Abdullah asked. "Pardon me, but you look flushed—maybe your blood pressure is up. After all, today's especially hot."

"Yes, *ustadi*," Nazih almost whispered. "I really don't feel well. Thank goodness Mr. Bob Downey sent a car for me and my assistant, Ali. We wouldn't have made it back from the desert on our own. Especially not with all the artifacts I found."

"How could we leave you and your assistant on your own, dear *ustadi* Nazih?" Bob said with a smile. "You found an entire hoard worth millions of dirhams! You might say you've outdone Abdullah Al-Qaabi."

"No, no, Bob, *ustadi* Nazih and I are not competitors!" the young Abdullah objected firmly. "As you know, near Abu Dhabi I recently discovered an ancient pearl town 8,500 years old. That's my specialty—ancient ruins—not the applied-art objects that Dr. Nazih focuses on. So I'm truly happy for you, my colleague Nazih! And I wholeheartedly congratulate you on this historic find. Abbasid gold and silver coins—this really is the discovery of the century!"

"You don't know the half of it, my friends: I also found the personal golden diadem of Princess Zubaidah!" Nazih boasted, pride gleaming in his eyes. "It's adorned with some of the purest diamonds and sapphires."

Everyone present warmly congratulated their talented and celebrated colleague.

"So where is the treasure, *ustadi* Nazih?" Bob Downey asked, his eyes shining. "Do you have it with you? I don't see it anywhere. We need to register it and place it in the collection of this esteemed museum as soon as possible."

"For now, I've left the valuables in your car," Nazih admitted. "My assistant Ali and I were so exhausted, we simply couldn't lift the heavy case. Ali's sitting out there in the vehicle, keeping an eye on the coins—just in case."

"Isn't that a bit excessive, sir?" Bob exclaimed. "Were you in some kind of danger?"

"Yes, my friends," Nazih sighed. "Somebody... shot at us! I don't know who—people in a big black SUV. We barely escaped. I was so afraid for our lives."

Bob himself, along with Ali, brought the suitcase containing the ancient Arab coins inside. Once Nazih laid them out on the head of collections' desk, everyone gasped.

"As you can see, dear experts, these gold dinars and silver dirhams—around fifteen hundred years old—have been extraordinarily well preserved," Nazih said, describing their general appearance. "And among them is one truly unique specimen: a silver dirham from Caliph Harun's wife, Princess Zubaidah. Its value at auction could reach... two million U.S. dollars."

"Come now," Bob Downey said with a laugh. "Is that even possible? As far as I know, Abbasid coins don't go for more than three thousand bucks."

"Yes, but not in this case," Nazih replied, shaking his head. "This particular dirham is the only one of its kind in the entire world—left to us by Princess Zubaidah herself!"

"In that case," Bob remarked, "we can't display such a rare coin for general viewing! I propose we keep it in storage, under my strict supervision. And I already know what we'll do: our friends at the Abbasid Palace in Baghdad have requested interesting exhibits the Arab world hasn't yet seen. This will be a one-day guest exhibition, and I'll use that opportunity to temporarily transfer not only the precious silver dirham but also Princess Zubaidah's gold diadem— along with the other Abbasid-era coins."

"Transfer them?" Nazih exclaimed. "But where to, and why, Bob?!"

"It must be done, Nazih," Bob said, without so much as a muscle twitch. "I'll take them to the most secure facility in the Emirates—I know the perfect place, and I'll tell you more about it later. Since no one aside from the few of us knows these treasures once belonged to Princess Zubaidah, I'm certain they'll be far safer during transport than if they remain here in our city. Once we've done everything possible to guarantee their absolute security, only then will we put them on public display in this museum."

After weighing the pros and cons, his colleagues—who had long trusted Bob's impeccable record—unanimously agreed with him.

* * *

Baghdad, Iraq, a café near the Abbasid Palace, a few days later

Following a curt exchange of greetings, Gharib and his "clients" got straight to the point regarding their new "job."

"Mr. Gharib," Sanya began, "could you—as usual, for a good price—give us the latest code to the display case holding the Abbasid Palace's gold coins? And, as you so skilfully did last time, arrange for our unhindered entry into the museum at night?"

"Alex and Johnny, this has become far more risky since that previous theft," Gharib confessed, though he also hoped to use these words to raise his price.

"Our line of work always carries risk," Vanya said calmly. "Otherwise, we wouldn't be making so much money. Same goes for you—thanks to us!"

"I understand," the tour guide murmured. "And how much will you pay me?"

Vanya scribbled an enticing figure on a piece of paper and passed it to Gharib. A grin spread across his face.

"By the way," Gharib recalled, "tomorrow the Palace is receiving some ancient exhibits from Sharjah for a special display, including a truly rare coin—Princess Zubaidah's dirham—and her diadem made of pure gold, studded with diamonds, rubies, and sapphires! What's more, the exhibition will only be on display for one day."

"Well, there you go—destiny's handing them to us on a silver platter!" Sanya said, suddenly more enthusiastic.

"And we need to act fast," Vanya added. "Are you in, or should we find someone else with a bit more nerve?"

"They've beefed up security at the Palace," Gharib warned. "No one but me would even consider taking such a risk. Honestly, even I don't want to lose my job—or end up in prison. I'm not sure what to do…"

Feigning disappointment, Vanya made a show of standing up to leave, with Sanya following suit.

"No, no, please, don't think I'm backing out!" Gharib said nervously, stopping them. "I need the money—desperately!"

"Of course you do," Vanya smirked.

"That's what we thought," Sanya said, nodding in satisfaction with the air of a boss.

"As soon as the director gives me the code to the display case holding Zubaidah's coin—plus the code for the case with the gold dinars from the Palace reserves—I'll get them to you," Gharib explained. "We'll meet tomorrow at seven in the morning by the Palace's seldom-used side entrance, which is normally locked. They'll start ramping up security at eight, specifically for these 'guest' exhibits—extra guards have been brought in from other sites in Baghdad. I'll arrange uniforms for you so you can blend in as security staff. The one snag is that you both look very European."

"No problem," said Vanya. "We'll just pull our caps down low to cover our faces."

"All right," Gharib agreed. "But be extremely careful—keep a low profile. Neither of you speaks Arabic, so stick to a few simple English phrases only if absolutely necessary. But silence is best. If any of the other guards ask a question, just nod. You can manage that. Move in on the displays only when no one else is around. I'll give you the signal. You'll open the locks, and come nighttime, just like before, you slip back in, open the cases quietly, and take what you want. Do everything you can not to get caught by our director or the police. And… I'm begging you—whatever happens, I must remain above suspicion!"

"Naturally," Sanya agreed confidently.

"Count on it," Vanya confirmed, signalling "okay" to Gharib with his hand.

11

Baghdad, Mesopotamia, Abbasid Caliphate, 810 CE

"Mother, as the best and most beloved of your three sons, do I not have the right to expect your support?" asked Prince Ma'mun, the second son of Caliph Harun, who had travelled from ar-Raqqah to Baghdad on business.

"What are you talking about, my son? And why this line of conversation?" Princess Zubaidah responded, as though she had no idea what he meant. Ma'mun noticed that, for some reason, she had chosen to wear her magnificent gold diadem set with diamonds and sapphires to their meeting.

It seems Amin tricked her, Prince Ma'mun thought, *leading her to believe she has a royal share of authority in this Caliphate—some power, at least over her own jewellery! Ridiculous. Amin himself has no real power here.*

"Amin wasn't born to rule the Caliphate, Mother, but I was!" Ma'mun declared heatedly. "Give me your full support—speak well of me wherever you go, praise me to our subjects, raise me up! I will remember that once I ascend the throne… Especially since I hear Amin occasionally treats you with disrespect."

"Well… he's gotten better," his mother said with a slight smile. "Amin has granted me a respectable allowance—enough for me to live quite comfortably."

"Oh? And what of it?" Ma'mun sneered. He had never once wondered whether she had anything to live on; he had always assumed his father, Harun, had left her more than enough wealth.

"Amin even allowed a coin to be minted with my name on it," Zubaidah explained. "A silver dirham! It's so beautiful… It really was a kind gesture."

"When I become Arab Caliph, Mother, I'll let you mint a hundred kinds of coins with your name!" Ma'mun promised, tossing out grand assurances without the slightest intention of keeping track.

"What do you want from me, my son?" Zubaidah sighed wearily, placing little faith in his promises.

"Get a hold of Father's turban from Caliph Amin—or rather, the so-called Caliph, for now!" Ma'mun demanded excitedly. "The one set with that lemon-sized pearl. I adore it… Such a treasure should belong only to a true, strong Caliph! That is, to me!"

Zubaidah looked her son over carefully, evaluating him, and paused before replying.

"You can have that marvellous turban with its perfect pearl once you become Caliph," Zubaidah said after a moment's thought.

"How can you not understand, Mother?!" Ma'mun flared. "I want that exquisite pearl now! Before my dear elder brother hides it away somewhere!"

"Well, I'll consider it," Zubaidah said evasively, unsettled by Ma'mun's near-regal anger. "If there's some way I can help, I'll let you know… And now I have no doubt that very soon, you'll be the one to become Caliph of Arabia, Ma'mun."

* * *

Marakanda, Hazrat Khizr Mosque—the residence of Khorasan's governor, 811 CE

Sumptuously dressed, Caliph Amin paced nervously through the most luxurious guest chambers—lodgings provided by his Khorasan governor, Mahan—casting anxious, dissatisfied glances at the man. His gaze betrayed both displeasure and fear.

"Mahan, I'm worried! You know that last year my brother Ma'mun and I locked horns, sparking a civil war in the Abbasid realm. I appointed you as the ruler of Khorasan and, in a special gesture of trust, put you in charge of my forty-thousand-strong army. Why, pray tell?!"

"To subdue your bro—uh, Prince Ma'mun, my lord," Mahan replied. "And to prevent him from usurping your throne."

"Exactly!" Amin shouted. "So why are you hesitating? Why is Ma'mun still alive? And free! I even know he's gathered an army!"

"Don't worry, my lord," Mahan ventured, trying to stand his ground. "Ma'mun's forces are quite small—no more than five thousand soldiers."

"Yes, but their leader is that fearless Tahir," Amin reminded him. "He lost an eye fighting the rebel Rafi ibn Layth, yet he never turned against the Caliphate or the Abbasids. He remains loyal. Though… what am I saying? If only I had such a brave commander! I would… But no, the cunning fox Ma'mun snapped him up somehow! What did he entice him with, do you think?

Promised him uncountable riches? Or perhaps dangled your post in front of him—eh, Governor of Khorasan?"

"I hope not, my lord," Mahan said, frowning. "I'd certainly find out if that were the case."

"Oh, you know nothing," Amin said, waving him off. "Enough. Get out of here—go back to your quarters! And think hard about how to crush Ma'mun and that Tahir."

"I'll be bringing silver chains to bind Ma'mun and deliver him back to Baghdad," Mahan retorted confidently. "And as for Tahir… we'll handle him too!"

* * *

Western Khorasan, Rayy, Abbasid Caliphate — Tahir's military headquarters, 811 CE, sometime later

"Congratulations on a great and glorious victory, my dear friend!" Prince Ma'mun exclaimed, patting Tahir on the shoulder. He was ordinarily sparing with praise. "And thank you. You're so powerful! How did you do it? My troops are few compared to the army of Amin and Mahan. When their forces approached Rayy, the entire province was thrown into panic—even I considered fleeing. But you weren't afraid of the risk at all, leading an attack on their huge army! In the end, Mahan was crushed—killed—and his men scattered in terror throughout the west."

"I'm glad, my lord, that I was able to be of service," Tahir replied. He was content but still catching his breath after the gruelling battle. "Even my father, Husayn, didn't want me to go to this war— he feared for my life. But by the grace of the Almighty, it's ended well for us. Your position, Your Highness, is now stronger, and so

I also congratulate you on your victory. Your main opponents have lost manpower, their military leader, and Prince Amin's prestige has taken a severe blow."

"Thank you for not calling him Caliph in my presence," Ma'mun noted, pleased.

"You are forever my only Caliph," Tahir declared, professing his loyalty.

"So, what are your strategic plans now, my greatest warrior and best of friends?" Ma'mun asked, clearly hoping for continued support in the war.

"I'll march west, my lord," Tahir explained. "I need to defeat another force of twenty thousand men under Abd al-Rahman ibn Jabal. After that, there will be further battles near Persian Hamadan and Mesopotamian Hulwan. I'm certain this will help secure the throne for you, my lord!"

"Thank you, Tahir," Ma'mun said with a smile. "If you like, I'll send couriers with a message to your lovely wife Benu, letting her know you're all right."

"Yes, please, my lord," Tahir replied in a subdued tone, trying to hide his emotion and longing for his wife while in the prince's presence. If only he could fly home to his loved one that very moment! "May God reward you for your kindness."

"Come now," Ma'mun said, patting Tahir's shoulder again. "You deserve it. Without Mahan, my brother Amin—his disheartened army in shambles—is doomed. Yes, for now, he clings to power, but I'm convinced he'll lose it soon. He's unfit to be ruler of the world. I am the Caliph of Arabia—me, not him or anyone else! Do you agree with me?"

"Yes, my lord," Tahir answered mechanically, his mind drifting to his wife and two young sons, whom he already missed terribly.

"Amin hadn't even settled on the throne before he minted gold dinars bearing his name," Ma'mun remarked. "I want my own gold! Coins with my name! I want them now! I'll speak to my friend, the head of the mint in Sharijah (modern Sharjah)."

"Excellent, my prince," Tahir nodded. At that moment, he resolved to send a messenger to his family himself, realizing the prince—busy as he was—might easily forget to do so.

12

Tashkent–Samarkand, 2023

Feeling overwhelmed by everything that had happened, Sharaf headed downstairs, wondering what he should do next: stay the night at the hospital—if that was even allowed—or find some affordable temporary lodging.

He took out his phone and opened the internet, thinking he might try to find a nearby hostel with good guest reviews, given that paying for a hotel seemed like an unnecessary expense. In a way, he was glad he had taken Said's advice not to spend too much of his limited funds on gifts for the doctor's family. Plus, he still had some cookies left—the ones he never got to give as a present and could now eat himself. He was a bit hungry, since he'd last eaten quite some time ago at lunch with Said.

Munching on a couple of cookies, Sharaf carefully searched

for suitable accommodations. One hostel's photos and service descriptions caught his eye more than the others: the price and advertised quality seemed balanced, and it was located nearby. Still, he worried whether the staff would speak English. After all, it was a hostel, not a hotel, and he didn't speak either of the local languages. But to the pleasant surprise of Tashkent's guest, when he called, the hostel administrator picked up and spoke decent English.

Check-in went relatively smoothly, despite it being the high season for guest accommodations. It was already late at night, which meant fewer arrivals. Sharaf booked a room for three nights and was delighted to find that, in the communal kitchen, tea with sugar and dried bread rings were available at no extra charge.

Exhausted by the day's dramatic events, he fell asleep almost immediately.

At eight in the morning, after grabbing the breakfast included with his stay, Sharaf rushed back to the hospital to check on Said's condition.

However, there was no new information; his biological father's status remained "stable but serious," and he had not yet regained consciousness.

Not knowing what else to do, and in no mood to wander around an unfamiliar city, Sharaf decided to return to the hostel.

His attention was drawn to some photographs on the wall above the reception desk: lovely pictures of Uzbekistan's ancient cities—Bukhara, Samarkand, and Khiva—with a sign above them that read "Экскурсии – Excursions."

Just then, he noticed a charming young woman standing near the reception desk, jotting something down in her notepad. Seeing this strikingly beautiful lady, Sharaf felt a pang of guilt at the realization that, ever since arriving in Tashkent, he hadn't once thought about his own beloved, Jahiza.

When she lifted her head and noticed Sharaf, the receptionist said something to him in Uzbek. Mistaking him for a local—he resembled Said Mumtazov—she assumed he was a native of the country. But when Sharaf didn't understand, she switched to English:

"Sir, sorry—I realize now you're a foreigner. May I ask where you're visiting from?"

Sharaf replied that he was from Qatar's capital city and was here as a guest.

"Wonderful! Would you like to visit one of the oldest and most beautiful cities in the world—Samarkand—today?" the young woman offered. "I started signing people up two days ago, but there are still three spots left. This tour is for international visitors, conducted in English. We won't be gone too long—we leave in about an hour and should be back before dark, around seven or eight in the evening. How does that sound?"

"I'd love to go, miss," Sharaf said with a smile. He was thinking how, at this point, he could do nothing more for Said, nor could he count on any assistance from the doctor's family. Meanwhile, he really needed to push forward with his quest for Khorasan's treasures!

After weighing the pros and cons, he decided not to pass up the chance. One concern remained:

"Excuse me, miss—this excursion must be expensive?"

The woman seemed surprisingly perceptive, guessing that this foreign guest might not have a lot of money. She replied:

"How about this: you just pay for your seat on the bus—that covers the driver's fee. As for my services as a guide, I won't charge you this time."

"That's… not really right," Sharaf said, embarrassed.

"It's perfectly all right," she insisted. "By the way, you can just call me Barno—that's my name. I'm a tour guide with a travel company; we partner with many hotels and hostels across Uzbekistan. And this way, I can get in some extra English practice, which I can always use to improve my spoken fluency. Will you agree to that?"

"Yes, of course, miss," Sharaf answered. "My name is Sharaf, from Doha—I'm a student. I'll be happy to help however I can. To be honest, visiting Samarkand has always been a huge dream of mine! Thank you so much for this opportunity."

"Excellent," Barno said with a smile. "Then be at the hostel exit in exactly one hour. Our bus will be waiting on the main road outside."

13

On the road, Barno and Sharaf had the chance to chat. Sharaf told the young tour guide a little about himself and his family. Then, without revealing his main goals or mission to this pleasant yet entirely unfamiliar person, he began asking her questions about the history of Khorasan—especially about its wealth and the most renowned figures who had possessed it. Barno shared what she knew with her foreign guest.

"Strange that a foreigner would be interested in Khorasan," she remarked. "Not all locals here know the history of their own region! Where does your interest in it come from?"

Sharaf grew flustered. For the first time, he wondered if he should tell this kind girl about the purpose of his journey—maybe she could help him even more. But he held back for now.

At that moment, Barno said something that left him momentarily speechless:

"I'm sure that on the territory of what used to be Khorasan— that is, somewhere in Samarkand, Bukhara, or Khiva—a great many treasures are hidden, especially from the era of the Arab Abbasid dynasty and the Turkic Tahirid dynasty. But… you'd need a map to find them."

Barno showed the foreign tourists Samarkand's most noteworthy sights: Registan Square, the Shah-i-Zinda architectural complex, the Gur-e-Amir mausoleum of Amir Timur and the Timurid dynasty, the Mirzo Ulug'bek madrasa, the Tilya Kori madrasa, and others. Despite her youth, she was an experienced guide who spoke with passion, enthusiasm, and an engaging style.

After the tour, the guests were free to explore the marvellous ancient city at their own pace.

Nearly all the tourists on this excursion had come in pairs or as part of a group. Sharaf, however, was alone. Noticing he seemed a bit at a loss, the perceptive Barno offered to keep him company— making it clear from the start that their relationship would be strictly professional and purely friendly, and that crossing those boundaries was absolutely out of the question. Sharaf, quickly grasping her point, blushed and immediately assured her he would never do anything to offend such a kind and lovely girl.

They walked around the city for a while, taking several selfies at Sharaf's request as keepsakes, then stopped at a café. Despite his modest budget, Sharaf—being a polite young man—paid for both of them. It was a late-afternoon snack: tea, pastries, and cakes.

Barno thanked her companion.

Suddenly, she glanced around anxiously and said with a hint of fear:

"Sharaf, for some reason I feel like someone is watching me," she confided in her new friend. "It's such a strange sensation… I can't see anyone obvious, but… it's like someone's following my every step. Have you noticed anything like that?"

"No, miss," Sharaf replied in surprise.

A moment later she said,

"I'll step away for just a minute to freshen up. Please wait here for me, and we can head to our bus together."

"Yes, of course, miss," Sharaf answered, smiling as he calmly finished his pastry.

However, the young foreigner's composure began to evaporate about ten minutes after Barno had gone to the restroom. He decided to wait a bit longer, thinking perhaps she felt unwell from the heat or the food. But after twenty minutes passed and she still hadn't returned to the café hall, Sharaf grew genuinely worried. He got up and headed toward the restroom himself. For a minute more he waited outside the door, anxiously asking each woman who exited—first in English, then in Arabic—whether they had seen a beautiful girl inside with long chestnut hair and green eyes. None of them, failing to understand him, gave anything but a shrug or a shake of the head.

At last, despairing and deeply concerned for his young companion and guide—whom he already admired and felt fond of—Sharaf did something he had never done in his life: he burst into the women's restroom and inspected every inch of it.

But Barno was nowhere to be found. Sharaf circled the café twice, all in vain. She was simply gone—no sign of her, no trace.

Now thoroughly alarmed, Sharaf decided to head alone to the bus parking area, clinging to the faint hope that perhaps some silly misunderstanding had occurred and Barno, forgetting him for a moment, had gone there by herself.

The entire group was already assembled, and the driver, spotting Sharaf, grumbled something in annoyance.

"Sorry, sir, for being late," the young man began apologizing, guessing the cause of the driver's irritation. The driver, who spoke no English, didn't understand him. "I was waiting for our guide, Barno. We walked around the city together, then ate at a café. But all of a sudden… she disappeared. And she's not here either? Barno! Barno!!"

Hearing the familiar name, the driver responded,

"She's not here! What are you shouting for? I have no idea where she ran off to."

A polite, good-natured man in the group, who apparently spoke some Russian and English, translated what the driver was saying for Sharaf.

"My shift ends at six!" the heavy-set driver behind the wheel was shouting. "And it's already past five. That means we won't get back until nine, and I won't be home before ten. It's a disgrace to keep waiting around so long! Suit yourselves, but I'm leaving. The entire group is ready to go. Maybe Barno got held up by something urgent… I don't know. I'm calling for departure!"

"In that case—yes, please go," Sharaf told him through the translator. "I'll stay and look for Barno. I can't just leave. I'm worried something might have happened to her. If I find her, we'll hitch a ride back to Tashkent."

Everyone agreed to this arrangement. The tour bus of foreign visitors departed for the capital's hostel, leaving Sharaf alone on the square, consumed by a single thought: Where was Barno? What had happened to her? Where should he look?

He suddenly wondered if all this might have something to do with him. Could someone have learned about his treasure map and abducted Barno in order to blackmail him somehow? But for the moment, the young man from Qatar had no answers.

14

Baghdad, Iraq, the Abbasid Palace, 2023, the same period

The Palace guides—including Gharib—were busy talking to the throngs of visitors about the priceless historical items on display, brought in from Sharjah: the golden diadem belonging to Princess Zubaidah and a unique silver dirham stamped with her name in her honour.

"The crowns of Arab princesses—the wives of the Caliphs— often called *tiqa-tiara*, or *diadem*, represent a symbol of feminine beauty, power, and wealth. They were widely used in the Arab world and held the status of official regalia. These diadems appeared during the heyday of Arab culture in the ninth century, when the Abbasid dynasty's rule over the Arab Caliphate made it the centre of Eastern civilization. You can see that this diadem of Princess Zubaidah dates to the early ninth century and was fashioned from gold and numerous precious stones, including diamonds and sapphires."

As a wave of visitors flooded the Palace on this remarkable day, gazing with keen interest at the artifacts behind their impregnable, thick-glass showcases equipped with electronic lock codes, the Palace staff continued their commentary:

"According to legend, Caliph Harun's famous widow, Princess Zubaidah, secretly wore this diadem so that her greedy sons, Amin and Ma'mun, wouldn't seize it from her and give it to one of their wives. The crowns and diadems of Caliphs' wives were widely known throughout the Arab world and were even exhibited at fairs and public events in those days. They were used for various ceremonies—weddings, ruler inaugurations, and other festive occasions. Over time, these crowns became symbols of beauty and femininity. They came to be recognized as some of the most exquisite and luxurious objects crafted in the Arab world—true emblems of their owners' high status and wealth. Enjoy them, dear visitors, for this exhibit is here for one day only and will return to Sharjah tomorrow."

* * *

That night, after the last visitor had gone, Palace guard Haidar suddenly "sprouted up" like a mushroom near the display cases holding the precious exhibits from Sharjah. He was startled to see... two tall, fair-skinned "guards" standing beside the cases, wearing the exact same uniform as his own—two men clearly not of Arab origin. Haidar instantly realized he had never seen either of them before; he knew exactly who was on duty that night, and these two were definitely outsiders.

His shock deepened when he noticed the men—completely ignoring the blaring alarm—swiftly but carefully removing the

Palace's most valuable exhibits from the cases and packing them into a black rucksack.

"Stop the thieves!" Haidar shouted into his radio, forgetting to specify his exact location. Deep down, he assumed the other guards would know precisely where the criminals would strike on a night like this.

Haidar charged toward the tall Europeans.

"Hey! Stop! What do you think you're doing?!" he yelled in Arabic.

Sanya and Vanya, the impostor "guards," didn't understand the words, but his gestures and tone made the meaning unmistakably clear.

No sooner had Haidar grabbed Vanya's arm—while simultaneously trying to land a punch on Sanya's face—than Sanya fired two bursts of pepper spray directly into Haidar's eyes. Roaring in pain, the real Palace guard let go, and Vanya easily pulled himself free.

Strong and well-trained, Sanya quickly recovered from Haidar's initial strike.

Before the stunned guard could collect himself, the two thieves bolted for the exit. The other two guards on night duty, Muhammad and Bahautdin—exhausted from a gruelling day and half-asleep—rushed around with flashlights in a confused attempt to find the burglars, but to no avail.

By the time they reached the main entrance, the intruders had vanished without a trace.

Sanya and Vanya sprinted to the car they'd rented earlier through a car-sharing service. Vanya jumped behind the wheel, and they sped away from the Palace so fast that, within minutes, they were back at their hotel.

After catching their breath and sipping some tea, the partners-in-crime decided to take a closer look at what they had stashed in their backpack. Sanya was visibly thrilled with their "fat" haul.

"Let's see our awesome 'catch'!" he crowed, beaming like a kid in a candy store.

"We almost got caught!" Vanya said more cautiously, though he too was pleased. "I'm worried that guard might've gotten a good look at us. If he tells the police, we're finished—prison for major theft! We'd lose our client, Kudrat, and all our plans for cruises. Our whole future would go down the drain."

"Stop whining. Nothing's going down any drain," Sanya snapped back, grinning as he unzipped the backpack.

He pulled everything out and laid it across the table.

"Gold, Vanechka! This is our gold!" the thief exulted. "Wait… what the…?"

"Hey, Sanyok—did you try to dupe me?!" Vanya snapped when he saw something was off. "Fess up: where and when did you swap out the 'real' gold for this junk? These are copper coins! Or maybe aluminium? And what's this scrap of metal that looks like a headband? That's supposed to be the Arab princess's crown?!"

"A diadem," Sanya corrected. "It was supposed to be gold, with diamonds and sapphires—an Arab relic. Ninth century."

"I know!!" Vanya shouted. "The question is, where did this switch happen?! Huh?!"

"I don't know, Vanechka, I swear," Sanya protested, nearly in tears, just as baffled. "You saw it yourself: from the moment we grabbed *this* out of the Palace display cases, I've been in full view of you. I didn't do this! Why accuse me? Maybe it was you?!"

"What—*me*?" Vanya glowered. "Stole the real jewels from right under your nose? Are you insane?"

"You're the one accusing me," Sanya whined, looking offended. "I'm just as stunned as you are!"

"Could someone else have 'scouted' us in the Palace beforehand?" Vanya wondered aloud. "If so, we need to get out of Baghdad before the cops nab us. First flight back to Tashkent!"

"But how?!" Sanya moaned. "We're leaving empty-handed—with no gold? I hate this idea!"

"And do you want to rot in an Iraqi prison?" Vanya retorted.

"No, I don't!" Sanya admitted. "But maybe we can go back to the Palace? Please, Vanechka…"

"Man, that guard really clocked you hard," Vanya muttered, hastily packing his things. "Must've rattled your brains."

"Huh? Why do you say that?" Sanya asked.

"Because you're talking complete nonsense," Vanya shot back. "I bet the place is already swarming with security and police. If we don't hurry, we won't escape!"

"Don't worry—we'll escape just fine," Sanya insisted. "I just can't stand leaving all that real gold behind! Maybe I ought to learn how to pray like these Arabs… so we catch a break someday."

"You'd better pray Kudrat doesn't wring our necks for this fiasco," Vanya sneered. "If the cops arrest us, we'll keep quiet. But he'll be furious we didn't get the map he wanted. That was the real job."

"We'll figure something out in Tashkent," Sanya responded, also hurrying to pack for their getaway. "We'll plan our next move—where and how to find the second half of Kudrat's map."

15

Baghdad – The Road to Jalak (Damascus), Abbasid Caliphate, 812 CE

By now, Caliph Amin was desperately trying to shore up his forces by forging alliances with Arab tribes from Jazira and Syria.

"Salih, travel to Syria with Mahan's son, Hussein," Amin said to one of his most trusted warriors. "Mobilize your units."

"Yes, my lord," the old warrior replied obediently. "But…"

"But what?"

"As long as this Hussein doesn't let us down!" Salih said, voicing his concern. "I don't really trust him. There's something odd and unreliable about him. It's unclear what he's really after."

"I think he's trying to earn my favour so he can become governor of Khorasan," Caliph Amin said confidently, "just like his father Mahan."

"Well… you would know best, my lord," Salih replied evasively.

* * *

Late one cool night, Lubana slipped quietly into her and the Caliph's chambers, approached the bed, and stroked her royal husband's hair. She asked:

"My lord, my habibi, things… aren't going so well for us, are they? Maybe our son and I should leave—go somewhere far away while this bloody civil war continues here?"

"Are you afraid for yourself, my habibti?" Amin asked, with a note of disapproval.

"No, not for myself—for our son," Lubana replied calmly. "And for you as well, my dear. Why haven't you been able to defeat that upstart, Prince Ma'mun? After all, your army is much larger!"

"Because he has one talented and bold strategist. They call him the one-eyed Tahir," the Caliph replied. "He's foiling my every plan and keeping me from winning this war. And that, unfortunately, isn't the end of it. I'm not even sure I should tell you this, my dear—after all, you don't really understand politics. But let me try to simplify. My efforts have failed in part because of longstanding conflicts between the Qays and Kalb tribes. Then there's the Syrians' unwillingness to get involved in this civil war. But more than that—the Abna', the entire Khorasan army, refuses to cooperate with Arab tribes or make political concessions. It seems the people of Khorasan feel their interests are not being properly represented. So my attempts to gain Arab support have backfired—they've been unsuccessful. And then there's this Hussein—nothing but a hypocrite, a coward, and a traitor!"

"Why is that?" asked Lubana. "And who is this Hussein?"

"In Khorasan, I had a governor—someone who managed things effectively—named Mahan," Caliph Amin began to explain to his wife.

"Yes, I recall," Lubana nodded. "But wasn't he killed in the war?"

"Yes, by Tahir's warriors!" Amin exclaimed, agitated. "They showed no regard for the fact that Mahan served our Caliphate faithfully! Well, Mahan had a son—Hussein ibn Ali. By all logic, he should be on my side, flying my banners, avenging his father's death at the hands of those Ma'munite jackals—especially Tahir!

Wouldn't you say so, Lubana?"

"Certainly, my habibi," Amin's wife agreed. "So what is he doing instead?"

"I've heard that Hussein openly—without shame or pretence—supports my brazen brother Ma'mun," Caliph Amin said heatedly. "Ma'mun, who so shamelessly and dishonourably dares to claim my throne, even though, praise be to the Almighty, I am still alive! As we've discussed, our father explicitly commanded all of us—his sons—not to break the line of succession by shedding blood. But Ma'mun is willing to spill innocent blood without end, all for the throne. And I know why."

"Why, my dear?" Lubana asked, fighting off drowsiness. "Perhaps he's just power-hungry?"

"Possibly that too," Amin snorted, "but that isn't the main reason. Gold! Treasure! That's what he covets and prizes above all else. Word has it he's even placed an order at the Mint to produce gold dinars bearing his name—sidestepping me! Can you imagine? With the Caliph still alive! But no matter. Damascus has an excellent mint as well. I'll have them strike new gold coins with my name—they'll be the most valuable in the Caliphate. I should have seized part of the rich inheritance we all received from our father, Harun, by force. But I spared him and our younger brother. Ma'mun doesn't appreciate my generosity; now he's waging war against me, spreading lies that I'm a bad ruler who doesn't care about the people! As if he'd actually look after his subjects if he becomes Caliph!"

"I'm afraid his issuing gold coins is not a good sign, habibi," Lubana said worriedly. "Today, Prince Ma'mun mints his own dinars; tomorrow, at this rate, he'll be seated on your throne. And if anything should happen… oh, no—pardon me, husband, I don't want to say it. But if it does… where will our son and I run then?"

16

Baghdad, Iraq, the Abbasid Palace, the day after the theft

Before the sanctuary of culture and art opened its doors, the Palace Director and Head of Security, Basil, gathered all the staff in his office—guards, guides, and the other employees hired just for the day of the guest exhibition from Sharjah.

"Friends, colleagues!" Basil began ceremoniously. "First of all, allow me to thank all of you for your fine, responsible, and conscientious work—and for your vigilance! Thanks to you, I'm pleased to say the exhibition went smoothly. Everything is in good shape! All the guest exhibits have already been collected and packed for transport, and in an hour, when the special vehicle arrives, they will be returned home."

Everyone present applauded and nodded approvingly.

Gharib tensed up, still not understanding what was going on.

How can it all be 'in good shape'? he wondered anxiously. *Nothing was stolen? Could it be that Alex and Johnny didn't manage to pull it off? They promised to hand me two gold dinars and the main part of my fee! Something must've gone wrong, and they failed… But Basil seems calm… Maybe… Maybe that's for the best. I may lose out on the money, but at least I keep my job!*

The director continued, "Additionally, I'd like to extend heartfelt thanks to all of our partners from other cultural institutions who helped with security and guided tours for this one-day exhibition.

Friends, thank you all so much. Right after this meeting, you can go to the accounting department to collect your pay for this challenging day's work, then head back to your offices."

Gharib brightened even more when he saw Basil glance at him as warmly and pleasantly as he did at everyone else.

All right, no problem! he thought. *I can think up a hundred other ways to swipe the gold from those displays some other time. It's just a pity the Sharjah exhibit leaves today... but at least the director and the security guys aren't suspecting me of anything!*

When the meeting ended and everyone began to disperse, Basil asked Gharib and three of his guards—Haidar, Muhammad, and Bahautdin—to stay "for a moment." Gharib was caught off guard, but seeing the director's calm, friendly expression again, he relaxed. Still, he was puzzled: Why would Basil want to speak with them? And why was he, a guide, included with the guards?

"Friends, pull up a chair," the director offered.

Gharib sat. To his surprise, the three guards took seats around him in such a way that they blocked all possible exits, effectively surrounding him. He stiffened.

"Are you afraid of something, dear sir?" the director asked with a smile.

"Me?!" the guide stammered. "N-no... I... I'm not afraid. Did... did something happen?"

"You tell us!" the director said, still smiling. "You probably know better than anyone."

"Me?!" the guide repeated, now sweating with fear. "No. I don't know anything."

"Really?" Haidar asked in astonishment. "Not even about the break-in last night?"

"A br-break-in?!" Gharib's face turned red. "A break-in... here at the Palace?"

"How did you guess?" Muhammad whistled. "Or did you actually know?"

"N-n-no, I... I didn't know... I don't know!" Gharib stammered, his shoulders slumping. "But you yourself said, Mr. Director—Master Basil—that 'the exhibition went smoothly,' that 'everything's in good shape.' So... then...?"

"Yes, indeed," Basil replied. "I am quite grateful to Haidar and the others for coming up with a way to protect the valuable exhibits—both ours and the ones on loan. Otherwise, I wouldn't be able to repay Sharjah for these jewels for the rest of my life! Right now, all of the guest exhibits have been securely packed and concealed until their departure for the Emirates. So well hidden that even I, if I didn't already know exactly where they were, wouldn't be able to find them. I see you're surprised they're all still here—that the thieves failed to steal them, right?"

Gharib stayed silent, not knowing what to say anymore, realizing that nobody here believed his denials.

"May I, *ustadi* Basil?" Haidar asked the director.

"Yes, of course," their boss nodded.

"When your thieving associates, disguised as security guards, opened the electronic locks to the display cases containing those precious artifacts—using the codes you gave them—" Haidar began, "our system administrator's server instantly received break-in signals indicating that those locks had been tampered with. Do you see?"

"N-no," Gharib admitted. He truly didn't understand how it worked technically—and was terrified that the director and guards now knew everything about him and would turn him in to the police.

"The plan was," Muhammad joined in, "that yesterday, once you had done your routine daily cleaning of the display case containing the Palace's gold dinars—because you're the one responsible for that—we'd have our system admin change the electronic lock code on the server. That way, any attempt to open that lock with the wrong code would instantly send a break-in alert. In fact, the server receives a signal whenever someone opens a lock, even if the code is correct—it just shows up as a green light. For an incorrect code, it lights up red. Which is exactly what happened yesterday."

"And as for the visiting exhibits," Basil continued, "Princess Zubaidah's golden diadem with precious stones, and that one-of-a-kind dirham stamped with her name. As you know, Gharib, no staff members—especially guides—were permitted to open the display cases containing them. In fact, none of the guides were even told their lock codes! I alone had the genuine codes, at least at first."

"But that left us with a question," Haidar went on. "How do we catch the thieves, and you, their accomplice? Because the danger of someone stealing those newly arrived valuables was real. Such risks always exist with knowledgeable criminals."

"And most importantly, how do we preserve the diadem and that priceless silver dirham belonging to the princess, so we can return them safely to Sharjah?" Bahautdin added. "Especially if we have a cunning 'rat'—an inside man—right here in the Palace?"

"Which is why," Haidar explained, "I suggested to Master Basil that immediately after the exhibit—where, of course, the genuine and very precious pieces were on display—we do a switch, replacing them with fakes provided by the Sharjah Archaeological Museum, just in case we needed them. We swapped them out swiftly, without you, Gharib, or any other employees noticing…"

"Yes, because we suspected the thieves could be among the

guards," Basil interjected, "but we weren't sure which ones."

"Indeed!" Haidar nodded. "Then, Gharib, suspecting you above everyone else, we deliberately gave you the correct codes for the two most important display cases with the visiting exhibits—but only after the exhibits had been swapped! And we programmed the locks so that if someone used that code to open them, the server would receive an alert with a red light, just as if the code was wrong. We were able to preserve the exhibits and confirm that you were the one acting as the thieves' lookout."

"Didn't it strike you as suspicious, Gharib," Muhammad asked, "that all the guides were explicitly told not to touch those two display cases or open them under any circumstances—and that none of them were given the codes? Yet you were an exception. You must have been sure nobody suspected you, am I right?"

Gharib lowered his head in shame.

"So what about th–those two 'guards'?" he asked.

"You mean your thief friends?" Bahautdin sneered. "Unfortunately, they escaped. But you've seen them face-to-face! If you don't want to end up in jail as their accomplice, you'll help us track them down, right?"

"You're… not going to turn me over to the police now?" Gharib asked in amazement.

"For now, no," the director replied, shaking his head. "We don't want extra publicity—that would damage the reputation of our fine Palace. But you are, of course, fired. And if you don't want to end up in prison, you'll do your best to help us catch the thieves. Agreed?"

"Of course," Gharib said, relieved that things were turning out more or less okay for him. "Tell me, do I… have a chance to redeem myself? I swear I'll turn over a new leaf!"

"Not at the moment," Basil answered. "But in time… perhaps

I'll think about it. Once I really see that you've changed your ways—stopped being so greedy and dishonourable, and no longer slander others without shame or conscience. You're aware that because of you, I unjustly fired an honest man, our guide Ikram. Naturally, I'll apologize to him and offer him his position back. As for you, Gharib—go on your way and think about your actions. I suggest you don't leave the city; we may still need you."

"Forgive me for everything, colleagues," Gharib croaked guiltily. "I'd be happy to help you capture the thieves. But they basically didn't steal anything of value, right? They only got some cheap fake jewels. And… they're foreigners. I don't even know what country they came from. All I know is… their English was awful! I could barely understand them. But I promise: if they ever come back to Baghdad and show up here, I'll let you know right away."

***

Samarkand, the day Barno disappeared

Evening was falling, and Sharaf suddenly thought of going to the authorities.

Checking his phone's navigator for the nearest police station, he went inside, trying to explain everything to staff who spoke neither English nor Arabic. He decided to show them on his phone a photo of Barno from their pictures together that day.

The duty officer reported to the investigator, Captain Ibrahim Salimov, that some young foreigner—who spoke neither Uzbek nor Russian—seemed to be looking for a girl he knew, since he kept shoving her photo in the duty officer's face.

Luckily for Sharaf—and to his great relief—it turned out

Ibrahim Salimov spoke a little Arabic because his mother had taught that language at an institute.

"So this girl is missing?" the investigator clarified. "What's her name?"

"Barno," Sharaf replied. "But I'm afraid I never got her last name."

"Do you know the address of this café?" asked Ibrahim. "All right. My shift's actually over, but if I just leave you here by yourself, my mother wouldn't understand when she finds out. She once had a work trip to Doha, and whenever she couldn't find something, your hospitable, caring people always helped her out, pointing her the right way. Let's go, Sharaf—right now, we'll drive to that café in my car. I know they work late there, until about eleven in the evening. I'll ask the management for permission to look at the security camera footage. Let's hope we learn at least something about your young woman today."

Sharaf started to say that Barno wasn't really "his" girl, that his beloved Jahiza was waiting back in Doha for his "heroic feats" on her behalf. But he realized this wasn't the time to talk about romantic matters with a stranger—more so, a police officer. Now was not the moment for heartfelt confessions. A person was missing! A good person. A sweet, kind girl, even if Sharaf himself didn't know her well.

"They don't have cameras in or right outside the restrooms," Ibrahim said, "but look here, Sharaf—these are recordings from the café's exit. Tell me—is that Barno?"

"Yes… it seems to be," Sharaf said uncertainly, because it looked like she was either drunk or in a deep sleep, which surprised him. "Actually… Yes, that is her. But what—are those men dragging her into their car? Are they taking her away by force?"

"Looks that way," Salimov nodded. "Seems they drugged her or got her intoxicated with something. And… I'm afraid you were right to be worried. It very much looks like a kidnapping."

"How… and where will we find her now?" Sharaf asked anxiously.

"I'll run the car's license plate in our system," Ibrahim said. "We're going on a search!"

On the one hand, Sharaf was relieved to at least have some information about Barno—a glimmer of hope for her rescue.

On the other hand, it was still unclear where she was, who might be holding her captive, or who had taken her—and why, for what obviously criminal and devious purpose. Who could she have angered? Or what might she know?

It's my fault, Sharaf thought, deciding for now not to voice his suspicions to Captain Salimov. *On the bus, as I was rummaging in my bag for a bottle of water, I pulled everything out—including that ancient piece of fabric with the map! I never imagined one of the nearby passengers or tourists might have spotted it. But maybe they did. Maybe Barno was abducted by someone planning to force me to hand over the treasure map of Khorasan… Or maybe I'm talking nonsense. Still… what if it's true?… Barno, where are you? What's happened to you?*

17

Baghdad – Tashkent, 2023

Sanya and Vanya had no intention of hiding from their influential boss, Kudrat Valiev. Working for him still seemed profitable—at least in the long run.

But the two of them were dumbfounded when, at Tashkent Airport, they were "cordially" greeted by a pair of brawny thugs. These tall, muscle-bound men quickly hauled them over to a black SUV, bending them in half as they went. Their "welcome speech" for the pair of travellers just returned from Baghdad was brief and convincing: "The boss is waiting for you!" With that, the goons shoved skinny Sanya and Vanya into the car and drove them to Kudrat's hotel room.

Following what Kudrat considered a "useful lesson" involving four powerful fists, he told the bruisers:

"All right, that's enough. I think they've got the idea."

Sanya and Vanya were dumped on the floor and doused with water from an expensive crystal vase.

Once they'd come to their senses, Sanya dared to ask:

"Boss, sorry, but how did you—"

"How did I find you?" Kudrat laughed. "Easily! True, I couldn't reach you on the phone while you were gallivanting around Baghdad, my enterprising duo! But thanks to the bug I installed on your phones, I always knew exactly where you were. That's how my best men met you at the airport. I think I don't need to remind you now that you don't even have the right to sneeze without my permission, do you? Huh?! Let alone visit places I specifically forbade you to go?"

"Sorry, boss!" Sanya mumbled, embarrassed.

"So," Kudrat went on, "what were you two doing at the Abbasid Palace again? Eh, fools? Thought you'd swipe something else behind my back? I told you to stay low, stay quiet in Baghdad. Didn't I say: *just* check out that library of ancient manuscripts, quietly locate the map? And what did you do? You must have visited that Sharjah jewel exhibit, right?"

"But… how did you kn—?" Vanya blurted, stunned.

"Remember, I always know what you're up to," Kudrat said sternly. "I hope you didn't get hauled in by the police? Didn't show up on their radar somehow? Otherwise, we'd be having a very different conversation!"

"No, boss, all good," Sanya lied.

"We kept a low profile, boss, don't worry," Vanya echoed, improvising. "Sanyok and I are squeaky clean in Baghdad."

"Okay, let's leave that," Kudrat said, waving dismissively. "On to business. These boys of mine, Thor and Sher, rummaged through your luggage, and I see that the second half of my ancient treasure map on cloth still isn't there. Correct?"

"Yes, boss, that's right," the hapless pair admitted.

"But we need that map—badly," Kudrat said, putting pressure on them. "In fact, it's imperative. So, here's what we'll do. Zulfiya! Come here, please."

A slim, beautiful young woman emerged from the adjoining room of Kudrat's luxury suite.

All the men except Kudrat stared at her, wide-eyed.

"Stop drooling, all of you, right now!" Kudrat barked at the four. "This is Zulfiya. We can't manage without her, because she's a very knowledgeable historian. She works as a research associate at one of Samarkand's museums, and she's agreed to help us search for the Khorasan treasure map. Sanya and Vanya, from this moment on, you'll be looking for the second half of the map with her. No, you're both under her orders now, and she'll report directly to me about the results. I'll also assign Sher and a car to you. He'll drive. Understood?"

Sanya and Vanya nodded, still reeling from the beating they'd just taken from Kudrat's henchmen, the sudden appearance of the beautiful Zulfiya, and the shock of being placed under the command of a woman only slightly older than themselves.

"Sher, you'll keep an eye on these two crooks," Kudrat said with a grin. "No need to watch over Zulfiya. As for you two—if you so much as lay a hand on her, you'll regret it. Got it? Good. Now all of you, get out."

Sher, Zulfiya, Sanya, and Vanya stepped outside.

"Where to?" Sher asked Zulfiya right away, not even glancing at the two men still doubled over in pain.

"What happened to you?" the young woman asked them, not realizing they'd been badly beaten before she came in. "Whoa, you're both bleeding! Sher, I think these two need to go to a hospital immediately."

"Boss didn't say anything like that," Sher replied, shaking his head. "But we can take them home."

"All right," Zulfiya agreed. "At least do that—bring them home. And… see if you can give them some first aid. Buy iodine, painkillers, something… But we need to discuss our plan. Then again, okay—let's meet tomorrow. Let's say at ten in the morning.

Sanya and Vanya—does that work for you?"

"Yes," Sanya nodded. "Zulfiya, you're so kind…"

"We'll meet at the entrance to the National Library," Zulfiya added more firmly.

"What?! The library again?" Vanya groaned.

"Of course!" the young woman replied with a smile. "Where else can we find the sources we need? Both you and I have combed through everything on the internet—we came up empty."

"Yeah," Sanya agreed. "You're right. No problem, we'll come by tomorrow."

"Thank you… for freeing us—today," Vanya told her. "At least we can rest."

* * *

Major Zakir Bakhromov of the Tashkent police came home in a foul mood. His new case was stuck at a dead end: his subordinates still couldn't find any witnesses from the scene of the accident involving the well-known doctor, Said Mumtazov. Meanwhile, journalists had already spread news of the incident throughout the country. He was also in a bad mood because, for several days, he hadn't been able to reach his son by phone.

Yet, to Zakir's surprise, his son Davron was sitting in the living room having dinner, with Davron's mother fussing around him.

"So you finally showed up, you little punk?!" Zakir roared the moment he saw him. "Where've you been all these days, huh? Hanging out again at some friend's dacha—one of those druggies? I told you that crowd would only lead you to disaster! And this is all your doing, Madina—spoiling him, feeding him from a gold spoon, giving Davronchik anything his heart desires. The most expensive things, a new foreign car that costs as much as a decent apartment, total freedom in everything! Have you any idea, Mother, what trouble our son's gotten into?!"

"What's happened, *adasi*?" Madina asked her husband anxiously. Then she turned to her son. "Davron, what's your father talking about? Are you in trouble?"

"Other people have misfortunes—nothing ever sticks to him," his father answered for him. "Come on, Davron, get yourself into my room. We'll have a man-to-man talk. Don't worry, Mother, he'll be fine. We just need to talk."

But when the nineteen-year-old "kid" dragged himself reluctantly into his father's room, Zakir lost control and delivered a ringing slap to his only son's face.

"What was that for, Dad?!" Davron howled. "What did I do wrong?!"

"He's actually asking!" Zakir hissed angrily. "When you hit someone on the road—driving into oncoming traffic—and then fled the scene, did you leave your brain behind? You couldn't at least call me to give me a heads-up? Or did you forget your father's a GUVD investigator? It's a good thing I suspected something was wrong when you didn't come home! I found the right video from a camera installed at a house near that road. Want to watch yourself mowing someone down? Actually, two people—though, thankfully, the second one, the passenger, wasn't hurt."

"I'm sorry, Dad," Davron said, bowing his head fearfully. "I was wasted. I hardly remember any of it."

"Or maybe not just wasted—maybe high?" Zakir pressed. "Obviously, I'll try to sweep this under the rug, because you're my son. But I can't guarantee some other officer won't dig up which car it was and who was at the wheel. Do you have some broke friend with no connections who, for the right price, would be willing to take the fall? Do you? You know—say you loaned him your car that evening, just for a spin?"

"I don't know," Davron mumbled. "I'll have to think about it."

"Think? Are you even capable of that?" scoffed the elder Bakhromov. "All right, here's the deal: you need an alibi. You're going to tell everyone that at the time this happened, you were at home. Got it? I'll say the same if anyone asks, and I'll warn your mother. Our word will outweigh any witnesses not on our side. Meanwhile, don't drag your feet finding your 'culprit.' The case might get bumped upstairs, and then it'll be much harder for me to fix it. I'll… look for a scapegoat myself too. Though… you know, son, it might do you good to spend a year in prison—clear your head, gain some life experience. Instead of going to the institute."

"Dad, no, please!!" Davron pleaded desperately.

"All right. I'm just scaring you. So that next time, you'll actually think before you do something."

* * *

The next morning, after the previous day's meeting, Zulfiya, Sanya, and Vanya gathered at the National Library of Uzbekistan. Sher had driven Zulfiya there. Kudrat Valiev had tasked him with keeping an eye not on her, but on the two unreliable characters in his view. Thus, Sher entered the library with them as well.

Leading the three men to a quiet corner where no one else could overhear, the young woman gave them their assignment:

"We need to find all the books we can about the history of the ninth-century Arab Caliphate. I think the cloth map we're after might have been mentioned among the possessions or war spoils of that era's most prominent Caliphs—Amin and Ma'mun—as well as among items belonging to their wives or concubines. By the way, the books might also mention large, notable treasures."

"Diamonds?" Sanya's eyes lit up—he was still dreaming of wealth.

"Yes, diamonds, and many other gems and precious metals," Zulfiya nodded. "But most importantly, keep an eye out for references to the turban with a pearl the size of a lemon!"

"Wow!" Sher whistled in awe, hearing about that treasure for the first time.

"But these books could be bursting with mentions of various riches belonging to the Caliphs and their retinue," Vanya pointed out thoughtfully. "Do we actually need all of that? We mainly want the map!"

"Agreed," the young woman said after a pause. "But let's start there and see how it goes. Let's get to work! And don't forget about the Caliphs' wives…"

18

Baghdad, Abbasid Caliphate, March 812 CE

Sensing her husband's complete failure and the defeat of his forces in the protracted civil war, Lubana, wife of Caliph Amin, secretly sent a messenger to the woman she hated more than anyone in the world. She wrote a brief message using the most respectful epithets.

Upon reading the letter, Ma'mun's lawful wife, Umm Isa—daughter of his uncle al-Hadi—gave the messenger her reply, in which she "magnanimously," or rather condescendingly, permitted the first lady of the Arab Caliphate to visit her personal, almost regal, chambers in one of Baghdad's wealthiest homes.

"We are fortunate, Lubana, that my husband—our great Caliph Ma'mun—knows nothing of your current visit to me," said Umm Isa, seizing the opportunity to slight the wife of the reigning Caliph Amin by deliberately referring to Ma'mun as the Caliph and her own husband. "Both princes are off waging war with their armies right now. Men are simply insufferable, wouldn't you agree? All they ever want is to strike someone, wound someone, inflict harm, and then gallop around on horses, brandishing swords and daggers!"

"Perhaps they see it as a matter of honour, dear relative," Lubana observed. "I hope you don't mind my calling you that? After all, our husbands are blood brothers, and—"

"They are blood enemies," her hostess cut in. "Yet here you are, writing me letters asking for a meeting and coming to me as though we were close friends."

"Forgive me for that, most esteemed Umm Isa," apologized the 'first lady' of the Caliphate, realizing that due to Amin's mounting military defeats in the war against Prince Ma'mun, she would likely lose that distinguished title within days. "And I thank you for... your courage and your mercy toward me and my child! As you surely understand, I have come here not by chance, but out of necessity—because there is no one else I can turn to for this."

Even before their meeting, the clever Umm Isa had guessed what the nearly toppled 'queen' might request. But she feigned ignorance:

"A request of me?" She assumed a look of surprise. "What could I possibly do for you, my dear?"

Lubana could sense the thinly veiled hostility in those final words—so much false courtly courtesy—that she had half a mind to stand up proudly and walk out. At that moment, however, two of Umm Isa's young sons—Muhammad al-Asghar and Abdullah— ran into their mother's chambers, playing cheerfully and trying to draw their strict mother into their game. She tousled their hair briefly before telling them to go play with their nanny in another room.

That scene would have meant little, had it not reminded Lubana of her own small son—now nearly unprotected, with nothing 'royal' about him anymore.

"Most honourable lady," she said, swallowing her pride and humbling herself further before this brazen upstart married to the rightful ruler of Arabia, "the supporters of Caliph Amin are resisting bravely and stubbornly, defending every inch of land in this city. And yet… if Caliph Amin should lose this decisive battle over Baghdad tonight, then—"

Catching Umm Isa's angry look, Lubana quickly corrected herself:

"Forgive me, dear lady. I meant: when my husband, Prince Amin, loses the main battle and surrenders Baghdad to your husband, Prince—Caliph Ma'mun—might I hope that he will spare me and my young son? After all, the boy is his nephew."

"Our family ties are utter nonsense," Umm Isa retorted harshly. "You know that perfectly well. But… if you do exactly as I command, perhaps I… perhaps I will help you and your son escape and remain safe."

Despite her companion's sheer audacity, Lubana once again

swallowed her resentment. She was not accustomed to hearing such an imperious tone—not even from her husband. And yet here it was—from some upstart…

"As you say, esteemed lady Umm Isa," the Caliph's wife responded softly. "What must I do?"

"Go back to your palace right now," Umm Isa said, "and fetch from Prince Amin's large trunk the turban of their father, Caliph Harun—the one with that magnificent pearl the size of a lemon and all its precious stones! That will be my gift to my beloved husband Ma'mun. And in return—just so—I will be pleased to give you an address where you and your son can hide for a long time, safely out of reach of the sword of justice."

Bowing to thank her so-called "benefactress," Lubana departed, burning with anger inside—but there was no alternative.

Without difficulty, she located the invaluable item in the Caliphal palace, then gathered her son's and her own belongings for a long journey and returned to Umm Isa.

Without the slightest shame or hesitation, Umm Isa took the royal turban with the largest pearl in the Caliphate. True to her word, she sent her "friend" and the boy to a safe, protected location.

That same evening, thanks to Hussein ibn Ali (son of the former governor of Khorasan, Mahan) and his loyal commander Tahir, Ma'mun completed the siege of Baghdad and took the city. By the next morning, Hussein had proclaimed Ma'mun the new legitimate ruler of the Arab Caliphate—a short-lived coup d'état against Amin. Ma'mun's generals occupied most of Iraq.

However, a countercoup led by other factions among the Khorasan "abna" restored Amin to the throne. But his wife and child did not return to him. Lubana believed that, in any case, returning would be far too dangerous.

* * *

Marakanda, Khorasan, Abbasid Caliphate, September 813 CE

Benu could not hold back tears of joy as she welcomed her husband Tahir home from the war.

"Habibi, my dear!" she exclaimed, throwing herself into his strong embrace. His rugged face—despite its imperfections—had always looked handsome to her.

"My habibti!" came the warrior's gravelly baritone as he whispered tenderly in her ear. "How I love you! How are you? How are the children? Are they well? I've missed you all so much…"

After Tahir had washed off the dust from his long journey, changed his clothes, eaten, and rested, he went out into the courtyard to play with his little sons for the first time in quite a while, then savour some peaceful time with his wife.

"Don't cry, my dear," Tahir said gently to Benu, recognizing that she was still afraid he might leave again for another extended campaign. "I don't think there will be any more wars for quite a while."

"I've already heard, habibi, that Prince Ma'mun has taken power in Baghdad…" said Benu.

"Tss!" Tahir warned quietly. "Habibti, we can't speak like that or we'll lose our heads. From now on, our master is Caliph Ma'mun. He is now the ruler of Khorasan and all of Arabia."

"Tell me how it happened," Benu asked. "How did it turn out that Caliph Amin lost the civil war to his middle brother, who then took his throne?"

"I'll skip the political and military details, habibti," Tahir said, enjoying truly good home-cooked food prepared by his beloved wife for the first time in ages. "In short, the urban poor of Baghdad defended their city in a partisan war for over a year. Under the blockade, famine set in. By early autumn, our troops had gradually seized key defensive positions. That revolutionary situation— combined with starvation and our military experience—led to Baghdad's downfall during our siege. I convinced some of the city's wealthy men to cut the pontoon bridges over the Tigris, isolating the city from the outside world. That allowed Ma'mun's forces to occupy the eastern suburbs."

"And that brought you victory?" Benu asked.

"Yes—though not immediately," Tahir explained. "As commander, I later launched the final assault. But before that, as you can imagine, there were multiple offensives against the army of the Cal—uh, Prince Amin. By the time my army—Ma'mun's army—approached Baghdad, the rift between Amin and the Khorasani troops had only deepened. Desperate, Amin turned to the common people of the city for help, arming them. But the Khorasanis no longer trusted him. They deserted en masse to my side. And about a year ago, in August 812, when Ma'mun's and my army first arrived at Baghdad, we already controlled certain districts and fortifications."

"Why didn't you initially support Caliph Amin, as duty to your sovereign and fatherland might demand?" Benu asked bluntly, knowing her loving husband wouldn't condemn her for such a daring question. "I remember how Ma'mun invited you to lead his then-tiny force against the Caliph. But… why did you accept?"

"Maybe you also remember, habibti, my saying: 'Amin was never a strong or wise ruler.' He always behaved frivolously and irresponsibly toward the people of the Caliphate, neglecting affairs of state in favour of constant entertainment and debauchery. I never respected him."

"Yes, I know, habibi, that Amin became unpopular long ago—unloved throughout Arabia," Benu said with a nod.

"You also know," Tahir continued, "that I, your husband, have long aspired to become governor of our Khorasan. That's why I aligned with Ma'mun when he called me. And as you see, I didn't lose. When he was still governor of Khorasan, Ma'mun built strong ties with the local landowning aristocracy. In contrast to Amin, who relied solely on the Arab elite, Ma'mun supported the interests of us Khorasanis and the Persian-speaking nobility. The weak-willed, careless, irresponsible Amin simply wasn't as mindful of Khorasan's welfare as Ma'mun is. And our new Caliph Ma'mun values me highly, considers me a friend—which is important. He might well entrust me someday with the honourable position of governor of Khorasan!"

"I would be so delighted about that, my habibi," Benu said with a radiant smile.

Tahir embraced and kissed her tenderly.

"Tell me, habibi… what about Amin? Is he still alive?" Benu asked apprehensively.

"Yes," Tahir nodded. "For the moment. But Prince Amin abandoned his army and fled."

"And his wife and child?" the kind-hearted woman nearly wept. "Are they… alive?"

"I don't know anything about them," Tahir sighed. "We didn't see them during the siege of the palace. Maybe they, too, managed to slip away somehow. That would be for the best—for them."

19

Samarkand, 2023

After running Sharaf's details through every database and finding nothing criminal in him or his associates, Captain Ibrahim Salimov of the Samarkand police invited the young man from Qatar to stay at his home for a couple of days—while Salimov continued searching for any leads on the missing Barno.

Sharaf gratefully accepted his new older friend's offer. He called the Tashkent hostel, where he'd left some of his belongings, to let them know he'd be staying in Samarkand for a while and would definitely return in a few days. The person on the other end said that, despite it being the busy season, they'd hold his spot and that he could come back anytime he liked.

While Salimov hunted for the car used by the bandits, Sharaf decided to do his part to help. At the hostel, he had obtained Barno's home phone number; she had been working with the hostel on behalf of her tour company for two years.

Not wanting to frighten her family, and knowing that his Arabic wouldn't suffice for a normal conversation with them, Sharaf asked Ibrahim to make the call instead.

The next morning, after the captain's family had provided Sharaf with a tasty, hearty breakfast and left for their daily activities—everyone except Ibrahim himself—Salimov, having learned some new information about Barno, decided to share it with Sharaf.

"First off, let me tell you a bit about this young woman's household," he began. "Her mother picked up the phone. I said I was a Samarkand friend of Barno's and passed along a greeting from her. She seemed a bit surprised, thanked me, and explained that she was sure her daughter was simply off on another work trip. It seems the girl travels around Uzbekistan with tour groups all the time and can't manage to call home every day."

"How could she 'not manage to call every day'?" Sharaf asked in surprise. "Does she live apart from her parents?"

"No, they live under the same roof," Captain Salimov answered.

"That makes it a bit odd that a young, unmarried girl wouldn't at least call her mother once a day," the Qatari said. "Even I, traveling in a country so far from home, make sure to send my mom at least a short message every day so she won't worry and knows I'm alive and well. Now and then I even call my—well, never mind. Still, here we have a girl effectively without a man's protection all day, yet her mother isn't concerned that it's been over two days since she last heard from her? I don't get that."

"Yes, it does seem strange," Ibrahim agreed, thinking aloud. "It appears things might not be so good in that household. Another oddity: the mother assumed I was calling to give her news about her husband. From what I've gathered through my sources, Barno's father, Fahriyar Tursunov, disappeared about a week ago, and his wife Rasima—Barno's mother—filed a missing-person report at their local police station."

"But she's not worried at all about a daughter who's stopped calling her," Sharaf pointed out. "That's both sad and ridiculous. Maybe she's not Barno's real mother?"

"Actually, based on their birthdates, they're only 17 years apart," Ibrahim replied. "So yes, it's entirely possible that Rasima is her stepmother. You're pretty sharp, Sharaf! If you knew Uzbek, I swear I'd recommend you join us as an investigator."

"Thank you, *ustadi* Ibrahim," the young man from Qatar replied modestly. "What about the car those men used to force our poor girl inside? Have you found it?"

"Unfortunately, not yet," Captain Salimov said, shaking his head. "But my team is still looking. The trouble is, the car is registered to an elderly woman in Fergana. Evidently, that was just to throw us off. The criminals are mocking us—law enforcement—in case we started looking for the kidnapped girl, which of course we did. The grandmother told our officers that some scary man showed up and, handing her a wad of cash, 'convinced' her to go with him to a dealership. There, they used her ID to register a brand-new foreign car, which he drove off immediately. Obviously, she has no idea where he went. I'm sure the bandits have already swapped out its plates. So it's going to be tough to track that car now."

"So what can we do?!" Sharaf asked in despair, fearing for Barno.

"Don't worry about it, young man," Ibrahim said, placing a reassuring hand on his shoulder. "The old woman gave us a description of the man, and we've drawn up a composite sketch. We haven't found him in our databases yet—maybe he's managed to avoid the police so far, and has never been taken in. Our facial-recognition software didn't get any matches either—likely he's never 'shown up' on social media. But we've sent out a description of him nationwide. We'll catch him any day now."

"But he wasn't alone, right?" Sharaf pointed out. "There were at least two of them. Why would they even need a modest tour guide? I can't figure it out. Although… No, I have no idea."

"Yes, there might be an entire gang," Ibrahim replied. "And you know, if Barno's father is missing, maybe her abduction is somehow connected to his disappearance."

"Do you think these criminals might have kidnapped him earlier?" Sharaf asked.

"Could be," said Ibrahim. "Or it might be something else—maybe they're using the girl's kidnapping to blackmail or flush out her father. Maybe he owes them money? That was my guess, since criminals sometimes abduct people over unpaid debts."

"This is awful," Sharaf said, distressed. "Please, *ustadi* Ibrahim, keep me informed about your investigation, won't you? And if you need my help—just say the word! I'm actually in love with another girl back home in Qatar. Her name is Jahiza. I hope she's waiting for me in Doha, missing me the way I miss her. But I think, *ustadi* Ibrahim, for this Uzbek girl, a near-stranger—Barno—I… I'm willing to do a lot. I don't know why. I guess I'm just afraid for her fate… for her life."

Captain Salimov nodded in understanding, took one last sip of tea, and then headed off to work.

20

Tashkent, the same period

Malika and her mother, Sitora, were almost constantly taking turns keeping vigil at Said's bedside in the hospital. He remained unconscious after his operation. As Ibrahim had nearly revealed, Sharaf was indeed calling his biological father's number regularly to check on his condition. Since Said still wasn't able to answer the phone, sometimes one of the ward nurses would pick up. They would update Sharaf on the condition of Dr. Mumtazov, who had been moved from intensive care to a regular room.

Sharaf was worried about Said and longed to see him again as soon as possible. Yet he felt he couldn't simply abandon Barno in her predicament—he had to help her, somehow free her from the bandits' clutches. If it wasn't already too late.

Time passed. Mumtazov was receiving the necessary treatment at the hospital. One fine day, he finally regained consciousness, with Malika at his side.

"Daddy, thank God!" the young woman exclaimed joyfully. "I'm so happy!"

Her delight almost immediately turned to dismay, however, when her father, studying her closely, asked:

"Excuse me, but... who are you? And where am I?"

Malika realized this was no joke, no light-hearted prank, but genuine amnesia.

She called her mother, telling her that her father had woken up, carefully hinting that they were facing some "difficulties" at the moment—though she didn't mention his memory loss over the phone.

When Sitora arrived and saw her husband, she was heartbroken to find that the beloved man she had lived with for many years did not recognize either her or their daughter. He regarded them as strangers.

"Don't worry," Said's doctor, Erkin Davlatovich, tried to reassure them. "It's temporary retrograde amnesia. We're giving Dr. Mumtazov all the necessary medications. He'll need time to recover fully. I'm confident everything will turn out all right."

It turned out that Zakir Bakhromov, the investigator in the traffic accident case, had instructed Erkin Davlatovich to notify him the moment Said Mumtazov regained consciousness. The doctor, unable to disobey, complied with the major's request, warning him that any interrogation—or even casual conversation—with the victim likely wouldn't be productive, since the patient, after a serious head injury, had not yet recovered his memory. But Major Bakhromov said he would come to the hospital immediately regardless.

Entering Mumtazov's ward, Major Bakhromov greeted him and his family politely and just as politely asked the women to step outside into the corridor.

"Is that necessary?" Malika asked with a frown. "My father hasn't done anything wrong, so this isn't an interrogation, is it?"

"That's correct," Zakir responded curtly. "But—"

"In that case, I'm sure there's no reason we can't remain here," Malika interrupted firmly. She didn't trust the major and feared he might exploit her father's fragile condition to slip some paper in front of him to sign. "If you disagree, Major Bakhromov, then summon my father to your station with a formal notice. But only once he's fully recovered—because right now, not only can't he get out of bed, he can't be moved at all! And no one knows how long his full recovery will take."

"I understand, miss," Zakir Bakhromov conceded reluctantly. "So be it—I'll accept your first option. All right then, Said Yahyaevich, do you know who hit your car and caused the crash? Do you know why the driver fled? Who did this, and why? Was it an accident or a planned crime?"

"Sorry, but I don't remember anything," Said admitted.

"Don't remember, or don't want to say?" Zakir pressed.

"Are you out of your mind?!" Sitora burst out. "My husband suffered serious injuries and lost his memory! Instead of looking for the criminal, you're sitting here wasting time. By the way, have you checked any cameras at the accident site?"

"Yes, we have," Bakhromov replied, suppressing his irritation. "They show nothing."

"How is that possible?" Malika asked, astonished. "'Nothing'? Not even footage of a car slamming into my dad's Chevrolet? Someone told us—you saw him yourself. He was sitting beside my father in the passenger seat at the time of the crash! And you practically jumped down his throat for no reason… Anyway, that guy—Sharaf, I think—told us the oncoming car, the one that caused the accident, was a white Toyota. You can see that clearly even in the dark! So there's not a single recording or witness? Strange."

"We're looking," the major replied tersely.

"We know how you 'look,'" Sitora muttered wearily. "You've probably already decided to 'bury' this case, haven't you?"

"I think we should all calm down," Malika interjected, trying to defuse the tense exchange. "Sir, please forgive us, and try to understand my mother: my father still feels very weak; he's had major surgeries and only just regained consciousness. And as you can see—he's lost his memory. He doesn't even recognize us. And here you are, grilling us with questions. Can you imagine how we feel right now?… My mother only meant that we're counting on you to find the culprit. And that… you'll punish him according to the law."

"Young lady, we always do everything by the book," Bakhromov replied more calmly, rising to his feet. "That's our job. I've been in this service for a quarter century."

He decided he'd done enough for one day. He badly wanted

to figure out exactly what Said might know—and whether his testimony could threaten Zakir's son in court—but realized he wouldn't get anything from the victim in his current condition.

"In that case, we're lucky you're the one handling this case," Malika said, now sounding conciliatory. In truth, she had serious doubts about the investigator's professionalism and integrity. She disliked lying but hated open conflict even more.

"All right, mommy," the major said rudely to Sitora, dropping all courtesy. "You'd best thank your clever daughter. Next time, watch what you say—and the accusations you throw at law enforcement."

"Yes, we understand, Comrade Major," Malika nodded. "Goodbye, all the best. As soon as my father recovers and regains his memory, we'll let you know—if he remembers anything important."

"What a character," Sitora sighed, looking at her daughter once Zakir had left. "Unpleasant man."

* * *

Sharjah, UAE, Archaeological Museum, the same period

The opening of the museum exhibit showcasing newly discovered ninth-century Abbasid-era artifacts—unearthed by Nazih Abu Jali—was a great success. Among the prominent guests was none other than His Highness the Emir of Sharjah. The event also drew leading experts in Emirati history and archaeology, as well as numerous local residents and tourists.

Showing special respect to Nazih as the "star" of the ceremony, the museum's young head of collections, Bob Downey, offered to keep Nazih's backpack—in which he usually carried important belongings—in his office. Nazih gratefully accepted.

The archaeologist planned to stop by the exhibit daily, at least briefly. First, he couldn't get enough of admiring his invaluable 1,500-year-old discoveries. Second, people—both acquaintances and strangers—kept coming to congratulate him, and Nazih quite enjoyed the attention.

The day after the exhibit's opening, with fewer visitors around, Nazih once again approached the display case containing Princess Zubaidah's jewelled diadem. Suddenly… he noticed something was wrong.

In the next moment, the seasoned archaeologist realized that what he was looking at was a convincing replica—not the original. He was certain that just yesterday, at the opening, the diadem had been genuine. Which meant someone must have swapped it out afterward.

Alarmed and distressed, he hurried to check the ninth-century coins as well.

To his shock, the gold dinars and silver dirhams of the Abbasid dynasty—including Zubaidah's dirham—were also nothing but fakes.

"What a disgrace!!" the archaeologist cried out across the exhibit hall, unrestrained in his outrage. "Who switched them?! Who dared?! What kind of outrage is this?!"

The museum director, Dari Irshad, decided to close the museum immediately. He apologized to visitors for the sudden, "entirely accidental" mix-up and, without providing details or defending himself, simply said:

"I believe, my friends, that you'll be able to return to our museum very soon—possibly even tomorrow. My apologies once again, and thank you for your understanding."

Then Dari turned to the famous archaeologist and said:

"Ustadi Nazih, please excuse me, but what you're claiming leaves me confused and deeply concerned! You see, in this exhibit—within a museum personally entrusted to me by His Highness—there should be no question of any fakes. Are you certain about what you just declared in front of everyone?"

"Yes, my friend, unfortunately I'm absolutely certain," Nazih replied quietly but firmly, on the verge of tears at the thought of his discoveries vanishing without a trace.

"Come, let's examine the main display cases together," Dari suggested. "I'm not as well-versed in archaeology as you are, ustadi, and just peering through the glass, I might not notice much. Plus, we're only allowed to remove such priceless items from their cases under the most extreme conditions defined in the museum's bylaws. But I do trust you as a top-level specialist. Still—let's take another look."

"All right, esteemed Dari," Nazih agreed without protest.

When the two of them, joined by Bob Downey, returned to the display cases, Nazih again cried out in despair. Agitated, he pointed out the unique identifying features of the authentic items, which were entirely absent in these skilfully forged artifacts.

Bob Downey suggested they try to find the thief themselves, but Nazih—devoted to truth and justice—vehemently disagreed.

"My friend, we're not detectives, and we have no investigative experience," the archaeologist said passionately to Bob. "It would be useless. We'd only waste time. And in case you haven't realized, I'm extremely worried about my finds! They're collectively priceless!"

"All right, ustadi," the museum director relented. "If you insist…"

"Yes, I beg you," Nazih pleaded.

So the director called the police.

Both Nazih and everyone present were taken aback when, after examining the crime scene, collecting all necessary prints, and photographing what he needed for his report, the officer turned to Nazih and said:

"Mr. Nazih Abu Jalil, you are under arrest—on suspicion of stealing museum exhibits, items classified as 'extremely high-value property.' We found your prints in the valuables storage area and on the key to it. Please do not resist and come with us immediately."

Slapping handcuffs on the stunned archaeologist—who had no idea what was happening—the officer led him away to his vehicle.

"Well, Nazih, couldn't settle for your legitimate share of the finds? You wanted it all—and right away?!" came Bob's condemning voice from behind him.

Nazih looked back as he was escorted outside. He thought his friend Bob Downey was mocking him… The archaeologist was baffled and dismayed.

21

Baghdad, Abbasid Caliphate, 814 AD

A former Zoroastrian from Kufa who had converted to Islam— the vizier to Caliph al-Ma'mun, Abu al-Abbas al-Fadl ibn Sahl ibn Zadhanfarukh al-Sarakhsi—was meeting in his lavish palace office with a renowned military commander of the Caliphate from Khorasan.

This visitor, Tahir ibn Husayn, had no idea that it was the vizier himself who had orchestrated his family's arrival in the Caliphate's capital.

Upon entering, Tahir greeted the vizier courteously, as custom dictated, though with a certain grimness. This did not in the least trouble the second-most-powerful figure in the Palace—and indeed in all of Arabia—after the Caliph.

"Esteemed son of Husayn," Sarakhsi began calmly, "you must be angry with me, I imagine? Perhaps because, in addition to my post as head of the state divan, I personally command the Caliphate's army as well? Despite the fact that, during the princes' civil war, it was you who led our sovereign's forces!"

Tahir said nothing, revealing only a trace of surprise at Sarakhsi's perceptiveness.

"Perhaps it was the will of the Almighty and of our Caliph, my lord Vizier," Tahir replied diplomatically, working to restrain his emotions. "No doubt that is why Caliph al-Ma'mun has called you *Dhu'l-Ri'asatayn*—'the master of two offices.'"

"Indeed," Sarakhsi nodded. "But as for your resentment of me—perhaps you were unaware, or have forgotten, that during the war, before each battle, I served as the Caliph's chief adviser on all military manoeuvres—both offensive and defensive. I was always his principal counsellor and right hand!"

"Yes, I know," Tahir replied with difficulty, suppressing his displeasure. "You charted our army's route by the stars—you were already the Caliphate's chief astrologer! You actually know very little about warfare. So what else could you do but rely on dubious celestial or magical predictions?"

"I see your point, my friend," Sarakhsi replied imperturbably. "Nevertheless, do you know that many here believe in the stars?

And the stars never mislead them."

"So, what then did they foretell about your fate?" Tahir asked, still in an ironic, sarcastic tone. "An eternal rise—or a fall from your fabulous heights?"

Any other subject of the Caliph might have been executed for such irreverence toward the state's second ruler—and, in effect, its true governor. But Tahir was confident that Caliph al-Ma'mun considered him a friend and would never permit anyone to take his head, even at the vizier's command. Still, Tahir genuinely could not understand why the Caliph had so elevated and embraced this ignorant Sarakhsi, awarding him not only the two most prestigious positions in the realm but also vast wealth and inherited estates—while appointing his brother, Hasan ibn Sahl, as minister of finance.

"The stars have prompted me… to speak with Caliph al-Ma'mun about… you," Sarakhsi emphasized, hinting at his role as a benefactor in his companion's destiny. "About how you have endured the Almighty's trials long enough—working without comfort, wealth, or renown in that disreputable position in Raqqa."

Sarakhsi smiled, each word further surprising Tahir.

"I received word via a messenger, carrying an order from our Caliph, demanding I come here to the Palace immediately, with all my belongings," Tahir explained. "That order… did you give it?"

"Yes. I considered it my duty to free you from that 'hole' you never deserved," Sarakhsi said with an air of self-importance. "Just to remind you—it wasn't I who sent you off there after your great victories; it was the 'grateful' Caliph al-Ma'mun! And your old job, as governor of the northern portion of Mesopotamia in the Jazira region, doesn't really suit you—though I hear the Qataris hold you in high regard. Still, that's not your level, Tahir. You should be made governor of Khurasan… but not now—later. I suggested to the Caliph that, given your talents as a warrior and leader, you would be more useful here in Baghdad for the time being. Would you be willing… once again to command the Caliph's army, to lead it into campaigns if need be? Would that position suit you?"

Tahir had never expected that his adversary and chief political rival would so abruptly decide to become his patron.

"What's the catch, esteemed Sarakhsi?" Tahir asked, carefully observing his counterpart, trying to discern what lay behind the courtesy and crafty smiles.

"There's no catch at all, my friend!" the vizier objected. "I simply find it difficult to manage both offices myself, that's all. And if, by chance, we need to march our army out against our enemies, I… well… My strengths lie in intellect, in manoeuvring the 'chess pieces,' in strategy, as you just mentioned. Meanwhile, we do need military campaigns and victories in Khurasan and the surrounding areas to ensure the security of the Caliphate's eastern borders. This is necessary in order to—"

"I understand: to bring more mercenaries and military slaves into our Caliph's army," the seasoned commander interjected.

"That's correct, Tahir," Sarakhsi agreed. "But as you know, I don't like to venture out onto the battlefield myself. Besides, I'm far more useful right here in the Palace. If you agree to my generous proposal, you'll live like a sheikh—I promise. However…"

"You have a condition, do you not?" Tahir surmised.

"No, not a condition—rather a… request, my friend," the vizier corrected him. "For every unsuccessful campaign, you will bear full responsibility before the Caliph and the people. But all glory for any successful campaigns must go solely to me—as your leader and the one who inspires you. In that way, you serve me, and I serve you. So, do you accept? If yes, you can assume the new post immediately."

"Yes, I accept, my lord Vizier," the warrior said after a moment of thought, drawing a heavy sigh.

Tahir was hardly thrilled about the plan. He detested deceit and prideful self-importance. But he knew all too well that, right now, Sarakhsi wielded far greater power than he did. If Tahir refused, the vizier would swiftly order the deaths of both him and his family. He felt little fear for himself as a warrior, but he trembled for his beloved wife and cherished children.

"And if you handle it all well," Sarakhsi added, "then I'll name you administrator of all the natural levies in the southern region of Mesopotamia."

* * *

Bukhara, Khurasan, Abbasid Caliphate, 817 AD

Caliph al-Ma'mun had decided that his elder daughter's wedding would be held in the ancient city of Bukhara.

The Caliph's younger daughter, twelve-year-old Sabika bint al-Ma'mun, along with her serving women, was helping prepare her older sister for marriage in the palace residence. That sister was the still very young Umm al-Fadl bint al-Ma'mun, whom Sabika simply called "Fadliyah."

The bride was trying on sumptuous wedding attire and expensive jewellery, all gifts from her regal father for the occasion.

"Why so sad, my dear sister?" Sabika asked gently once the serving women had left the room. The two girls could not even trust their own attendants, who would brazenly report every move the princesses made to the Caliph or his vizier. And their mother, Buran bint Hasan, dared not interfere in such matters. "Well, I understand you, Fadliyah. You had your heart set on some handsome young prince! But our father has decided to marry you off to that old, bearded ram, Ali al-Rida. Worse still, some of that imam's brothers—far from virtuous—have already risen against the Abbasids! How can we make sense of Father?"

"I would indeed oppose this dreadful marriage alliance," Fadliyah replied, "but you know I can do nothing against Father's will. He is not only our ruler but the ruler of all Arabia. And that nearly fifty-year-old cleric, al-Rida—he was invited here from Medina itself! I'm still so young and not well-versed in politics, but I've heard our father recently decided to get closer to the descendants of Abu Talib—the Alids. I don't know why."

"I've also heard that Father has declared that foul al-Rida— your fiancé—his heir, *wali al'ahd*," added Sabika. "And he's already ordered silver Abbasid dirhams minted in Isfahan bearing al-Rida's name as the heir to the Muslim covenant. Isn't that too great an honour for an outsider—and virtually an adherent of a different persuasion? Why would he do such a thing? Maybe he's deliberately provoking the local nobility?"

"Yes," Fadliyah confirmed. "Father commanded that after his own name, the coins should bear the name of this old man, reading: 'al-Rida, Imam of the Muslims.' I wonder how our relatives will react—our brothers, and Uncle Muhammad al-Mu'tasim, younger brother of Uncle Amin and of Caliph al-Ma'mun? Especially since our grandfather, Caliph Harun al-Rashid, had established a proper order of succession for all three. Is it even possible to break that?"

"Our father already broke it when he overthrew and killed Uncle Amin," the precocious Sabika reminded her. "And now, look—he's breaking it again!"

"If only the two of us could be completely free from men's authority," Fadliyah murmured dreamily. "How I'd love to rule on my own, like Khutak-Khatun, Bukhara's queen from more than a century ago. Although… no. I recall she met a bad end: the Arabs killed her, led by someone just as vile as al-Rida—Salm ibn Ziyad. As for me, I'm neither that strong nor that brave. I'll have to obey Father. So be it, for me. But Sabika, my little sister, I've heard something that frightens and pains me far more: that our father has promised al-Rida that you would be wed in Medina to his, as-yet-underage, son. The only advantage is that he isn't old—unlike my future husband. Oh, how I hate him! One day I may even kill him."

"And yet, I truly wish happiness for both of us," Sabika said sorrowfully.

* * *

Merv, Satrapy of Margiana, Abbasid Caliphate, early 818 AD

Tahir's wife, Benu, was waiting at home for her husband with a hot and appetizing meal.

When he arrived and they, together with their children, had enjoyed their dinner, Benu began questioning Tahir about the events that had everyone talking—not just in the city, but throughout Arabia.

"Is it true, habibi, what people are saying?!" the woman asked anxiously, having sent the children to sleep in their room.

"What do you mean, my dear?" Tahir did not immediately join the conversation. The Caliphate's military commander knew all too well what she was referring to, but he did not wish to spoil the evening with such a grim topic.

"They say that Caliph al-Ma'mun's son-in-law, al-Rida… was truly killed?" Benu asked for clarification. "How could that be? He was the Caliph's closest confidant! The heir to the throne and ruler of the entire Caliphate!"

"That is precisely why he was killed," Tahir surmised. "The fact that our Caliph so greatly elevated someone from the Alid line—a figure foreign to many—clearly provoked retaliatory anger among most members of the Abbasid dynasty. And now, al-Ma'mun's enemies are accusing him and his advisors of anti-Arab policies. Besides, al-Ma'mun and I still haven't managed to defeat that endlessly rebelling Persian, Babak, from the village of Mimadh near Bilalabad. So, the Caliph is going through a difficult time. And just today, his enemies proclaimed Ibrahim ibn al-Mahdi—Ma'mun's uncle, a true Abbasid—as Caliph. Not here in Merv, of course, but in Baghdad, as is customary."

"Ibrahim? The poet and musician, son of Harun al-Rashid's brother—Caliph Muhammad ibn Mansur al-Mahdi?" Benu asked in surprise.

"The very same," Tahir nodded.

"He does have some decent songs," his wife remarked, "but does he know anything at all about governing?"

"Certainly not," Tahir replied, almost in a whisper. "What kind of Caliph could he possibly be? I suspect Ibrahim is merely a puppet in the hands of the Abbasid nobility."

"Once, at a reception with the Caliph, I noticed how fiercely his young wife looked at al-Rida," Benu said. "Poor girl! He was old enough to be her grandfather. At that moment, I thought how fortunate I am with you, habibi. We suit each other in age, and we share a mutual love—and are dearly loved in return."

"That is true, my sweet habibti," Tahir said gently. "But you don't think that poor Fadliyah ordered her servants to kill her so-called 'beloved husband,' do you?"

"Didn't she, my habibi?" Benu asked, uncertain.

"Oh no, my dear," Tahir shook his head. "She had nothing to do with it. Let me tell you, as a seasoned warrior: I'm sure there are far more powerful forces behind al-Rida's death. He should never have interfered in another clan's affairs, let alone claimed the succession. Many people resented that. He was punished. Just like Vizier Sarakhsi."

"Yes, I know he too died under suspicious circumstances," Benu nodded. "So he was killed as well? And he's the one who gave us this lovely, cozy house here in Merv! I'm very grateful to him for that. What happened to him, habibi? Who would do such a thing?"

"Sarakhsi was found dead in his bath at Sarahs, in northern Khorasan," Tahir recounted. "He was accused of attempting to seize the Caliphate and restore the Sasanian state. Reliable sources told me that Sarakhsi refused a large sum of money from the Caliph and resigned to pursue an ascetic life. But between us, Benu, I believe Caliph al-Ma'mun himself—fearing revolts and conspiracies—ordered Sarakhsi's execution, and then had al-Rida eliminated as well. All of it, despite his strong friendships with both of them… Today, Ma'mun announced al-Rida's funeral. They say the loud wailing of the grieving Caliph can already be heard beyond the Palace walls. He mourns the dead man deeply—though he's the one who had him taken out! Now why the sad face, my dear?"

"I'm afraid for you, my habibi," Benu confided, her voice full of concern. "In this land, those in power don't value human life. You see? The Caliph is capable of turning even on his closest friends!"

"Nothing bad will happen to me," Tahir laughed, trying to reassure her. "I'm a strong man and I fear no one." Then his face grew grave. "But if one day, for no reason, without any warning, I suddenly disappear—if I fail to come home—and if anything strikes you as dangerously suspicious, then… I beg you with all my heart, my habibti: flee at once! Save yourself and our children! Just as the wife of Caliph Amin did, whom Ma'mun executed, and as the vizier's wife did too."

Benu rested her head heavily against her husband's chest. Then, another thought came to her:

"What do you think will happen to Vizier Sarakhsi's great wealth?" she inquired, usually disinterested in such matters. She was simply curious who would inherit the vast riches of the second-most-important figure in the Arab Caliphate.

"Obviously, his wife and chi—" Tahir began, then cut himself off. "Though… as ruler, Ma'mun could rightfully claim it for himself, since he already possesses limitless Caliphal treasures! Perhaps it's no accident that I once saw him with a map…"

"A map?! What kind of map?" Benu asked, surprised.

"A map of the Abbasid treasures, drawn not on paper as usual, but… on pieces of silk cloth!" Tahir clarified. "Rather like the one you told me about, the one you saw with that tailor Maruf from the village of Vedar near Marakanda. Remember him? He sewed belts."

"Of course I remember him. My goodness!" Benu exclaimed. "So now the chief riches of the Abbasid Caliphate—and that treasure map on cloth—might belong to Ma'mun… or else to the new Caliph, Ibrahim? That's the question. And moreover: is this Ibrahim ruthless? Might he be dangerous to us all? How will we live under him…"

22

Doha, Qatar, 2023

Jahiza's mother, Fatima, went upstairs in their lavish mansion in the city center and knocked softly on her daughter's door before entering. She wanted to check on her before bed and wish her a good night. The woman didn't always do this—just tonight, since Jahiza hadn't even stopped by to see her parents after coming home from a party with her girlfriends. Fatima sensed something was wrong.

Indeed, the moment she saw her daughter, she gasped in horror and clapped her hands to her face.

"Good God!! What's happened to you, child?! Why are you in such a state?!"

Jahiza was sitting on the floor in an expensive but torn dress, her hair disheveled and her makeup smeared from crying. She just kept trembling and letting out quiet moans, giving her mother no answer—though Fatima already understood nearly everything.

"Did this happen at that elite nightclub a couple of blocks away? The one for 'gold card' holders, right?" her mother asked.

With a dull look, Jahiza glanced at her mother and lowered her eyes in affirmation.

"And who is he? Who is that scoundrel?!" Fatima persisted. "He came on to you, didn't he?"

Without speaking, the girl nodded and whimpered softly again.

"You said you'd be there with your girlfriends!" her mother continued, unrelenting. She helped her daughter up from the floor and sat her in a soft, comfortable armchair. "How could this be? How could they let this happen?! If it were up to me, I wouldn't let friends like that anywhere near you!"

"I w—went to the ladies' room," Jahiza stammered weakly, still twitching from the shock. "He… he… attacked me from behind, all of a sudden. And… Mom, he… ra… ra…"

"All right, all right, no need, my little girl," Fatima cut her off, hugging her tenderly. At her mother's touch, however, the girl flinched again and twitched, causing Fatima to lament even more: "Oh dear, oh dear, what is the world coming to?! My poor child! I'm going to tell your father everything. You know he's got extensive connections—he'll definitely find that bastard and wipe him off the face of the earth!! Don't you doubt it. And wash your face—look at you! A girl from our family must always look respectable!"

Having learned what had happened to his only beloved daughter—whom he had cherished and pampered from birth—hotel-chain owner Sarwan al-Tawil decided not to file a formal police report. However, he phoned a friend of his, a senior police officer—Colonel Rashid Khatib—and suggested they meet.

Over a 'cup of coffee' at a restaurant, Sarwan briefly explained the situation to Rashid and asked him to assign one of his most trusted subordinates to quietly investigate the young rapist—discreetly, without drawing public attention. In return, Sarwan promised that if the job was done well, he would generously reward both Rashid and the operative under his command, who in this case was to act strictly as a private investigator. The colonel agreed and assured him he would help.

***

Samarkand, around the same time

Sharaf couldn't afford to call Jahiza from abroad—it was too expensive for him. He sent her his regards through his mother whenever his stepfather managed to get hold of him by phone, and he texted her several times a day through a messaging app.

For a while, she replied, albeit briefly. But in recent days, she had stopped even reading his messages. This upset and worried the young man. During one of his phone conversations with his mother, he asked her to find out if everything was okay with Jahiza, explaining why he was so anxious. He didn't mention that, judging by the messenger's activity, Jahiza appeared to be logging in, suggesting things were at least tolerable on her end. Even so, he let his mother know he was concerned about his "fiancée."

He couldn't tell anyone—not even his mother—that he couldn't stop thinking about his new acquaintance, the tour guide Barno, who had been kidnapped by unknown criminals.

Meanwhile, Captain Ibrahim Salimov wasn't sitting idle. Together with his operatives, he had conducted several investigative operations and located a place where three bandits were hiding out—and where, in Salimov's view, Barno might be held hostage.

"May I go with you to apprehend these criminals?" Sharaf asked his new policeman friend.

"Certainly not," Ibrahim replied firmly. "It's far too dangerous. The bandits are likely armed. I'll tell you something else—my team and I aren't going to play heroes either. We're calling in the Mobile Special Task Unit—a specialized takedown force."

"But Barno might need medical help!" the young Qatari fretted.

"Maybe she'll need me too!"

"You forget you're not a doctor, but a future lawyer," Ibrahim reminded him. "So you, more than anyone, should respect law and order. Don't worry—we'll handle it the right way. If necessary, we'll call an ambulance. Then I'll call you, and if the girl's all right, you two will see each other soon."

Sharaf had been raised not to argue with his elders; he could make suggestions, but never contradict or debate. So, he complied.

* * *

Tashkent, around the same time

Zulfiya, Sanya, and Vanya spent a long time combing through the National Library for anything that might lead them to clues about the ancient Abbasid treasure map on cloth. Almost daily, Kudrat Valiev demanded progress reports from Zulfiya and her tag-along driver/overseer Sher, who also kept an eye on the two thieves.

Eventually, their boss began losing patience.

"We've come to believe that Caliph Amin never hid any royal treasure," Zulfiya told Valiev. "All the most valuable items ended up in the hands of Caliph al-Ma'mun. Still, during our research, we tracked the period when Ma'mun temporarily lost royal power. It's possible he hid the treasures somewhere he stayed—perhaps in Merv. And maybe that's exactly where we ought to look for the second half of the map…"

"Merv? Where's that?" asked Kudrat, whose knowledge of geography and history was limited.

"Merv, also called Gyaur-kala, is one of the oldest known cities in Central Asia. It stands on the banks of the Murghab River in the southeastern part of Turkmenistan, about thirty kilometres east of the present-day city of Mary, near Bayramaly," Zulfiya explained.

"Excellent!" Kudrat interrupted. "So you can all go off to Turkmenistan."

"Please hold on, boss," Zulfiya stopped him. "Let me finish. All right. Merv was the capital of the Persian satrapy of Margiana and later of the Turkic Seljuk Empire. The ruins of Merv are now a World Heritage site. It's believed that ancient Merv was once the largest city in the world, with a population of over half a million. After the Arab conquest of Central Asia in the seventh century, the city experienced a second flowering as a launchpad for expansion northward and eastward. Under the Abbasids, Merv became a major centre of Arab scholarship, hosting as many as ten libraries. The city was home to immigrants from across Arabia, Sogdiana, and beyond. From 813 to 818, Caliph al-Ma'mun made Merv his temporary residence, effectively making it the capital of the entire Arab Caliphate. But—"

"What else?" Valiev grumbled impatiently. "Hurry it up—I haven't got all day."

"As I said, in 817, Caliph Ma'mun lost his authority, and it passed to his paternal uncle, Ibrahim ibn al-Mahdi. Then, when power in the Caliphate returned to Ma'mun, Ibrahim refused to swear loyalty to him and went off to Rayy, where he declared himself Caliph. He stayed there for about two years while Ma'mun waited for him to come around, like the rest of his subjects. But Ma'mun grew tired of waiting and marched with cavalry and infantry to Rayy in pursuit of Ibrahim. When Ibrahim heard the news, he had no choice but to flee to Baghdad and go into hiding, fearing for his life. Ma'mun then offered one hundred thousand dinars to anyone who revealed Ibrahim's whereabouts."

"Wow! That much?" Valiev exclaimed. "Well, that's interesting."

"Yes," Zulfiya nodded. "And who knows? Maybe during Ibrahim's reign, his associates managed to take Caliph Harun al-Rashid's riches away from Ma'mun. That means we should probably be looking in Baghdad after all—where Ibrahim ruled!"

"I've had it with this Baghdad!" Kudrat erupted. "But... if that's where the treasure is, then fine—fly there again! Find out anything you can about that... what's-his-name... Caliph Ibrahim!"

"Sure thing, boss! Will do," Sher answered for them all. "I'll buy tickets for all of us today—and keep an eye on these guys so they don't pull any more stupid stunts!"

23

Baghdad, Abbasid Caliphate, 819 AD

After several months of siege, Ma'mun took control of Baghdad, and Caliph Ibrahim fled. A few days later, he was found—not to be killed, but imprisoned in a dungeon.

The military commander, Tahir, was friends with the warden, Parza. Parza conveyed a request from one of the highborn prisoners: to meet and speak with Tahir. When Tahir's wife, Benu, learned that the prisoner was Caliph Ibrahim ibn al-Mahdi, she did all she could to dissuade her husband from visiting him:

"Habibi, you know how severe the returned Caliph Ma'mun can

be!" she began to lament. "He's furious with his uncle Ibrahim, who seized the throne through conspiracies and held it for nearly two years. Maybe you shouldn't get involved in these political intrigues? It's so dangerous for you—for all of us! Ma'mun himself gave us this house in Baghdad—only temporarily, but still a good one. No worse than what we had in Merv. But just as he gave it to us, he could take it away at any moment—for any sign of disobedience. And our lives, too!"

"In large part, you're right, my habibti," Tahir replied. "But I'm a warrior. I'm not used to being afraid or hiding behind screens and curtains. A man of noble birth hasn't exactly asked for my help—only for a meeting and a conversation. It would not be right to refuse him. Have you considered that, if tomorrow he were to become caliph once more, his servants might kill me for showing no compassion toward him? But it's not even about that."

"Then what is it?" Benu asked, close to tears, fearing the wrath of Caliph Ma'mun, who had risen anew from the ashes.

"I'm sorry for this aging Ibrahim," Tahir admitted honestly. "I'll go talk with him. At the very least, I'll find out if he needs anything. Please prepare some good food for me to take to him. Who knows what conditions he's being kept in? It's certainly not the Palace, and he's used—if not to luxury, then at least to comfort and good meals. And he hasn't turned to any other influential figure in the Caliphate—he turned to me. That means something."

* * *

"Thank you for coming, honourable Tahir," the deposed Caliph Ibrahim said. "Please, have a seat. I have always respected you, and I was not mistaken. Given my circumstances, I must say—you are a bold and courageous man. If Caliph Ma'mun finds out you've visited me, he might take revenge on you and your loved ones."

"I'm hoping he doesn't find out," Tahir replied, likely reassuring himself more than anyone else. "The warden here is a longtime, trusted friend of mine. He would never betray us."

"That's good to hear," Ibrahim nodded. "I believe you are a trustworthy man. So, if you'll allow me, I'll briefly recount the story of my flight after my nephew Ma'mun reclaimed the throne. Then, as a wise man, perhaps you can tell me whether I have any hope of saving my life—or whether I must resign myself to the fate of Sarakhsi, al-Rida, and the other great souls who have passed on."

"I'm listening closely, honourable Ibrahim," Tahir said.

"When I heard about the reward my highborn nephew Ma'mun had placed on my head, I panicked and was thrown into turmoil," Ibrahim began his lengthy account. "At midday, I left my house in disguise.

"At first, I had no idea where to go and ended up in a dead-end alley. I exclaimed, 'Truly, we belong to God, and to Him we shall return! I've doomed myself! If I go back home, they'll suspect me—looking as I do, like a man in disguise.' Then, at the end of the alley, I saw an African slave standing by the gate of his house. I approached him and asked, 'Do you have a place where I can hide for a little while?' 'Yes,' he replied, and opened the gate. I entered a clean house with reed mats and leather cushions. The slave, Yusuf, led me inside, locked the door behind me, and left."

"He left you right after letting you in, honoured sir?" Tahir asked in surprise. "That's strange! A hospitable host doesn't behave like that!"

"You're absolutely right, honoured one," Ibrahim agreed. "I suspected him as well. I thought he must have heard about the reward and had gone to report me, so I'd be arrested in his house. I was furious. But then, suddenly, the African slave returned—with a porter who had brought everything I could need: bread, meat, new cooking pots, spoons and plates, a new cup, and pitchers.

"Slave Yusuf took the cargo from the porter, then turned to me and said, 'May my life be a ransom for you! I earn my living by bloodletting, so that people may be healed. I know you won't scorn me for how I make my living. These are items no one has used before you. Use them as you wish.'

"Now, I was in dire need of food, so I cooked myself a good meal—my nurse had taught me how. Then Yusuf said, 'O my lord! My station is not such that I can ask you to sing, but there is a debt you owe me. If you would honour me, your servant, I will see that you receive worthy gifts.'"

"I know, honoured Ibrahim, how musical you are and how beautifully you sing," Tahir remarked, only now remembering, since he hadn't heard Ibrahim's songs in some time. "You have a rare voice and marvellous talent. But how did the slave know it?"

"I asked him the same," Ibrahim answered. "I didn't think he knew who I was. I said, 'And what makes you think I sing well?' The African replied, 'Our lord is well known for it! You, master, are Ibrahim ibn al-Mahdi—the Caliph until yesterday—the one for whose head Ma'mun has offered one hundred thousand dinars! But don't be afraid! You are safe here with me.'"

"When Yusuf said that, he grew great in my eyes, and I became certain of his noble spirit. So I agreed to grant his request. Taking up the lute, I tuned it and began to sing—about my separation from my son and family, and about how God might exalt and richly bless this Yusuf.

"He was overcome with extraordinary joy. I believe that, in that moment, his entire life seemed blissful to him! When happiness seized him, Yusuf cried, 'O lord! Will you permit me to say what has come to my mind, though I am by no means practiced in that art?' And I replied, 'Do it. You've shown yourself noble, my dear friend, and you've chased away my sorrow. Do whatever your heart desires.'"

"And what did he do?" Tahir asked. "I hope nothing untoward?"

"No, not at all!" Ibrahim exclaimed. "He sang me a song he had composed himself! Though he was practically illiterate, the song was splendid—about honour and dignity, about death and life, and about trusting good people. Hearing Yusuf's words, I was utterly astounded, and my boundless delight led me—yesterday's Caliph—to bow before a slave! Euphoric, I dozed off and didn't awaken until evening.

"And my thoughts returned to the greatness of this bloodletter's spirit and his propriety. I took my sandalwood casket, which held gold dinars, tossed it to the slave, and said, 'I entrust you to God! I'm leaving. Please, take whatever you need from this chest that bears my emblem and use it for your needs. Accept this as my gift.'

"But Yusuf returned the sandalwood casket to me, saying, 'O my lord! We poor souls in your presence are worth nothing. But I follow my own nobility. How could I accept money for the good fortune that chance has brought me—that you've come to stay with me here? And if you reject my words and throw your money at me again, what reason would I have to go on living?' So I slipped the casket back into the pocket of my robe and left."

"When I reached the house's gate, Yusuf said to me, 'O my lord! You would be safer hiding here than anywhere else, and it's no burden for me to have you stay. Remain with me until God delivers you!' And I went back inside and said, 'On the condition that you spend from what's in this chest.' The African slave agreed to that.

"I stayed with him for a few days, living well—though he never took a thing from the chest. Eventually, I deemed it improper to remain under his protection. I felt ashamed of imposing on him, so I left. Changing into women's clothing—shoes and a veil—I walked out of his house. Once on the road, I was seized by intense fear and attempted to cross a bridge, only to reach a flooded patch of ground.

"Suddenly, a soldier—one who had once served me—spotted me. He recognized me and shouted, 'There's the man Caliph Ma'mun wants!'

"He seized me, but to save my life I pushed him, knocking both him and his horse down on the slippery ground. People rushed toward him while I tried to flee as quickly as I could. After crossing the bridge, I found myself on another street. In front of a house, I saw open gates and, within them, a woman.

"I said to her, 'O mistress! Take pity on me—save my life! I'm a man in fear.' She answered, 'Peace and comfort to you—come in!' She told me her name: Dilbar.

"She led me into a room, laid out a place for me, and brought me food. 'Let your fear subside; not a soul will learn about you,' she said. And for a time, that's how it was.

"But suddenly, there was a loud knock on the gate.

"The woman went out and opened it—and in came that very soldier I had pushed on the bridge. His head was bandaged, blood soaked his clothes, and his horse was nowhere in sight.

"'Hey you, what happened to you?' asked Dilbar. The soldier said, 'I caught a man, but he slipped away from me.' He recounted what had happened, and the woman took a piece of cloth, tore it into strips, and bandaged his head. Then she prepared a place for him, and he lay down, injured. She came back to me and said, 'I suspect you're the one that soldier was talking about… but you'll be fine.' And again, she treated me with kindness."

"I stayed three days at Dilbar's place. Then she said to me, 'I fear that man may harm you if he finds out who you are and reports you to your pursuers over the very thing you dread. Save yourself!' I asked her to let me wait until nightfall, and she agreed. That night, I dressed in women's clothing again and left.

"I went to the house of Shahida, a freedwoman who might have been freed by me personally. On seeing me, she began to cry and lament, praising Almighty God for my escape.

"Then she left, as though intending to go to the market to prepare a feast for me. I took it as a good sign. But I had scarcely blinked before I saw the Caliph's guard, 'the Mosuli,' approaching with his servants and troops—and leading them was a woman.

"I looked carefully and suddenly realized it was Shahida—the mistress of the house where I was hiding! She walked at the front of the soldiers. I had no time to flee, nor at that point did I think it fitting to run. And the lady of the house turned me over to her 'guests.' In that moment, it felt to me as though I were staring death in the face…"

"Ah, yes, I understand all too well," Tahir said sympathetically.

"They took me to Ma'mun in whatever clothes I happened to be wearing. So then—tomorrow morning, he will summon a gathering of all his officials and order his guards to bring me before him. I suspect you, revered Tahir, as one of Ma'mun's closest men, will certainly be at that gathering. If you believe I still have any hope of survival—if you are inclined to show me even a bit of mercy—please speak a word in my defence! I'll be forever grateful, beyond measure."

"I need nothing," Tahir replied with humble calm. "I won't promise anything in vain, but… let's see how it goes. I'll do all I can."

"Thank you with all my heart," said Ibrahim, placing his hand over his chest and bowing.

The next morning, Caliph Ma'mun did indeed hold a gathering of his highborn subjects who served at the Palace.

By Ma'mun's order, they brought his uncle Ibrahim into the throne room. Entering, Ibrahim saluted Ma'mun as Caliph. But Ma'mun cried:

"May God grant you no peace and no long life, Uncle!"

"Don't be hasty, Commander of the Faithful," Ibrahim answered. "Only Almighty God has the authority to bring vengeance or forgiveness. Yet clemency is closer to piety. God has placed your pardon above every pardon, just as He has placed my sin above every sin. If you punish me, you act with justice; but if you forgive me, you act with mercy."

After that, Ibrahim recited verses about how his own offense against Ma'mun was great, but Ma'mun's offense would be greater still if he responded with cruelty. He called on Ma'mun to be gentle and forgiving.

"If I haven't proved myself worthy in my deeds, then you, in your deeds, should show that worth," he concluded.

Then Ma'mun turned to his son Abbas, to his brother Abu Ishaq, and to all those closest to him, asking:

"Well?! What do you think about this matter? What shall I do with my uncle Ibrahim?"

"He deserves death!" nearly all answered in one voice, disagreeing only on how to execute the man who had so recently been Caliph.

Ma'mun looked at Tahir, noticing his silence, and asked:

"What do you say, our illustrious warrior?"

"O Commander of the Faithful!" Tahir replied, "if you kill him, there will be many like you who kill many like him. But if you forgive him, I doubt we will find anywhere another man like you, who forgives one such as he! If we cast our arrow, will it not strike us? And we know you as our gracious and compassionate master."

Ma'mun nodded to him and said:

"Then let it be so! If my friend wishes to anger me, I will pardon him and absolve him of guilt. For I fear that otherwise, I might have to live without my friend. I shall show mercy to him—and to myself as well! Uncle, I have no reproach for you on a day such as this. May the All-Merciful God forgive you. I too forgive you and restore to you your property and estates."

Ibrahim raised fervent prayers on Ma'mun's behalf and recited verses of gratitude and praise. After the assembly, he approached Tahir and discreetly expressed his thanks for his advocacy and friendship. Tahir remained silent.

The Caliph, upon learning the full story of his uncle Ibrahim's flight, ordered generous rewards for the African slave Yusuf and for the woman Dilbar, who had mercifully sheltered both Ibrahim and the soldier who had been his enemy.

He punished the soldier. Ma'mun commanded that the soldier's house and all its contents be given to Yusuf, bestowed upon him an honorary robe, and decreed that he receive an annual stipend of fifteen thousand dinars. As for Dilbar, Ma'mun showed her great respect, telling her to come to the Palace and saying:

"You are a wise woman, and you'll be useful in the important affairs of state. You will receive a weekly salary from us and live at the Palace."

Afterward, Ma'mun ordered that Shahida—the freedwoman who had revealed Ibrahim's whereabouts to the guards and handed him over—be brought before him. At that moment, she was at home, expecting a grand reward from the Caliph.

When she stood before Ma'mun, he asked:

"What prompted you to do such a thing to your master Ibrahim?"

"I love the sound of gold coins," Shahida admitted.

"Do you have a child or husband?" asked the Caliph.

"No, my lord!" she replied.

Caliph Ma'mun ordered his servants to give her one hundred lashes and imprison her for life.

I wonder, Tahir suddenly recalled, *which Caliph ended up with the turban that had a pearl the size of a lemon? I didn't see it on Ma'mun today. Did Ibrahim take it in secret, or not? Is he truly honest and noble? I still don't know everything about him…*

24

Samarkand, 2023

Having freed Barno with the help of his operatives and a special task group, Captain Salimov took her to the hospital and called Sharaf so he could come visit her. The bandits they had apprehended were temporarily placed in a detention centre. Investigator Salimov summoned them one by one to his office at the police station. What they said was later retold to Sharaf by Barno herself, when the young man came to see her in her hospital room.

"Thank you, Sharaf, for worrying about me," said the girl, whose overall condition was still far from good. "And thank you so much for the fruit. But why did you spend so much? There's enough here to feed the entire ward!"

"Eat as much as you like and get well soon," Sharaf said with a smile. "You've gotten so thin during those terrifying days! And you have injuries, too. Those scoundrels beat you? It's outrageous!"

"Captain Salimov said that as soon as you feel better, you need to file a report against them. Then he will take all necessary measures. Naturally, everything will be done lawfully and in accordance with the principles of justice. But why did they kidnap you? Why did they need you?"

"My father, Fahriyar Tursunov, has been missing for more than a week," Barno began. "He's just a regular college instructor who got sick of being poor. So a few months ago, he decided to start his own small business—open a stall in one of the clothing markets."

"His own business?" Sharaf asked. "But that's a good thing! A worthwhile venture."

"Yes, if you have plenty of your own money," Barno remarked. "And most important—this I know from reading books by successful, wealthy entrepreneurs—is that a person must have the necessary knowledge. Without knowledge of basic business principles, strategies, and an understanding of how finances work, a novice entrepreneur can easily be duped. Or he might quickly 'go broke' and lose everything. I guess that's what happened to my father. I was caught up in my own job and didn't know what problems Dad was facing."

"Did your father try to borrow money from official sources—banks?" the Qatari inquired.

"Of course," Barno nodded. "He prepared the paperwork, but he had no initial capital, and the banks wouldn't approve a business loan for him—likely because we had nothing to offer as collateral. Our apartment isn't worth much, and on top of that, my mother flatly refused to sign off on mortgaging our only property as security for a loan."

"She was right," Sharaf noted. "What would you have done—live on the streets?"

"We don't even own a car," Barno went on. "But it turns out one of Dad's acquaintances, Victor, was somehow connected with those bandits—I found that out from the bandits themselves. This Victor introduced Dad to their boss, Gosha. Dad borrowed money from those frightening people at a huge interest rate. But… they gave him the money instantly. That's what appealed to my father. I didn't get involved in his business and don't know the details. But Dad's business failed, and the gang put him 'on the clock,' so to speak."

"I see…" Sharaf sighed sympathetically. The young man felt awkward that, in such a complicated situation, he hadn't been able to help this good girl and her family.

"Gosha is a thug," Barno said, shuddering at the memory. "But fortunately—at least—he never let any of them harass me as a woman. Even so… it's a wonder I made it out alive. They beat me often and hard. It hurt so much…"

"And thank God you're alive! Now it's all behind you."

"I hope so…"

"And where is your father?" Sharaf asked. "Have you seen him at all lately?"

"No," Barno shook her head. "I suppose he's gone into hiding somewhere, without a thought for me or my mother. Though… she's living her own life, too. She doesn't care about me."

"I gathered as much from the conversation my police friend, dear Ibrahim, had with her," Sharaf said candidly. "But why is that? Forgive me—could she be drinking?"

"No—what makes you think that?" asked Barno in surprise.

"Well, generally people love their kids, worry about them, and take care of them," Sharaf explained. "Unless they're drug addicts or drunkards. Sorry…"

"It's fine," the girl smiled. "No. Actually, my mother isn't my birth mother. She's been raising me since I was five, but she never managed to love me like her own child. My real mother died twenty years ago of a serious illness."

"I see," the young man replied with sympathy, nodding. "Please don't despair, dear Barno! We'll figure something out. We'll find your father."

"You said that captain is your friend, right?" Barno said anxiously. She so wanted to trust the pleasant Qatari youth.

"Captain Ibrahim Salimov?" Sharaf clarified. "Yes, he's my older friend, a good and decent man. He's the one who found you! Well then, why don't we ask him to find your father too? After all, those bandits who were looking for him are in custody now, so presumably his life is no longer in danger. And eventually he can repay his debt to them, right?"

"Yes, of course," Barno brightened at this new hope. "I'll work hard myself to help Dad pay off that horrible debt! If only they'd stop all those 'daily penalties' and usurious interest rates that go through the roof!"

"I'll do what I can to help," Sharaf said with a smile. "I am, after all, a budding lawyer. We'll sort it out! But please, get well soon. And promise me that later you'll also help me with one very interesting and mysterious business. Deal?"

"You said that in such a way it almost sounds like it involves some ancient map and old Eastern treasures!" Barno laughed, not realizing how "on target" she really was.

"Who knows, who knows?" her new friend said with a mysterious smile.

* * *

Doha, Qatar, the same period

Someone knocked on the office door of hotel-chain owner Sarwan al-Tawil.

"Come in!" he called out.

"Good day, Mr. al-Tawil!" the visitor greeted as he entered. "My name is Fahad. I'm a private detective, here at the request of my boss, Colonel Rashid Khatib."

"Please, sit down, Fahad," said the influential businessman in a clipped but polite tone. "I'm listening. Did you manage to learn anything concrete about this... hmm... young man? Do you have pictures?"

"Yes, here they are, Mr. al-Tawil." Fahad was a bit nervous, seeing the kind of powerful man he was dealing with, but he strove not to disgrace himself and to speak clearly and to the point. "His name is Nizar Abbas. He's twenty-seven years old and unmarried. And—"

"That's good," Sarwan cut in. "If he's not married, it'll be simpler to handle him! Does he work anywhere? Or is he just some idle brat with wealthy parents? Because I heard he goes to that super-elite private club. But I doubt he's anybody important. So where did he even get a 'gold card'?"

"Now we come to the main point, Mr. al-Tawil," Fahad said, smiling over his investigative success. Indeed, the detective was proud of having uncovered information about these people. But now he worried he might pause too long and anger this other man of power—Sarwan al-Tawil. "This fellow, Nizar Abbas—the one you're interested in—is the son and junior partner of Mr. Najib Abbas! In fact, Nizar himself helps manage the biggest commercial institution, *Abbas Bank*, alongside his father. He's head of the finance department. He's also... on the Board of Directors."

The detective figured that even a man as savvy and powerful as Sarwan al-Tawil would need at least a few seconds—or even minutes—to process the information that had just come crashing down on him.

25

Baghdad, the same period

"This city is so huge!" Sanya whined. "Where on earth are we supposed to find anything here connected to Caliph Ibrahim?! Vanya and I already scoured everything in the old manuscripts library on our last trip. Zulfiya, if it's not a secret, where are you planning to look for this ancient Arab map?"

"Exactly," Vanya chimed in. "Because it's been fifteen centuries since Ibrahim's time. That's nearly one and a half thousand years! In all that time, even gold could've turned to dust… Though no, that's not right. Gold stays in perfect condition forever. If only we could get our hands on those hundred thousand dinars that the generous Caliph al-Ma'mun offered for Ibrahim's head…"

"Only Ma'mun, 'His Majesty Generosity,' didn't give them to anyone—he kept them for himself," Zulfiya smirked. "Where they've ended up now, only the Almighty knows. But perhaps the answer lies in that same map we're looking for? And so far, we don't even know who in the Abbasid dynasty ordered it to be made— Amin, Ma'mun, Ibrahim, or one of their descendants…"

"Unlikely to be Amin," Vanya reminded her. "You yourself said that after him, everything went to Ma'mun."

"Exactly! And see, you're always saying the right things!" Sanya all but sang, gazing open-mouthed at the young woman. "You're so clever, Zulfiya! And so beauti—"

"Shut your mouth or a fly will get in," Vanya teased, cutting Sanya off when he noticed his friend's growing admiration for their "kind of boss in a skirt."

"Where to now?" asked Sher in a plainer tone, nearly echoing the thought that Sanya and Vanya had just expressed.

This muscle-bound man, who had been authorized by Kudrat Valiev to pay for and oversee all the expenses of the small group, had rented the cheapest yet most convenient car from a car-sharing service and was now standing around idly.

"Let's think," Zulfiya proposed, speaking to everyone at once. "What if we look up antique shops and stalls online and go check them out? Maybe, among the old stuff, we'll get lucky and randomly stumble across the second half of the cloth map we need?"

"I don't mind!" Sanya said eagerly—he tended not to argue with the beautiful young woman and preferred to agree with her on everything.

"Will there be a café there?" Vanya asked. "I'm starving!"

"We'll find one, you gluttons," teased the trim Zulfiya, who ate little and maintained an excellent figure. Her gentle jab included all the men.

Several days went by.

The "investigators" toured nearly all of Baghdad's antique shops and markets worth visiting. But no ancient maps turned up. They did spot one intriguing early-20th-century map painted on some sort of animal skin. It depicted the Abbasid Caliphate of the 9th–10th centuries. Zulfiya ordered them to buy it, and Sher—obediently—paid the seller.

"Maybe it'll come in handy," the woman explained. "Though of course, it's not really what we're after. But it's a pretty map. No idea whose hide it is—maybe an antelope's."

"Made of gold?" asked Sanya, who was seeing gold everywhere these days and still recalling an old cartoon with a similar story.

"Are you stupid?" Vanya glowered at his friend. "Why on earth would it be gold?"

"I suppose it's just plain old leather," Zulfiya said with a wry grin. She was amused by Sanya's naive spontaneity and Vanya's dead-serious manner. But from both their vocabulary and, more importantly, their behaviour and manners, she sensed they were both rather "questionable characters." Possibly even thieves. Sher also seemed like a "dark horse" to her. All of this made the young woman uneasy, yet she had to put up with them—Valiev had promised her a decent fee for the job.

Finally, in one small shop of old items at the Baghdad market,

Zulfiya suddenly noticed something that intrigued her. Looking more closely, she was delighted.

"What's got you smiling?" Sher grumbled. "Some half-rotted wooden box? So what? I could bring you a pile of those from any Tashkent market."

"Not any market—only the Old City," Vanya corrected the uneducated remark.

"How about you stop trying to sound clever and let her talk?" Sanya intervened on Zulfiya's behalf.

"All right," Sher said without protest.

Vanya just nodded in agreement.

Keeping her voice low so the seller—and more importantly, other prospective buyers—wouldn't sense her excitement, Zulfiya went on:

"Look at this chest—or more accurately, this small trunk. It's made of wonderfully fragrant wood—sandalwood. So, on its front wall there's a seal. Back when we were studying the 9th-century Arab Caliphate's history together, I remember seeing a symbol like this somewhere. I'm pretty sure it's... the personal seal of Caliph Ibrahim!! Which means this is precisely the little casket that, according to legend, Ibrahim gave to that hospitable African slave who fed him and sheltered him?! Can you believe it?! Right now I'm holding something that once belonged to a Caliph of the Abbasid dynasty! It looks like it was treated with resin, and that's how it survived to the present day."

"That's all well and good, but you've been told to find a map," Sher reminded them all sternly.

"We know that without you!" Vanya snapped. "Trying to lecture grown 'kids'..."

"Don't fight, boys," Zulfiya said to all of them with a smile, then asked Sher to pay for this item as well. Fortunately, because the seller didn't recognize the historical significance of Caliph Ibrahim's trunk, it wasn't expensive.

Once they were outside, Zulfiya told the men,

"I want to be honest. I'll admire it all I want and then hand it over to our Samarkand museum so others can admire it too. It's a piece of genuine history, after all!"

"What a woman you are, Zulfiya…" Sanya mumbled in awe. "Oh, what a woman!"

"Where to now?" Sher asked, directing the question exclusively to the woman, pointedly ignoring the two guys he found tiresome and useless.

"I think back home to Tashkent," the young historian sighed regretfully. "And then maybe we'll fly to Turkmenistan. Or… just go straight there. Right, Sher?"

"Sure, we can go straight there," Sher replied. "The boss already gave the green light for Turkmenistan, didn't he? Why waste time going back and forth, returning home empty-handed? Valiev won't exactly pat us on the head for that."

"And do we have enough money for all the flights?" Sanya fretted.

"Don't worry, there's money," Sher said, once again looking only at Zulfiya.

But on the way to the airport, Vanya and Sher got hungry again. No one else objected to grabbing a bite, so they stopped at a cozy-looking café.

While they were eating, Sanya noticed a jewellery store directly across from the window. Lying to everyone that he had to pop into the restroom, the incorrigible thief dashed off to admire the jewellery that had enthralled him since his youth.

However, Vanya spotted his friend through the café window. Making the same excuse to Zulfiya and Sher, he slipped off to the jewellery shop without the pair noticing.

"What'd you forget here, you 'Baghdad thief'?" Vanya whispered just behind Sanya's ear as the latter stared at some large-carat "diamonds" in gold settings.

Sanya jolted in surprise and hissed at his friend.

"Will you ever quit?" Vanya continued in a low voice. "Or are you planning to buy something?"

Sanya scowled in response.

"Dammit, Vanya! You scared me. I'm not going to buy anything. I just wanted to check out how the Arabs live—what kind of jewellery they wear, and what stones they use."

"They live well—very well," Vanya answered calmly on behalf of all Arabs, "and their stones are pretty impressive, too. Had a look? Good. Let's go!"

"What's with the bossing around?" Sanya hissed at his friend.

"Because I know you—I didn't meet you yesterday," Vanya replied, still speaking quietly so the Baghdad vendors, who wouldn't understand them anyway, wouldn't overhear. "We're already getting a decent wage from Kudrat. You're acting like a child. This is neither the place nor the time for your stunts!"

Just then, Sanya reluctantly turned around to follow his friend back to the café, where they'd likely already been missed by their "boss," Zulfiya, and the man overseeing them for Valiev—Sher. Vanya, smiling at the silliness of it all, gave his buddy a pat on the shoulder and took a big step toward the exit—when suddenly someone pounced on them both, punching and yelling:

"Grab them! Catch the thieves!! These foreigners wanted to rob our Palace!"

Sanya and Vanya had no time to explain or protest. They had to flee at once, or they'd be caught. They broke free of those surprisingly familiar hands, sprinted outside, grabbed Zulfiya and Sher, jumped into their car, and raced to the airport.

Only once on the plane bound for Ashgabat did the two friends breathe a sigh of relief. By then, they were no longer as frightened or tense. Almost in unison, they cried out: "Garib! That's the tour guide from the Palace! The scoundrel nearly got us!"

"You two are always getting tangled up in something," Sher grumbled from the seat beside them. "And then we have to yank you out!"

"Not this time—you didn't do a thing," Sanya retorted. "We saved ourselves, thank you very much."

Zulfiya glanced at them both, still confused about what had happened—why the four of them had bolted out of Iraq's capital like scalded cats.

But she decided it was best not to delve too deeply. The less you know, the better you sleep.

"As long as we're all alive and well, thank God," she said, leaning back in her seat and starting to doze off.

"Sanya, what was that guy holding in his hand?" Vanya suddenly remembered. "A newspaper or something?"

"You're the 'newspaper,' Vanya!" Sanya teased in return. "It looked more like a very old paper map."

"A map again?!" Vanya was surprised. "But so what if it's not the ancient Arab treasure map we need, right? Wait—didn't you rip a piece off it when you fought that Garib? Probably threw it away?"

"Why would I do that? Of course I kept it—just in case!" Sanya said proudly.

"And what for? So that one day you can brag to your grandkids how tough you are?" Vanya laughed. "Show me!"

"Here, look." Sanya pulled a small scrap of badly worn paper from the breast pocket of his shirt. "Something's written on it—looks like Arabic. But what do we do with it?"

"Let's ask someone on the plane to read it," Vanya suggested.

"It says 'oturu,'" read one friendly fellow passenger.

"What does that mean?" Zulfiya asked—the noise from her boisterous companions had robbed her of her nap.

"It means 'incense,'" the passenger translated.

"'Incense'?" Sanya and Vanya repeated. "Sounds nice!"

"You know," Zulfiya mused for some reason, "this word might not be random. What do you think, gentlemen? Maybe it's some sort of clue for us. Maybe it's a bit mystical, but… I have a feeling it's connected to the secret of the treasure we're looking for…"

26

Sharjah, United Arab Emirates, the same period

Mahshud al-Mualla, Head of the State Department of Tourism and Antiquities, could be soft and democratic only among his friends—historians and archaeologists. In all other situations, and with most other people, he was the "Big Boss"—always extremely serious and uncompromising.

Naturally, word of his friend, archaeologist Nazih Abu Jalil, being arrested reached Mahshud fairly quickly. He did not summon the famous museum's director, Dari Irshad, to his office; instead, he personally drove to the Archaeological Museum.

"Mr. Director, why did you not inform me yourself that Nazih was arrested?" Mahshud asked Dari, attempting to remain courteous and composed. "And why did you, without my knowledge… ahem… call the police? How could you?!"

"Forgive me, sir," Dari replied with his head lowered, "but Mr. Nazih… he's the one who called the police himself!"

"What?!" an astonished Mahshud repeated, raising his voice slightly. "What for? How could he be at fault?"

"I—I… don't know," stammered Dari, who was somewhat afraid of the influential Mahshud.

"What are you mumbling about?" the Big Boss scowled. "Answer directly, please: what happened at the museum yesterday? I know you had the opening of the exhibit with Nazih's new Abbasid-era archaeological finds just a few days ago."

"Yes, Mr. Mahshud al-Mualla," Dari Irshad nodded. "You personally visited the exhibit on opening day for a few minutes."

"Yes, because I'm constantly busy," Mahshud said, as if justifying himself. "But I did manage to talk business here with two or three important people. That's beside the point. So what happened yesterday? Everything was fine! Did you open a new exhibit—without my permission? But from what I can tell, it's all the same items!"

"It's the same exhibit, *ustadi*," the sweating director explained, clearly nervous. "Mr. Nazih came every day. I'm not sure why. Perhaps he was just basking in the glow of his fame and couldn't get enough—"

"You forget yourself, respected Dari," Mahshud cut him off

firmly, though not rudely. "My friend Nazih has every right to savour his fame. He's the most outstanding, most talented archaeologist in our country. And all his finds are unique. Why shouldn't he admire them one more time before you hide them away in underground storerooms and archives for years on end?"

"My apologies, sir," Dari said humbly. "Yesterday, when Nazih once again approached the display case with Princess Zubaidah's jewelled diadem, he cried out loud."

"So something frightened or alarmed him?" Mahshud suggested.

"He immediately claimed that all the treasures in the new exhibit were copies of the precious finds he'd unearthed! But that's a shocking misunderstanding! I can't comprehend how it's even possible. Who would dare do such a thing here, in a place frequently visited and patronized by His Highness himself? It's nonsense!"

"Dari, I'm still not clear: why didn't Nazih notice the substitution on the first day of the exhibit?" Mahshud asked sternly.

"Because apparently, on the first day, there was no switch," the museum director answered. Then, suddenly realizing what Mahshud was implying, he added: "Wait, *ustadi*! You think Mr. Nazih is innocent? That somebody framed him? And now he's locked up… in someone else's place?"

"Yes—in place of the real thief," Mahshud finished the thought. "It's just unclear how he got caught. Presumably, most of the valuables weren't found on him!"

"Indeed! But how did you figure that out?" Dari asked, surprised.

"Nazih and I have been friends for many years," Mahshud explained. "I know him very well."

* * *

Arriving at the police station where archaeologist Nazih was being held, Mahshud looked for the chief's office. A sign on the door read: "S. al-Iman."

"Greetings, Mr. Iman," he said, knocking and then entering. "I need to speak with you."

"Hello," Iman replied curtly. "Have a seat. I'm listening. Who are you, and what is the matter?"

"My name is Saud ibn Mahshud," the visitor said. "May I ask on what grounds my friend and colleague, Mr. Nazih Abu Jalil, is being detained?"

"Who? Oh, yes. He was brought in yesterday. We suspect him of stealing government property of especially high value," the station chief answered, just as unemotionally.

Mahshud was surprised by the man's demeanour, noting that he offered no special deference.

"Do you have any proof of his guilt?" Mahshud asked, striving to appear just as calm.

"Certainly," Iman replied, still stone-faced and without even glancing at the Big Boss of tourism and antiquities. "But that's part of the investigation. I can't discuss it."

"Hold on," Mahshud objected. "If this were really about some notorious crook or repeat offender, I'd not only agree with you but be glad to help lock him away for a long time."

"Commendable," Iman noted, sounding like a teacher giving a mark—though without a trace of emotion in his voice.

"But I'm not talking about myself," Mahshud continued. "Ustadi Nazih Abu Jalil is a world-renowned archaeologist, a scholar of international standing—"

"Excellent," the station chief interrupted in a monotone. "So what?"

"You don't understand—he could never have committed any theft! Not ever!" Mahshud burst out.

"No need to shout," Iman calmly advised. "Why not? They all say that, and then they steal. And we put them in prison."

"That's simply not who Nazih is!" Mahshud flared up again. "Sorry. But don't you get it? If he'd wanted to keep even all those Abbasid treasures for himself, he could have done it quietly— during the desert digs! He's the one who found them. If he wanted to, he could've just taken them on the spot, unnoticed."

"Ah, so he *could* have done it," the dense Iman concluded.

"No! That's not what I meant," Mahshud said, exasperated. "I meant theoretically. Archaeologist Nazih is an honest man! Someone obviously planted the items on him."

"His fingerprints are on them," Iman replied, his face unmoved. "They're also on the valuables storage and the key to it. The exhibits were found in his bag. His guilt is proven. So he'll do time."

Getting nowhere, and not being a relative of the detainee— thus lacking permission to visit—an irked and furious Mahshud left.

* * *

Nazih was transferred from the police station to a detention centre for further investigation. He was placed in a cell with hardened conmen, thieves, and repeat offenders. True, there weren't many inmates in that cell, but the cultured academic—though accustomed to discomfort during long field expeditions—found the atmosphere deeply unsettling at first. He eyed his cellmates warily and distrustfully, and they took every opportunity to taunt this man from a different world.

So when a guard told Nazih to prepare for a visitor, he was delighted, thinking perhaps his wife or son had come. In his distress, he'd forgotten that all his family members, except him, were vacationing in Europe.

Cut off from the outside world, Nazih had no way of knowing that they hadn't been able to reach him—and were growing increasingly worried. Once they finally got in touch with Mahshud, he explained to Nazih's wife, Samira, what had happened.

Samira asked their son, Ilham, to return home immediately. But that day, they were still too far away to visit the head of the family.

When Nazih was brought to the visitation room, he immediately recognized the visitor—and was quite astonished by who it was.

"Hello, dear *ustadi* Nazih!" the museum collections manager, Bob Downey, greeted him with exaggerated warmth and sugary politeness.

"Mr. Downey?" the archaeologist replied in surprise. "What are you doing here??? How did they even allow you in? My friend Mahshud wasn't permitted… yet *you*—?"

"Well, you see," Bob answered with feigned astonishment, "it's all about having the right connections! So I came to check on you—see how you're doing. Comfortable enough here?"

"Are you kidding me?" Nazih asked, scowling. "You were the one mocking me when the officers hauled me away at the museum! Why've you come now—to gloat?"

"Oh no, sir!" Bob declared, still in that cloyingly sweet tone. "How could I?! You're in serious trouble—no one jokes about that.

I brought you a little treat. Here: mandarins, grapefruit, and orange juice."

"All my colleagues know I've had a citrus allergy since childhood," Nazih reminded him. "Haven't you ever heard of that?"

"No, Mr. Nazih, no," Bob lied smoothly. "I can't possibly know everyone's allergies or ailments, now can I? Ah yes—my apologies, how could I forget? You're our big star! A super-famous personality! Everyone's supposed to know everything about you, worship and idolize you for your discoveries, right? Dance circles around you, pampering Your Highness! Forgive me for letting it slip my mind."

"So you came here just to torment me?" Nazih asked bluntly, his throat dry.

"No, no—what do you mean, dear scientist? Excuse me if I gave you that impression. I only sympathize with you. Clearly, you won't be getting out of here anytime soon."

"I've done nothing wrong," Nazih insisted in his own defence. "All they found on me were two of Caliph Ma'mun's gold dinars. That's it. But I didn't steal them—and *you* know that, don't you? Because *you're* the one who set me up, aren't you? And the rest of my Abbasid valuables—*you* have them, don't you?"

Bob Downey smiled with mock innocence.

"Shh, Mr. Archaeologist," he said, placing a finger to his lips. "Why shout it to the entire world? Perhaps you should first prove *my* guilt, and your *own* innocence—before spouting nonsense. Clear? I'll be waiting for you. On the outside."

Having figured things out, Nazih saw no point in arguing with this young man who seemed deranged to him. He knocked on the door and asked to be taken back to his cell.

Bob Downey, watching Nazih's retreating back, smiled contentedly.

27

Tashkent, Spring 2023

Major Zakir Bakhromov's son, Davron, liked hanging out with friends from his economics university. Most of them were privileged rich kids, many of whom had little interest in studying and loved burning through their parents' money.

Davron Bakhromov had lent money to one of his friends and classmates, Kamil Akbarov. Kamil came from a modest background. He secretly gambled, hoping to win easy money to keep up with his wealthier friends and avoid looking poor among them.

Davron didn't approve of his friend's habit, fearing he himself could end up in serious debt—or even in jail. But after Kamil's persistent pleading and whining, Davron—who never placed much value on personal savings and didn't know how to grow capital—lent him a large sum of money.

"Don't worry, I swear I'll pay you back in full, with interest!" Kamil promised.

"No need for interest," Davron replied, declining the offer. "What am I, a bank? Or a loan shark? Let's just call it a credit—a regular loan."

"Wow! I didn't even know you knew any economic terms," Kamil joked. "You're the one who mostly sleeps or chats during lectures and seminars. But it turns out you've learned a few terms anyway. Okay, as you say. Thanks, man."

Time passed, and Davron largely forgot about Kamil's debt. And Kamil never brought it up again.

***

The same period

Knowing his son had little interest in studying hard, working, or improving himself, Zakir repeatedly urged him to get serious. One day after work, he knocked on Davron's door, came in, and started a serious conversation.

"Davron, tell me: why did I enrol you in that prestigious university, huh?" asked the elder Bakhromov, starting off sternly. Then he changed tactics, choosing to ask questions only—for now. "I even pulled strings—and not for free, mind you—so you could pass the entrance tests and get in! I helped you, and you were admitted, thanks to my connections. And now you've been studying there for about two years. Any success to speak of?"

"It's all good," the young man answered lazily, offering no details. "What do you want, Dad?"

"I want that if anything happens to me, you'll be able to take care of yourself—and look after your mother! So that neither you nor she will be in need. And what are you doing instead?"

"Mom works anyway and makes decent money," his son objected.

"You're forgetting she's not getting any younger, and she can't keep working forever," Zakir explained, practically spelling it out. "Son, soon enough, we'll both need your help!"

"What—I'm supposed to become your nurse? I don't want to!"

whined the spoiled young man.

"Stop being rude to your father!" Zakir reprimanded him. "Not a 'nurse' or a 'caretaker,' but a loving, caring son! A real man, when it comes down to it. Decent kids do this: they at least repay their parents in some way for raising them, feeding them, and getting them educated."

"I never asked you to," Davron snapped. "It's what *you* wanted. And anyway, Dad, what's with all the lectures now? I'm heading out."

"That's all you ever do—go out and have fun. So I'm asking you, what knowledge are you getting at that university of yours? Do you know the laws of economics or business? They're teaching you how to run businesses and manage projects, right? How to handle finances and personnel effectively? What do you even know?"

Davron remained silent, finding his father's questions pushy and irritating.

"You like feeling like a 'big shot' around your friends and the girls, right?" Zakir asked bluntly. "Have you ever realized that your 'coolness' is just a soap bubble? You're only 'rich' because of your father's money!"

"Dad, I don't get it—have you gone stingy?" Davron asked, looking offended. "Don't feel like spending on your only son? You've got loads of cash! What do you need it all for?"

"Like any adult, I have plenty of needs," Zakir tried explaining. "You know I work hard, and my job is dangerous. I'm an investigator, which keeps me busy. Your mother and I have never even managed to travel abroad together! But you've been places. I'd like to travel too. And take your mom. We're people too!"

Davron said nothing. He had two impulses: put on headphones so he wouldn't have to listen to his father's 'nagging' and hurry off to a bar with his friends. But he feared his father's anger and the possibility of losing his allowance. He had no other source of income.

"So how do you even pass your tests if you hardly study and know practically nothing?" Zakir inquired. "When I was in school, I read a ton and studied on my own. What about you?"

"I don't cram," Davron responded lazily. "Why bother? Some students do it all for me—writing my term papers, seminar texts. I just pay them. And some of the professors too. I told you about that when I asked for money."

"Oh yes… I'd forgotten. But aren't there any who refuse or can't be bribed?"

"Sure, quite a few," Davron agreed. "But I find a way around it. I'm not that dumb."

"Really?" his father replied sarcastically. "I'm not so sure… All right, son, go. Rest… from your hard labours. I wish you'd grow up a bit—mentally, first. And learn how to make… ahem… I mean, earn… legitimately."

"Okay, okay," the son waved him off.

"You'll need to marry eventually. That day's not too far off," his father continued, sounding resigned. "I can't pay for your wife and kids your whole life, you know! Think about it, please. Okay? You get any of that?"

"Uh-huh."

"Right. We'll come back to this conversation another time!"

***

Tashkent, Summer 2023, after all the preceding events

After his conversation with his father about finding a "culprit" to take the blame for the accident in which Said Mumtazov was injured, Davron started thinking—and recalled Kamil's debt.

He went to his friend's house.

"How's it going, my man?" Davron asked, plopping himself down at the table, where Kamil's mother had set out tea and sweets.

She discreetly stepped away to give them privacy.

"All good, Davron," Kamil said with a nervous smile, sensing trouble. "Why do you ask?"

"Because you owe me a tidy sum of money," Davron said right away, getting straight to the point. "Remember? Kamil, you borrowed from me a couple of months ago. Shall I tell you how much?"

"No need, I remember," Kamil replied glumly, lowering his gaze. "I'm sorry, I don't have the money right now."

"Oh, poor thing! I feel for you!" Davron mocked. "So where'd it all go? I hope you didn't drink it away?"

"Are you kidding?" Kamil gave a sad smile. "So you're not mad at me? Of course, I didn't drink it away. I'm not a big alcohol fan, remember? It makes me sick."

"All right. So?" Davron persisted, expecting honesty.

"I owed some nasty people," Kamil mumbled. "A lot. You know how I gamble. Well… gambled."

"Oh? So you quit?" the young Bakhromov asked sceptically.

"Yes! I won't go near it again," Kamil assured him. "But I can't pay you back in full right now. I mean, I can… some, but not all. Sorry. If you could wait…"

"No, I won't wait," Davron said, intensifying the pressure without revealing all his plans. "Why should I?"

Kamil began sweating with anxiety and dread. Sure, Davron was a friend, but Kamil owed him a big sum. What if Davron rats him out to his father, the cop? Or maybe he already has? That'd be a nightmare. The Major would lock him up quick! And Kamil's parents likely wouldn't be able to help.

"I'll be right back!" Kamil said, placing his palms together in a pleading gesture. He scurried out of the kitchen like a guilty boy.

"Running away from me, are you?" Davron shouted after him, laughing.

But Kamil soon returned, a few bills in hand.

"Here—everything I've got," he said, offering the small bundle to his friend.

"No, keep it," the younger Bakhromov sneered.

"Why?!" Kamil asked, surprised. "Oh, right, I know—it's not much. But I'll scrape more together—I promise I'll pay back everything. I'll find a way. You believe me? I just need time. Could you forgive me? Please… I don't want to ask my parents! I'm too ashamed, you must understand."

"Yeah!" Davron suddenly exclaimed, loudly, energetically, even cheerfully. "I'm forgiving you, Kamil. Right now! Your entire debt."

Kamil was thunderstruck; he staggered and nearly collapsed onto a chair.

"H—How?" he stammered, unable to hide his shock. "You're joking again, right?"

"No!" Davron said just as brightly and enthusiastically. "But there's one small condition. If you agree, you owe me nothing—not a single dollar, not a single sum. If you refuse, my father will lock you up for your underground gambling. Also, for 'extortion'… or for stealing my money… Your choice!"

"What?!" Kamil exclaimed, more astonished than ever. "But I… You gave me that money voluntarily!"

"Prove it," Davron retorted shamelessly. "Everyone in our group saw me with those big bills that day, flashing them around. They also saw you hanging around me constantly… like usual."

"But that doesn't prove anything!" Kamil protested, still not realizing how pointless it was.

"My father will make sure it proves plenty," Davron replied. "He already knows everything."

The younger Bakhromov was lying; his father, Zakir, knew nothing about Davron's 'loan' to Kamil.

"All right, I get it. What do I have to do for you?" Kamil asked grimly, deciding he no longer had a friend named "Davron Bakhromov."

"Nothing special!" Davron quipped sarcastically. "Just go to jail on my behalf."

"What?!" Kamil cried out, even more shocked. "Are you… are you insane? Did you… break the law or something?"

"Cool it with the dramatic talk, okay?" Davron snapped, annoyed. "I got unlucky, is all. I collided with another car on the road. Some dude got hurt. He's in the hospital now, but he's alive—don't worry! Had some surgery, apparently. He'll be fine, so you won't get a big sentence. I'll even throw in some cash."

"You bastard, Davron," Kamil gritted through his teeth. "Did you at least help that person? Pay for his operation? Or at least for the medicine?"

"Don't act all morally superior," Davron scolded him. "What

do you care about that guy? He's alive, that's all you need to know! Anyway, here's how it goes. Remember your 'cover story.' You borrowed my car for a spin, to show off. Or you can skip mentioning a girlfriend if you want—your call. Then you got drunk, hit that victim. I'll check with my dad and message you the exact date and time of the accident. Got it? That's all you need to know. You'll go to the police and straight to my father. He'll write up a 'voluntary surrender' and a 'heartfelt confession.' The court will give you a reduced sentence for that."

"What?! Going to court??!" Kamil exclaimed in sheer despair. "This is a nightmare."

"What did you expect?" Davron asked, feigning surprise. "You ran someone over. Practically almost killed him, you might say."

"I did?"

"Yeah, of course you did. Caused him serious bodily…"

"Me?!"

"Yes, you!" Kamil's 'friend' nodded coolly. "If not, then pay me all my money. Right this minute! And you'll still go to jail for something. I told you."

"You're scum, Davron!" Kamil burst out indignantly. "Got that? A parasite."

"Hey, easy!" the investigator's son remarked without taking offense and gave his 'friend' a playful flick on the forehead, making him take the 'deal' seriously. "I'm your saviour, you see? It won't be a big sentence. My dad will add that you 'cooperated with the investigation.' You might get two years max. Then you'll be out in one on parole. That's worst-case. I bet you could even avoid prison entirely—just get a suspended sentence and a scare. We'll also try to 'butter up' the victim so he won't file charges. Everything'll be set! And you'll get money from me. A nice profit."

"Money from Daddy again?" Kamil sneered. "Not man enough to earn your own?"

"Don't piss me off, idiot," Davron chuckled. "We clear on each other?"

"Yeah," Kamil agreed reluctantly. "You've got me by the throat. Where else can I go?"

28

Doha, Qatar, the same period

"Greetings, ustadi Sarwan," said a young man on the phone, once the secretary of Mr. Al-Tawil, owner of a chain of hotels, connected him. "This is the assistant to the General Director and founder of Abbas Bank, Mr. Najib Abbas. My apologies—are you able to speak right now?"

"Yes," Sarwan answered briefly. "What do you want?"

"I have been asked to find out, most esteemed ustadi Sarwan," the young assistant continued, "whether you would do my boss the honour of joining him for lunch tomorrow at two o'clock in the afternoon at a restaurant on the waterfront."

"Oh? Whatever for?" Sarwan pretended not to understand.

"Ustadi Najib wishes to talk with you," the assistant replied with a polite, mildly surprised tone, as though it should be obvious why wealthy and busy businesspeople invite someone to a business lunch.

Sarwan did not reply immediately, making it seem as though he were weighing the invitation. He was making himself appear valuable.

"Well… all right, I agree," he finally said. "Tomorrow, two p.m."

Deep down, conflicting emotions were raging inside Sarwan.

On the one hand, as the father of his only and dearly loved daughter, Jahiza, he could not easily forgive the young man who had insulted her—and, by extension, the young man's entire family. Sarwan needed to react as a furious parent would.

On the other hand, as a practical businessman, he had long dreamed of having a major, financially strong partner like the owner of the most prosperous bank in all of Qatar.

Of course, like all major business figures in the country, Sarwan and Najib had known each other for years—but not closely, only superficially. They had met and politely exchanged greetings at various industry events—symposiums, business seminars, banquets, receptions, and so on. But Sarwan had never been able to forget the grudge he held against Najib.

A little more than ten years ago, when Sarwan was first attempting to scale up financially, he had visited Najib's bank—at that time not yet the largest—and asked him to become one of the chief investors in his hotels. Najib had refused the hotelier. Explaining his decision to his board of directors, the banker had said he did not consider that particular man's, meaning Sarwan's, business successful or promising, citing what he termed his questionable financial literacy and professional competence. Sarwan had not understood the reason for the refusal—and had harboured a deep resentment toward Najib ever since.

Today, despite the small chain of hotels Sarwan had built, business still was not going especially well. Many of the projects he and his associates had envisioned, to his dismay, had not yielded the hoped-for results. Customers, dissatisfied with the service in his rooms, were increasingly opting for the hotels owned and operated by his competitors. His entire operation had become far less profitable. A considerable portion of the foreign capital he had raised had gone up in smoke, leaving him owing penalties and fees to his international investor partners.

So his situation was actually far from rosy, contrary to what Sharaf and his adoptive father, Nazih Jaber, believed. Not even his wife and daughter knew about his problems; he kept them hidden and, loving them as he did, could never bring himself to say no to them about anything.

Hence, Sarwan had been looking for a way to skilfully and subtly secure an investment from one of the country's reputable and generous financial backers. But he hadn't thought about Najib Abbas in years. Being a proud Arab, he had no wish to be the first to ask for help or impose upon potential wealthy partners. He waited for a suitable occasion, tried to find ways—and had so far failed. He had once mentioned this briefly to his family in passing.

Now such an opportunity had practically fallen into his hands! Najib's capital!

It seemed like a fairytale, magic… "Open sesame!"… and a treasure chest just ahead…

"Interesting," he thought. "Was it mere coincidence that my daughter Jahiza was nearly dishonoured by that lowlife Nizar, the son of this banker Najib—or is it some sign from above?"

29

Samarkand – Tashkent, the same period

Barno was recovering quickly, and Sharaf, as her new friend, decided to take her by taxi from Samarkand to Tashkent. The young Qatari warmly said goodbye to Captain Ibrahim Salimov of the local police. Ibrahim invited him to visit Qatar in a couple of months, when Sharaf himself, he hoped, would return home.

Ibrahim wished Sharaf and Barno the best of luck and cautioned his young friends to be more careful in the future, especially in unfamiliar places.

"If you need me, you know where to find me," the captain said in parting. "Don't hesitate to ask! I'll always help in any way I can. And I'll do my best to find Barno's father if he's still alive. Then I'll let you know whatever I can find out. Well then… My regards to your mother—she raised a good son, polite and kind!"

"Thank you for everything, Ustadi Ibrahim!" Sharaf responded, beaming.

On the road to the capital, the young man told Barno he would need her help.

"Barno, I'll call you tomorrow and explain exactly what I need," he said with a mysterious smile, signalling with his gesture—due to the driver's presence—that he couldn't share any secrets just then.

"All right, I'll be eagerly waiting," Barno replied warmly.

That same day, after lunch, Sharaf headed to the hospital to see his father, Said Mumtazov. To his relief, none of Said's family members were in the room or corridor at that hour—but to his disappointment, "Doctor Mumtazoff" did not recognize him.

"Excuse me, who are you?" he asked the young man in a friendly tone.

Since Sharaf believed that, overall, his father's mind was clear—that he was speaking rationally—Sharaf recounted the entire story of their relationship from the beginning.

Said was overjoyed to "rediscover" his son. And when Sharaf, who better than anyone else knew the details of the accident they both had experienced, shared it all with his father, to the young man's surprise, Said… began remembering something.

"Well, this is remarkable!" exclaimed Said. "I just had a kind of flash in my mind. I remember how that white car raced straight toward us at high speed…"

"Yes, yes, it was a Toyota," his son confirmed. "And its driver fled."

"And how about you, son?" Said suddenly asked, concerned. "Were you hurt at all?"

"No, Father," Sharaf assured him. "I'm fine. Thank you."

They embraced. Sharaf promised he would continue visiting him in the hospital.

"I'll be sure to introduce you to my wife and daughter," Said said. "They've been here by my side all this time, and I couldn't recognize them. But now—imagine! I suddenly remembered them too! I think I've recalled almost everything. Which means I'm on the mend. And once I'm fully well, you must come to our home!"

"Yes, of course, Father! As you say!" Sharaf beamed. "But I might be out of Tashkent again for a few days on important business. If it's okay, I'll call you every day. Then I'll come see you."

"I'll be delighted, son," a happy Said replied.

Barno was still on medical leave and thus had free time. The next day, Sharaf invited her to a café where they could talk in peace.

"Barno, I'd like you to know the real reason I came to Uzbekistan!" Sharaf began. He spoke quietly so as not to draw attention to his words or let any outsiders overhear. "But what I'm about to tell you must stay strictly between us!"

"All right, of course," the girl answered at once, clearly understanding. She had no idea what he was going to say, but already trusted Sharaf, sensing that a responsible, serious person like him would never ask for secrecy frivolously.

Sharaf then briefly told Barno about his birth father, Said, about the accident the two of them had suffered, and about how Said had been hurt far more severely.

Barno listened without interruption, nodding now and then to show she understood.

He then went into much greater detail about how he had inherited a strange and astonishing ancient map—a map of Abbasid-era treasures, or more precisely, most likely of Khorasan and other territories of the Arab Caliphate of that period. Actually, it was not the entire map, but just half of it. And he revealed his main dream: to find the treasures shown on the map and bring them to Jahiza, his fiancée in Doha.

Until now, Barno had been listening silently, patiently, and attentively. But at the mention of a fiancée, it was as if a jolt went through her. She certainly had no claims on Sharaf, although she did find this nice young Qatari appealing. Realizing he had unintentionally been somewhat tactless toward this sweet Uzbek girl, Sharaf grew flustered.

"Forgive me if I… said something extra… or maybe not so pleasant," he tried to explain. "It's just that I've loved her for a long time. Though… sometimes I think I may not love her as strongly as before. Honestly, my time with you, Barno, seems to have changed something inside me. I feel so comfortable with you! It's like for the first time in my life I'm truly… happy. Sorry. We're just great friends, and I have no right to claim anything more. Besides, I owe loyalty to my girlfriend. Again, sorry!"

"It's fine, Sharaf," Barno said, smiling gently and deciding it best not to comment further on his words.

"Barno, you know the history of the ancient East very well—including Khorasan!" Sharaf said with excitement. "Tell me—would you be willing, while you're still on medical leave, to travel with me to a couple of places that might be linked to the treasures of Khorasan? Later, you could take some days off work or unpaid leave for the same purpose. And of course, when we find the treasure, I will reward you generously. I'm sure you won't regret it."

"Sharaf, all right—I'll think about it," Barno smiled. "I'd be interested in finding that treasure myself. Especially since you say you have a map—on cloth…"

"Oh dear! How could I forget to show it to you?" the young Qatari exclaimed, flustered, and pulled the ancient map out of his bag. "Yes, here it is!"

"Wonderful!" Barno said, peering at what, for both of them, was a set of entirely unfamiliar symbols—symbols Sharaf believed marked places and settlements of the ninth-century Arab Abbasid Caliphate. "But, Sharaf, I don't need any reward—don't even think about it. All I ask is that you cover our travel expenses and modest lodging, simply because my salary may not stretch that far. As for paying me for voluntarily helping you from the heart—that's completely unnecessary."

Sharaf warmly thanked this kind, unselfish young woman, inwardly surprised that such girls—or even people in general—could be so altruistic.

"I may later ask my parents for help as well," Sharaf said. "For the moment, my father, Doc Mumtazoff, gave me his bank card and told me to use it as I see fit. So I think we'll manage."

"Let's hope so," Barno smiled.

"By the way," Sharaf reminded her, "we only have half of this map, on scraps of cloth! And since I figure the treasure might be at the place where both halves meet, we absolutely have to find the other half, no matter what. But where should we even start looking? I've also read about the history of those Caliphs who might have possessed this map, and about the Tahirid dynasty that ruled Khorasan..."

"Under the Tahirids, Khorasan's capital was the ancient city of Merv," Barno pointed out. "Look, you can see it here on your half of the map. Maybe we should go there first? Maybe we'll find a clue about the second part of the map—or even the treasure itself?"

"Great idea!" Sharaf exclaimed brightly. "I'm lucky to have you. You're so good at world geography—you saw Merv right there on the map! Indeed, maybe we can find at least some lead for our search in Merv! I'll buy tickets today, and tomorrow we can set out."

Barno nodded in agreement, smiling.

30

Merv, Near the Cities of Bayramali and Mary, Turkmenistan, the same period

"This city is on UNESCO's World Heritage List as an ancient centre of the Great Silk Road," began historian Zulfiya, addressing her companions Sanya, Vanya, and Sher once they arrived by rented jeep at the ancient ruins of Merv. "Also known by other names—Margush, Margiana, or Maru—it was one of the largest cities of the ancient world and is now an open-air museum-reserve. Its origins are shrouded in mystery, but one thing is certain: the earliest written references to it appeared in the Avestan chronicles sometime between the eighth and sixth centuries BCE! Chroniclers called it 'the king's soul,' 'the mother of the cities of Khorasan,' and even 'the city on which the Universe depends.'"

"But practically the entire city was destroyed in the thirteenth century by the hordes of Chinggis Khan," Vanya reminded them. "On the way here, I read a booklet about Merv. In just three days, nearly seven hundred thousand captives were executed by Chinggis Khan! That's almost the entire population of the city. Merv itself was burned to the ground, and for several decades after that, it lay in ruins and never recovered. All its splendour and luxury disappeared almost instantly... So, what exactly are we supposed to look for here now?"

"History holds many secrets and riddles," Zulfiya objected.

"And believe me, there's no such thing as a past civilization about which not the slightest trace remains to this day. Somehow, something always survives—a bit mystically, perhaps. So, what does that imply?"

"And what does it imply, Zulfiya?" Sanya asked, nodding at her.

"That we must at least attempt to search here," Sher burst out, "if not for the treasure itself or a map showing its location, then for some hidden symbol pointing the way."

"Precisely, Sher!" Zulfiya smiled approvingly.

The travellers bought tickets for a guided tour around the city and, together with their guide, inspected almost all the main attractions: Sultan-Kala, the Shazriar-Ark citadel, the remains of the walls of the palace of ruler Abdullakhan (Abdullakhan-Kala), the ruins of fortresses and towers in Baramalikhan-Kala, the Kyz-Kala fortress ruins, various mausoleums, the Erk-Kala fortress ruins, the remains of a temple at Gyaur-Kala, and numerous leftover bathhouses, palaces, reception halls, and other structures.

Sanya, Vanya, Sher, and Zulfiya had no idea that at that very moment, the same ancient Merv landmarks were being explored by others who possessed the first half of the map—namely Sharaf and Barno...

Likewise, Sharaf and Barno were unaware that the second half of the ancient Khorasan and Abbasid treasure map they were looking for was "wandering" somewhere close by, not far from them...

Zulfiya and her companions asked their guide to show them a place they had heard about from other tourists: the main ice-house on the outskirts of the city.

"An 'ice-house'—or yakhchal—is an ancient tall conical structure made of clay bricks," the guide explained. "Inside, local residents would gather and store snow and ice during the winter months, creating a huge 'refrigerator.' Any traveller or merchant passing along the Silk Road through Merv, weary from the heat, could step inside that ice-house to cool down."

"Maybe inside the bricks of its interior walls, something's hidden?" Sanya whispered to Vanya, still searching for secret signs or markers.

"Unlikely," Vanya shook his head. "This building has stood for centuries. So many people have come and gone. What could possibly be left there?"

Zulfiya caught on to Sanya's line of thought but signalled with a look that there was probably nothing for them to find here—just an unusual, striking historical site, and nothing more.

"Pity," Sanya muttered softly.

Afterward, Zulfiya, having let the tour guide go, said to her companions:

"Did you know that one of the greatest figures in our history was buried here in Merv, though unfortunately no one knows anything about his tomb or mausoleum…?"

"Who do you mean?" Vanya asked, intrigued.

"It was the head of the Tahirid dynasty—commander under the Arab Caliph Ma'mun, governor and first emir of Khorasan: Tahir ibn Husayn!" the historian clarified. "He lived here when, in 821–822, he governed Khorasan for just under a year. Sadly, he was killed here in 822, presumably on Caliph Ma'mun's orders…"

"I guess that Ma'mun turned out to be quite treacherous and ungrateful to Tahir!" Vanya noted.

"Perhaps so," Zulfiya nodded. "Anyway, Tahir moved Merv's centre further west and erected a whole series of buildings along the Khurmuzfarra Canal. The first large structures that greet museum-reserve visitors today are the mysterious clay fortress-keshks—Big and Small Kyz-Kala, with semicircular columns forming the facades. Many scholars believe these may very well have been Tahir's constructions."

"I think I saw them on the way here," Sanya remarked.

"Yes, those were the ones," Zulfiya nodded. "Also, in the ancient settlement of Gyaur-Kala, archaeologists uncovered traces of a structure they believe to be the earliest mosque in Merv and all of Central Asia—the Benu Mahan Mosque, dating to the sixth century. In 748, Abu Muslim, leader of the Abbasid movement in Khorasan, led the Abbasids' supporters into Merv. He moved the government residence from the old city to the western side of Gyaur-Kala. A subterranean water reservoir is the only real landmark that lets us locate the remains of the complex, renovated in the ninth century by order of Caliph Ma'mun and through Tahir's efforts. There are still fragments of walls and a minaret base, along with semicircular columns embellished with carved Ganch ornamentation."

"Let's go check it out ourselves!" Sanya proposed.

To his surprise, even though they were already quite tired and worn down by the Central Asian heat, his companions agreed to an excursion to the Benu Mahan Mosque.

"But only if it's our last stop in Merv, all right?" asked Sher, who was usually calm and not prone to complaining. "We're all so exhausted."

"Of course," said Zulfiya, the leader of their expedition.

"Let's head there—mainly because next to that reservoir-well, it might be a bit cooler," Vanya added. "And we can buy more water somewhere along the way."

"Exactly!" Sanya backed him up. "I'm dying of thirst here. Constantly!"

When they approached the remains of what had once been the Benu Mahan Mosque, they spotted a collapsed dome.

"It's here," Zulfiya pointed out. "Let's go look over whatever's left."

"But there's nothing here!" Sanya lamented, disappointed that the Abbasid treasures he'd been dreaming of—already imagining himself holding them in his own hands—had not materialized.

Indeed, after the travellers explored the remaining ruins of the Benu Mahan Mosque and descended modern steps to the ancient underground reservoir with its musty smell, they thoroughly checked the inner walls of the old well. But no matter how hard they looked, they found nothing of note.

"Fancy a swim?" Sher teased the unathletic and frail Sanya.

"N–No way!" Sanya yelped in fright. "If you want to, go for it! I'm not going in! The water's almost ice-cold! Brrr! Besides, the well looks pretty deep. God knows how many meters down it goes."

"I'm just messing with you," Sher pulled a face. "I can't swim at all."

"What's with this childishness?" Zulfiya gently scolded them both. "Nobody is going anywhere. You'd just drown. Then how would I explain it to the boss?! I'm responsible for all of you here."

"So does that mean we have to go back to Tashkent empty-handed?" Sanya asked in despair. "I really don't want that! I'm scared. Kudrat's going to kill us!"

"He won't kill us, brother. We'll fend him off. But you've got to learn how to lose," Vanya tried to reassure him and the others. "This is hardly the end of the entire war! We can't give up yet!"

"Yes, it's time to head home," Zulfiya said with regret. "We've come up empty here. I'll report that to the boss myself and figure out how and where to continue the search. Kudrat's map shows some of the Persian Gulf countries. I think it makes sense for us to look for the treasure there next."

"You mean we're going back to Baghdad again?" Sher asked in surprise.

"No, why would we?" Zulfiya answered with a question. "The Persian Gulf countries aren't just Iraq—there are many others. I'll think about this secret sign—something about the word 'oturu,' which means 'incense'—then I'll study Kudrat Valiev's map carefully and decide exactly where we'll head next."

"But Vanya and I pored over it left and right," Sanya admitted. "Honestly, though, we couldn't make head or tail of it!"

"True," Vanya confirmed.

"I suspect that map is no simple matter," Zulfiya said thoughtfully. "It seems almost... mystical, you know? From what I can see, part of Khorasan is there—though not all—and a big portion of the ninth-century Arab Caliphate, but obviously not all of it, since we still only have half the map! Crucially, there are patterns and some symbols that are still unclear to me... but no direct, explicit clue about where the Abbasid treasure might be hidden! So what do we do with it? I'm not sure yet... But I trust a solution will come. For now, I think we should take a break, recharge. In the Arab countries—that are just as hot as Turkmenistan and Uzbekistan in the summertime—we'll need all the energy we can muster."

* * *

Meanwhile, no sooner had they left than Barno and Sharaf drove up to the ruins of the old Benu Mahan Mosque, with its underground reservoir, in their rented jeep.

At that moment, no one else was around but them.

Once they went down, to Barno's surprise, the young Qatari decided right away—holding carefully to the handle on the reservoir wall—to dip his head into the water.

"It's so cold! So refreshing!" he said, sharing his impression with her.

Before Barno could blink, Sharaf had already tossed off his travel backpack, quickly removed his shoes, taken a short running start in the cramped underground space, and dived elegantly into the icy water like a fish.

A few seconds later, cheerfully waving at her with the hand holding his flashlight, the young man... vanished beneath the reservoir's dark water.

Nearly three minutes passed while poor Barno had almost lost hope of seeing Sharaf alive again. In horror, she began thinking how she'd have to carry on alone in a foreign place without this new but already dear friend—when suddenly... Sharaf surfaced! Alive and well, and not empty-handed, either. In his right hand, he held... a dagger.

"Look, Barno!" he cried out, as happily as before his dive, jumping back up onto dry land. "I think this is a ninth-century weapon. As soon as I saw it by the beam of my flashlight, I recognized crucible steel. I once read that back then, here in Merv, there was a famous workshop that produced exactly this special kind of steel! They made it by melting down old blades and swords. This steel is softer and more flexible than typical damask. See? There's an Arabic inscription with a name: 'Tahir ibn Husayn'! And here—engraved is Caliph Ma'mun in a turban with an enormous pearl! Wow! I can't believe my eyes! What a lucky find!!"

"Sharaf, it's truly amazing!" Barno agreed. "The dagger's blade is covered in sediment, and there's moss on it, so it must've sat on the reservoir floor for centuries. You were so fortunate to spot it right away!"

"I'm a lucky guy," the young man said proudly, "but… I didn't expect it to go this well. It was just… something clicked when I saw this underground water. Maybe my intuition kicked in?"

"Yes, you did great, Sharaf. But how could you suddenly jump into the reservoir like that?" Barno scolded her friend, still shaken. "I was worried sick! And… how could you dare to dive with no mask, without any fear of drowning?"

"You don't need to worry, my dear companion," he replied with a smile. "Remember, I'm Qatari by birth—many of my relatives have been pearl divers in the Gulf for generations. I learned to swim and free-dive as a child. Plus, it was refreshing: Turkmenistan is so hot at this time of year. Now… I feel great!"

"Sharaf, so we're on the right track after all?" Barno asked, hugging him lightly once they'd both emerged from the underground space into the sweltering midday heat.

"Without a doubt!" Sharaf grinned. "But we still need to take another good look at my half of the map. We have to figure out where we go next. Because, besides this truly remarkable historical find—the emir of Khorasan Tahir's own dagger—I didn't see any other treasure underwater in that reservoir."

"Yes. We've basically 'ransacked' almost all of Merv," Barno added. "No sign of the Abbasid or Tahirid treasures here. Let's go back to Tashkent. Then we can examine your map more carefully! We got caught up in the excitement and adventure; I've only glanced at it so far."

"That's true," Sharaf agreed. "Oh, if only we could find the other half! I'm sure that would help us so much in our search! But where is it?… Who has it?… That's a big question. Maybe it's lying in the corner of some house, collecting dust."

"Or maybe someone else is traveling around with it—like us—and also searching for ninth-century treasure," Barno ventured.

"Really? You think so?" Sharaf asked, surprised by this new idea. "That… could be possible. You're brilliant, Barno. But… how do we find those people—or their map?"

31

Merv, Khorasan, Abbasid Caliphate, 822 CE

The faithful wife—now widow—of Tahir ibn Husayn loved all her sons. Yet now, even when her dearest child of all, Abdallah, arrived from Baghdad to attend his father's funeral, she neither rose to meet him, nor embraced him. She did not even greet him.

All three of Tahir's sons—Talha, Ali, and Abdallah—performed the required funeral rites. They feared their mother might wail aloud over the grave during the mourning ceremony, for they knew how deeply she had loved their father, and how greatly he had loved her in return. They knew her grief was immense, far greater than theirs. For Benu and Tahir had been one, indivisible. And yet, Benu did not shed a single tear. She was as if lifeless: voiceless, disconnected from all and everything—a statue of stone.

"Everyone deals with grief in their own way," said Talha, the eldest, to his younger brothers.

The other two nodded in agreement.

All three felt lost and crushed by what had happened.

"Where did we get so many fruits and sacks of grain?" Abdallah asked in surprise upon their return home. "Mother? This is enough food for an entire regiment!"

His mother remained silent, without so much as twitching a brow, as though she hadn't heard him.

"They arrived this morning from Caliph Ma'mun," Ali explained.

"They came along with 'the deepest and most sincere condolences to our family' on the loss of its head, our provider," Talha added.

"How dare he?!" Abdallah flared up with anger. "The entire city—no, the whole of Khorasan—is saying that this scheming fox himself ordered Father's death! Even in Baghdad, they whisper it, because many there knew and truly respected Governor Tahir!"

"Yes, we... caught wind of that," Ali concurred. Then, in a lowered voice, almost into his brothers' ears, he said, "It seems the Caliph had stopped fully trusting our powerful father, feared his influence and renown. He'd ordered his men to watch Tahir's every move. Moreover... Father, during his last Friday prayer at the congregational mosque, failed to speak the Caliph's name..."

"Which, in the Arab Caliphate, is considered treason and rebellion!" Talha whispered tensely. "All the more so because Father—though indirectly, in veiled words—declared Khorasan's independence from the Abbasid Empire. Clearly, Caliph Ma'mun wouldn't have liked that."

"And so—his immediate response is to kill a man—a brother?!" Abdallah fumed, less diplomatic than his siblings and unwilling to hide his emotions. "The cruel cynic! Now he sends us gifts. Throw them out, brothers! Personally, I won't eat a thing from that lot! What if they're poisoned too? Father had foam at his mouth. That means those carrying out the Caliph's order poisoned him! I don't want the same fate. May our father rest in peace, and may the Almighty watch over his soul!"

"Shhh, lower your voice!" Talha warned him with a gesture. "If you want Mother and the rest of us to stay alive, speak carefully, brother!"

"Father's last words before death were in his native Persian," Ali told Abdallah. "He said, 'Even in dying, one must have courage!' That's how he lived his entire life—just, brave, and courageous."

"In any event," Talha said, "people who commit such dark deeds know how to cover their tracks. How can we now find out who precisely gave the order for a swift end to the actual ruler of all Khorasan? And who exactly carried it out? Look at the faces of the Caliph's officials and servants: so charming, friendly, and filled with sympathy! Yet you, brother, are now like a father to us."

Abdallah was their youngest brother, though the age gap was not large. Talha and Ali knew, however, that Abdallah was the strongest and smartest of them all. From childhood, he had shown the makings of a leader—someone who could take responsibility for others. He spent more time with their father than the other brothers, eagerly learning military strategy, politics, and the art of governance. Soft-spoken and not inclined to commanding others, Talha and Ali followed Abdallah's lead in many everyday matters.

"In addition," Ali recalled, "the Caliph's messengers said Ma'mun is summoning you, Abdallah, for an audience. I asked them if they knew why he was calling you, but they got all flustered and said they didn't know. They're afraid of the Caliph."

"We figure it's pretty clear: Ma'mun wants you to take over as the Caliph's governor—i.e., to assume Father's position as governor of Khorasan! You're the most worthy among us. And after all, Father wrote his last guidance to you specifically! That means he saw you as his successor in that prestigious office."

"Indeed, brother," Ali nodded and turned to Abdallah. "Who else if not you? We belong to one of Khorasan's noblest families. Our ancestors owned Bushang and governed Herat for many years! You're the wisest, best-educated, and most capable of us all."

"I'm supposed to serve that jackal—after he dealt with my… with our father?!" Abdallah raged.

Young and ambitious as he was, he did want to become emir and governor of his beloved Khorasan, but he feared he wasn't ready for such a burden—and that one day they might condemn him to death just like they had done to their father. "You say I'm educated, dear brothers, but in truth… I'm still not knowledgeable enough for that job."

"Regardless, go to Baghdad today and meet with the Caliph. Then send a messenger to us with a letter—let us know everything that happens!" Talha urged him. "We'll figure out together what we're to do next, how we'll live… without Father. Ali and I will look after Mother! And talk to the people. If anyone has pressing needs, we'll help them however we can. We are, after all, the Tahirids—a new noble dynasty."

"That's right, Talha," Ali supported his brother, then addressed Abdallah: "Brother, we're all deeply aggrieved by the Caliph, but if he appoints you to govern our homeland, Khorasan and Mawara' al-Nahr, you won't refuse, right?"

"Certainly not!" exclaimed Abdallah. "Let that be our revenge on Ma'mun: I'll govern here as governor! And everything will be done our way, for the memory of Father."

* * *

Baghdad, Abbasid Caliphate, the Caliph's Palace, a few days later

When Abdallah arrived at the Palace, it was not Caliph Ma'mun—who had "invited" him—who received him, but Ahmad ibn Abi Du'ad, the chief judge (qadi). Since the death of Vizier Sarakhsi, Du'ad had become the most influential figure in the administration. The excessive power once held by Sarakhsi had led Caliph Ma'mun to act more cautiously, determined not to let any single official accumulate such far-reaching authority.

"The Caliph is very busy at the moment, honourable young man," the judge informed him, "and cannot receive you. However, he instructed me to speak with you on his behalf."

"As you wish, ustadi," Abdallah said, inclining his head. He hid his relief at not having to meet face-to-face with the man he loathed—the enemy of his entire family, who, by persistent rumour, had arranged the deaths of his father, his own brother Caliph Amin, Vizier Sarakhsi, and many others throughout the Caliphate.

They proceeded to the judge's office, where a servant offered Abdallah fruit, juice, and cool water. He politely declined to partake in anything.

"Caliph Ma'mun asked me to inform you that by his supreme command, you are appointed as his overseer—namely, the governor of all Khorasan!" the senior official announced to twenty-four-year-old Abdallah. "And also the administrator of Mawara' al-Nahr. The decree has already been signed. In His Majesty's estimation, none is more worthy than you to succeed your father in this state office."

At the word "father," Abdallah involuntarily flinched. This was not at all how he had wanted to become his father's "successor!" Not through his parent's death. Yet he thanked the judge for sharing such good news and, following protocol, asked him to convey his gratitude to the Caliph.

"Did you know, esteemed Governor," continued Qadi Du'ad, "that Caliph Ma'mun is aware of the letter your late father wrote you when he was still governor of Raqqa? I believe Tahir ibn Husayn intentionally made it public—indeed, I would say he made it part of the public domain. It is so magnificent that it likely has no equal anywhere. Even the Caliph himself read it."

"Truly?" Abdallah said, surprised. "I was aware it circulated widely, but I never imagined the ruler of all Arabia was familiar with it."

"How could he not be?" The judge smiled. "He must be informed of all significant developments in his realm! Having read it, Caliph Ma'mun said at a meeting of the governmental diwan: 'Our commander Tahir was wise. In his letter, he left out nothing pertaining to the affairs of this world: religion, governance, shaping public opinion, politics, strengthening the state and its subordinates, preserving the government, obeying the Caliphs, and supporting the Caliphate. He handled all these issues with great skill and provided guidelines for addressing them properly.' The Caliph then ordered that this letter be sent to officials in various regions so they might use it as a model and follow its advice."

"I'm grateful for this information, ustadi," Abdallah said, stroking his still-thin beard. "It pleases me to hear that my father's good name is not forgotten in the Caliphate!"

"Indeed, it is not, my young friend," continued the official. "Now, let us return to your appointment. You, honourable Abdallah, know your region better than anyone. Moreover, you hold a prominent position in the Caliph's army, and Caliph Ma'mun has personal ties to you. Hence, he can trust you. Is that not so? I trust you'll agree. But the question is this: I understand your home is currently here in Baghdad. What are your immediate plans? Will you relocate to Merv now? We need to know."

"No, I'll handle the administration from here," Abdallah replied. "Baghdad boasts marvellous libraries, and I wish to continue my education here. Meanwhile, in Merv, my deputies—my brothers Talha and Ali—will remain on-site. They'll report to me on every major issue, and they can handle the minor ones themselves. Naturally, I'll make frequent visits throughout Khorasan and Mawara' al-Nahr. At some later point, I may move to Merv permanently."

"Well then," the judge nodded, "we anticipated as much and have no objection. Let it be done however you sons of Tahir ibn Husayn find convenient—so long as peace and calm continue to reign in Khorasan and Mawara' al-Nahr, to the glory of the Almighty and of Caliph Ma'mun! Under no circumstances must you allow any revolt or rebellion, my boy! Never forget who your benefactor and your master is—Caliph Ma'mun. Do you understand?"

"Yes, esteemed Qadi," Abdallah replied submissively.

"Excellent!" Du'ad beamed. "The Caliph and I shall personally observe you and your governance closely—for the good of the state!"

"I understand, *ustadi*," Abdallah said with a bow and the hint of a smile. "Have no fear—Khorasan and Mawara' al-Nahr are in safe hands."

32

Sharjah, United Arab Emirates, 2023

Bob Downey had not been working just one or two years in the field of antiquities, artifacts, and valuables—he was deeply entrenched in the elite community that revolved around such items. He knew every museum, gallery, auction house, buyers' club, and antique shop in the country, as well as most of the major collectors.

After carefully assessing the situation following the incident at the Archaeological Museum—the theft of the exhibits and Nazih's arrest—Bob decided not to approach any potential buyers directly about the stolen collection (which he had, of course, stolen himself). Instead, he chose a different tactic.

Downey posted notices on popular specialty websites, suggesting that some intriguing valuables from the Abbasid era had surfaced in the city. He added that the person offering them for sale could be found on a "closed" marketplace site under the nickname *Salesman*. He wrote that only those seriously interested in a purchase should contact him privately; anyone random, idle, or suspicious would be blacklisted immediately.

A few days later, someone calling themselves *Merchant* wrote to Salesman. The nickname caught Bob's attention—especially because Merchant claimed to own a private museum of Eastern applied art in Spain, specializing mostly in fifth- to tenth-century artifacts. He expressed interest in Arab coins and mentioned that he happened to be in Bob's city at that very moment. He proposed a meeting on his yacht at 23:00 that same night, when it would be quiet and deserted. The yacht's name was *Madjrit*.

Naturally, Bob went to the first meeting with this unknown *Merchant* without bringing the treasures. He wanted to test the waters first—to see whether the customer was trustworthy, or if he might cheat him or, worst of all, turn him in to the police for handling stolen goods.

At the appointed time, Downey arrived at the dock, carefully looking for a boat with the somewhat unusual local name *Madjrit*, especially in that spelling.

Just as he approached the target vessel, a man of about forty— quite short, almost a dwarf, with a thick mane of dark chestnut curls and a disproportionately large beard for his frame—emerged from it.

"Ah, *Mister* Salesman!" he greeted Bob heartily in very broken Arabic. "How are you? Not too hard to find me?"

"Hello," Bob mumbled, somewhat taken aback, as he bent down toward the short man and offered a handshake. "I'm pleased to meet you. Sorry, but you're Spanish, aren't you?"

"Oh, *sí, sí!*" responded the yacht's owner.

"Well then, if you don't mind, we can speak in English," Bob proposed, switching at once to his native tongue. "I assume it'll be easier for you as well. I'm afraid I don't speak Spanish. I'm American by origin."

"Oh, good, of course—come on! Let's speak English," said the Merchant in passable English, inviting Bob inside the cabin. "Tea? Coffee? Something stronger?"

"No, thank you," Bob said, shaking his head. At the moment, he had other concerns.

He was focused on how to sell the valuables as profitably and quickly as possible.

In the light, something about the yacht owner's appearance struck Bob as strange—and not just his near-dwarfish stature. First, the Merchant's face looked more like a local Arab's. Second, the obvious opulence of the expensive, well-furnished yacht didn't match his shabby, not particularly fresh or branded clothing.

Ah well, every millionaire has their quirks, Bob told himself.

"Did you know that Spain's capital, Madrid, was originally a Muslim city?" the yacht owner suddenly asked.

"Really?" Bob was surprised. "No, señor, I didn't know that."

"Yes! It was founded by an Arab prince, Muhammad al-Awsat, in 855, and called exactly the same as my yacht—'Madjrit'!" the short man continued. "Translated from Arabic, that means 'a place with abundant water.' As an Ar... Spaniard, I really liked the word!"

"Yes, I'm familiar with it," Bob nodded. "I speak Arabic fluently. So you truly are Spanish?"

"Why do you doubt me?" the Merchant smiled, then added, "In fact, dear Salesman, you've passed my little 'face control' and earned my trust. So I'll give you my real name. I'm Señor Fernando Gonzalez. And you? Wait, let me guess! You're Bob Downey, right?"

Bob nearly dropped his jaw in shock at the unexpected unmasking. Panicking at being recognized, he jumped up, ready to leave at once.

"Wait, dear Mr. Downey, wait!" Gonzalez stopped him with a hand on his arm. Startlingly, the dwarf's grip was strong and firm, pressing painfully into Bob's forearm. "It's simple: the entire city is abuzz about the stolen Abbasid treasures from the Archaeological Museum. And you think I, as a big aficionado and connoisseur of such valuables, would fail to take note of the event and not do my own thorough inquiries on all potential or even improbable participants? You just don't know me, young man! Your only saving grace is that the police don't suspect you of anything—you managed to wriggle out of it skilfully, framing someone else who's completely innocent! Yes?"

Bob flushed, raising his head proudly. It pleased him that his cunning had been recognized, but he was terrified of exposure or, worse, arrest.

"Are you going to turn me in to the police?" he asked nervously.

"Why would I do that, old chap?" the short man laughed, his dark curls and big beard shaking. "We—well, I—can still make use of you. You haven't brought me the treasure yet! And even when you do, I won't turn you in… provided you behave nicely. I don't need any trouble either. These artifacts are stolen goods, after all! You understand that, right? So here's what I can offer you… say, five thousand US dollars."

"What?! What do you mean?!" Bob couldn't believe his ears. "Excuse me, Señor, but that's robbery! They're worth millions of dollars! You know that very well. There will be no deal."

"In that case… I'll hand you over to the nearest station," said Fernando calmly.

"But you promised not to!" Bob sputtered, confused.

"I promised not to—on the condition that we come to terms!" the short man explained matter-of-factly. "Otherwise, I have nothing to fear. The police have nothing on me. No evidence at all. I'd simply say I happened upon a swindler, a thief, a con man—meaning you. And that you tried to cheat me, to palm off stolen valuables. Once I discovered this, I was going to call the police right away, but I didn't have time. End of my story. Yours, however, is much darker. No future. Or rather, only one: sell me your 'trinkets'—for four thousand dollars. I just subtracted one thousand from the five. For your stubbornness. My nerves aren't free, you know!"

"You're the con man here, Señor Gonzalez," Bob said. "Someone like you belongs in jail."

"Look who's talking," Fernando grinned. "But you yourself? So, do we have a deal?"

Bob thought for a few seconds. Actually, he had been counting on netting at least five million for the gold coins alone, and another fifteen million minimum for Princess Zubaidah's diadem. But Bob had run out of luck: this man, looking more like an Arab than a Spaniard, knew Bob's face and name. Indeed, he could easily rat Bob out to the police—and then Bob would lose his money and, more importantly, his freedom. He had dreamed so long of heading to the Maldives or the Caribbean. He would be forced to agree to four thousand. And maybe... he could negotiate with the swindler for a fifth.

"I'll pay you... three thousand dollars!" the "buyer" shot back at the treasure "seller." "Not a cent more!"

Ultimately, Fernando and Bob agreed to meet and finalize the deal tomorrow, at the same place, around the same time.

Bob left feeling dejected. Even so, as he glanced back at the smug, self-assured dwarf, incensed by him, Bob resolved:

Just wait—within twenty-four hours I'll figure something out! I'll be the one who ends up rich!

33

Tashkent, the same period

Kamil Akbarov showed up at Investigator Zakir Bakhromov's office.

"Hello there, young man," Davron's father said politely yet sternly. "What brings you in?"

Kamil gave the major his name and briefly explained the reason for his visit.

From the very first words, Zakir realized that standing before him was the necessary "culprit" for his son—the one who would take the blame for the traffic accident that injured Said Mumtazov. *"The lineup has changed,"* he thought.

"Good that you came, Kamil," the investigator said more softly. "Yes, I more or less know what this is about: you're a friend of my son's, right? Mind if I address you informally?"

"No, we're just classmates," Kamil mumbled, his tone showing displeasure.

"All right, all right, I see," Zakir chuckled. "You're a bit upset with him. You'll get over it. What matters, boy, is that you're about to do the right, noble thing—admitting your guilt. And now you'll write a 'voluntary confession'…"

"But I…" Akbarov began, still hoping that his 'friend's' father might be kinder and spare him.

"Wait! On such-and-such a day, at such-and-such an hour,"

Zakir prompted Kamil, offering the "correct" version, "you borrowed my son's white Toyota just to take it for a spin, right? Then, not seeing well in the dark, you accidentally—that is, totally unintentionally, with no malicious intent—struck a car that was traveling at that moment in the oncoming lane. And then, panicking, you drove away. That's what you wanted to say, correct? My son explained it all to you in general?"

"W-well… yes," Kamil managed.

"And he warned you about the consequences of giving false testimony, right? That's a criminal offense, sonny!"

"I'm not your son," Kamil said sourly, feeling even more of Zakir's pressure. "I'm saving your son—with these lies."

"Don't say that! Although, of course, sorry," the major said with a grin. "Thanks for being such a… decent and smart guy! Good for you. Now then, Kamil, you need to put in writing everything we've just discussed. These will be your official statements. Don't worry: for now, they'll stay with me. I've got the file sewn up but shelved for 'lack of evidence,' meaning there's no formal case. Luckily for you…"

"Lucky for me?!"

"Who else?" Zakir replied, feigning surprise. "You're the one at fault in the accident! As I was saying: you were lucky the victim hasn't submitted an official complaint yet."

"Yes," Kamil sighed, "a complaint against me."

"And fortunately for you, the victim's relatives don't seem too familiar with legal procedures and haven't insisted on opening a case," Bakhromov continued. "Though his wife is no simple character—some sort of businesswoman, apparently. Attractive, strong-willed. I'm wary of that type; there's no telling what they might do… But that's a digression. One can hardly blame her! Her husband was badly injured. And those two women, his wife and daughter, had to pay for all the surgery and meds themselves!... So here: take this money, Kamil. Go to the hospital and find out if Doctor Said..."

"Doctor?" Kamil asked, confused.

"Yes, the victim is a doctor too," Davron's father explained. "A well-known one. Don't interrupt, please. Find out if he... eh... needs financial compensation for his injuries."

Saying this, he pulled a wad of sum-denominated bills from the top drawer of his desk and held it out to Kamil.

"Remember: it's for them, not for you!" the major warned him harshly.

"I know! That's not the problem. If I show up there... then they'll definitely 'put me away'!" Kamil blurted in alarm. "Maybe it's better if I don't go? I'm scared. Couldn't... you go yourself?"

"Think about what you're saying! In what capacity would I offer them money? You've nothing to worry about!" the major advised. "Apologize to them, especially the women—maybe let out a few tears. They both seem like sympathetic sorts. They'll see you as a sincerely repentant sinner and forgive you, I'm sure. Besides, the injured man is alive and almost well already."

"If things are like you say, then..." Kamil mumbled, at a loss.

"Of course, my friend! All will be fine. But! If you so much as utter a single word about Davron, well... you'll have only yourself to blame. Got that?"

"Yeah, I get it," Kamil sighed again. "I won't let it slip. Don't worry."

"You need to be the one who's worried," the investigator cautioned him again, with a slight menace. "But not now—later, if you foul up our plan for mercy. Though you won't foul it up, right?

Just keep your wits about you. I'll support you and help however I can. Now go! You're free for now."

* * *

Doha, Qatar, the same period

Najib Abbas, owner of the largest bank in Qatar, arrived at the restaurant where hotel-chain owner Sarwan Al-Tawil, who had arrived a few minutes earlier, was already waiting. Both men were understandably anxious: how would their meeting go? Would everything proceed smoothly?

"Greetings, Mr. Al-Tawil!" Najib called out in a warm, friendly tone as he approached the best table in the restaurant, where Sarwan was seated, extending his hand.

When the banker appeared, the hotelier rose to shake hands—less effusively, but still acceptably. Even so, the older Najib, well-versed in the psychology of personal interactions, sensed a faint chill and carefully concealed hostility from Sarwan. He noticed it but did not so much as bat an eyelid.

"Have you been here before?" Najib Abbas asked his companion. "They have a wonderful kitchen. The head chef always serves me personally! His dishes are outstanding—real masterpieces!"

Look at that—I just walked in and he's already showing off his social superiority! Sarwan inwardly fumed. *The chef serves him personally—what a brag! I've also been served by top chefs before—so what? Poser! He's just flaunting his millions.*

Aloud, however, he answered shortly:

"Yes, I know, Ustadi Najib Abbas... Thank you for inviting me here."

"Please, it's I who should be thanking you for making the time to have lunch with me!"

They both glanced at the menu and placed their orders.

Without waiting for the dishes—wasting no time—Najib Abbas got straight to the point of their meeting.

"My esteemed Ustadi Sarwan Al-Tawil, I'm aware you have some reason and grounds to harbour resentment toward me and my family," he said, speaking cautiously and unhurriedly.

"Oh really, Ustadi Najib Abbas?" Sarwan replied, feigning surprise, thinking that perhaps the banker did, in fact, feel some shame about personally offending him.

Meanwhile, Najib continued:

"Yes, I'm referring to the unpleasant incident which, for reasons quite baffling to me, took place at a bar involving my son Nizar and your daughter."

"Aha, so that's it!" said Sarwan, sounding a bit disappointed—despite the fact that this very issue was the main reason he had come today. "Yes, it's a rather distasteful matter, Ustadi Najib Abbas. Quite unacceptable in Qatar! You agree, don't you?"

"Absolutely, absolutely," the elderly banker repeated somewhat anxiously. "Though it's… so unlike my boy… You must understand, he's a kind, pure, decent soul."

He hated apologizing, making excuses, or humbling himself in front of anyone—and virtually never did so. But this time was "a special case."

"Suppose so. But on this occasion, your son… how to put it gently…" Sarwan said with calculated coolness, "couldn't restrain himself. And our faith calls for restraint, does it not? He insulted my lovely girl! So, what exactly do you propose?"

For the first time in about ten years, Sarwan felt power over his old adversary—this powerful man—and he relished and savoured it with every fibre of his being.

"Mr. Sarwan Al-Tawil, would it greatly offend you if I offered you and your daughter... a substan—or rather, a worthy... compensation?" asked Najib Abbas.

"So you're suggesting I sell my only daughter's honour for money?!" Sarwan flared up—though, in truth, it was partly for show.

"No, no, not at all!" the old banker said agitatedly. "Nothing of the sort was on my mind! Very well, then—perhaps you'd find it more acceptable if, for instance, our bank were to invest in your business? I believe you're in the hotel industry, if I'm not mistaken?"

If he's not mistaken! Still uncertain? You'd better have memorized me and my hotels for life! fumed Sarwan internally. *And where were you with this proposal ten years ago when I asked you for it?!*

Yet at the same time, he fully realized that now—perhaps more than ever—he very much needed exactly that investment from this very richest bank. He needed it like air! How could he possibly refuse?

"I have a counterproposal for you, Ustadi Najib Abbas," Sarwan said with a condescending smile, now thoroughly confident in the favourable outcome. "After all, your son did... in a sense... almost compromise my daughter's honour..."

"But he never actually did anything!" Najib Abbas objected.

"Yes, yes, I know—he didn't succeed, because a bar security guard intervened," Sarwan retorted. "But he certainly tried! And so, if he's an honourable young man, under our laws, he ought to marry Jahiza! And do so quickly, before any dirty rumours start spreading around town. You don't want publicity on such a delicate matter, do you? I imagine it would damage your bank's impeccable reputation.

Meanwhile, you and I—let's say we become business partners. I'm not necessarily opposed to it."

For a few moments, Najib Abbas remained silent. While the waiter set down their ordered dishes, he pondered his companion's proposal.

"All right," the banker finally said. "Please allow me a couple of days to make my final decision, Mr. Sarwan Al-Tawil. I'll call you myself with an answer."

"Thank you, Mr. Najib Abbas," Sarwan replied. "I'm glad we're starting to see eye to eye. But for now—let's enjoy our meal. Let nothing distract us from good food!"

However, deciding he'd had enough conversation for one day, the older banker rose unhurriedly in his slow, dignified manner, still smiling hospitably:

"I've just remembered some urgent matters, Mr. Sarwan Al-Tawil. If you'll excuse me, I'll take my leave. Do indulge yourself—on me. After all, we're almost family!"

34

Shanidar Cave, Mesopotamia, Abbasid Caliphate, 822 CE

"Abdallah?!" Caliph Ma'mun exclaimed. "How did you get here, my son?"

"I am not your son!" the new governor of Khorasan and Mawara' al-Nahr shouted furiously at the ruler of Arabia. "I had a father—

deeply loved by me, my mother, and my two brothers—Tahir ibn Husayn. But *you* personally ordered his murder! And now he is gone…"

"Who told you I gave that order?" Ma'mun asked with a smile, addressing the young viceroy. The Caliph brushed aside the arm of his closest bodyguard, who was already poised to skewer the audacious Tahirid with his sword. "Wait, young man. Outside this cave, my loyal soldiers are standing guard…"

"They're gone, my lord," Abdallah replied, eyes flashing, a spear in his hand. "My loyal, brave warriors took care of them."

With that, Abdallah pointed the spear at the king's bodyguard, who immediately dropped to his knees before him, pitifully begging:

"Don't kill me! Please don't hurt me, master! I have a wife and three little children!"

So it was with my father… Abdallah thought. He decided to spare the soldier, handing the torch over to Ma'mun to give him the chance to simply flee the cave.

"So it's just you and me now, Caliph," Abdallah said. "Give me the torch. I'll help you." *Id* had ordered one of his spies to track you, and that's how I know your every step. You visit this place often. So I came as well."

Ma'mun tried to read something in his adversary's eyes— something beyond resentment and anger—some hope of escaping this dilemma. Meanwhile, Abdallah ibn Tahir placed the torch in a bracket carved into the cave wall.

"I suppose you came here to Shanidar, before your next difficult military campaign, to hide your treasure! Isn't that right?" the Tahirid asked. "Though… this cave is so small. What could you possibly conceal here? Or was this… a trap?"

"You're quite the clever one, Khorasani," Ma'mun said bitterly. "You know everything. No wonder I appointed someone so young as governor over my dominions."

"These dominions will be of no further use to you," Abdallah said sternly. To Ma'mun's surprise, he pulled a second weapon from his belt—one the Abbasid instantly recognized: the sharp dagger that had belonged to his late friend and general, Tahir ibn Husayn.

"You intend to kill me with *that* dagger?" Ma'mun asked, startled. "Have you noticed the engraving—my portrait—on it? And by the way, do you realize that I have its scabbard? Without it, you can't... But never mind. Fear the Almighty! How can you raise your hand against your own ruler and benefactor?... Don't do this, Abdallah!"

Ma'mun himself wore a sharp sabre at his waist. Trained from childhood in the use of arms, he might normally have felt confident in a fight. But now he knew he was facing the son of Tahir—who until recently had commanded his entire army—and that Abdallah was far more skilled in every kind of weapon than the Caliph of Arabia. Surrendering to the young man was the safer option.

"When you ordered the death of my father—who had served you loyally for years, seeing you as a friend and brother," Abdallah said loudly, "did you never consider the consequences? That we, his sons—proud men—would inevitably seek vengeance for his life and blood?!"

"Forgive me, Abdallah," the ruler of Arabia murmured unexpectedly, lowering his head. Abdallah had been certain he would try to justify or exonerate himself, to twist and dodge as he'd so often done before. Instead, tears came to Ma'mun's eyes. "I miss my friend Tahir so much. Truly... I grew angry with him for wanting to be free of me and the Caliphate, to be completely independent."

"It wasn't for his personal gain," Abdallah observed, "but for Khorasan and its people!"

"Yes, I realized that later," Ma'mun nodded. "At the time, it seemed as though my patronage had become a burden to him. And yet I never meant to harm or belittle him—on the contrary, I singled him out above others and valued him more than most. And now… Indeed, I gave the order to poison Tahir—out of spite. Ever since, I've had no peace. If you can, forgive me, O Khorasani—and let your family do so as well. Let's settle this peacefully. We still have many wars ahead, which means plenty of spoils. I'll give you whatever you want from them—houses, gold, slaves, concubines."

For a moment, silence hung in the cave. Tahir's son pondered how to respond.

"All right," he finally said. "I'll spare your life, lord of the Caliphate. And I'll continue aiding you in warfare, as will all your vassals and governors. Naturally, I'll keep sharing my treasury with you—though let it no longer be a 'tribute,' but rather… voluntary gifts from all of Khorasan. And also—I, like certain other governors of Arabia, want the title of Emir of my lands: Khorasan and Mawara' al-Nahr."

"Oh, certainly, my boy," Ma'mun nodded. "As you say. You deserve it. Perfectly permissible. I'll see to it. Anything else?"

"Yes," Abdallah continued. "As Emir of Khorasan and Mawara' al-Nahr, I must be free to act independently. I must have the authority to make all significant political and strategic decisions for the regions entrusted to me—on my own."

"What—so you won't even consult your Caliph?" Ma'mun teased slyly, looking at the son of his late friend Tahir.

Ambitious as he was, the young governor remained silent.

Then, after a pause, he said wisely:

"In especially complex matters—if you permit—I will indeed seek your counsel, my lord."

"Excellent!" Ma'mun beamed.

The Caliph certainly had no intention of granting Abdallah—or any of his satraps and governors—too much freedom or power. But at this moment—when Tahir's dagger lay in the hand of that warrior's bold, hot-blooded young son—Ma'mun decided to challenge nothing.

Someday, everything in my domain will be on my terms again, he thought, for Ma'mun, too, possessed ambition and decisiveness in ample measure.

* * *

Al-Andalus, Iberia (Spain) – Merv, Khorasan, Abbasid Caliphate, 825 CE

Talha and Ali had received word from their brother, Abdallah, that after his campaign in Crete, he would soon arrive in Merv.

They understood that their young governor of Khorasan and Mawara' al-Nahr needed a respite—that he missed his mother and brothers, just as they missed him. So Talha, selecting the finest horses and accompanied by their friends, rode out to meet Abdallah at the city's outskirts. When they met, the two brothers embraced tightly and exchanged handshakes.

"Where's Ali?" Abdallah asked at once, worried.

"Don't fret, brother," Talha reassured him. "He's well. He's out inspecting those new irrigation channels and fields that you yourself ordered us to develop more rigorously."

"And rightly so!" Abdallah responded enthusiastically. "We need the highest crop yields. I instructed the legal scholars to formulate rules for water usage. Our people must not go hungry. We'll do whatever it takes to ensure they live in prosperity and security. Well done, my beloved brothers."

"You'll see Ali this evening," Talha said with a smile.

They rode home slowly, where a hot hammam awaited Abdallah, along with delicious home-cooked food. After washing up, the brothers sat down at the table and continued their conversation.

"We love you too, Abdallah," Talha said sincerely. "But please— tell us how your expedition in Iberia went, and why you chose to go there."

"I was asked to go by Caliph Ma'mun," Abdallah began. "But to make it clearer for you, I need to start from the beginning. You know, of course, that the current ruling dynasty of the Arabian Caliphate—the Abbasids—was preceded by the Umayyad dynasty?"

"Yes, of course," Talha nodded. "I recall our father—may he rest in peace!—teaching us about history. The Umayyad Caliphate conquered North Africa, part of the Iberian Peninsula, as well as Sind, Tabaristan, and Jurjan. Two branches of the Umayyads ruled from Syria until the mid-eighth century. That was the Damascus Caliphate. But in 750, the Umayyads were overthrown by the Abbasids in the uprising led by Abu Muslim, and almost all Umayyads were eliminated."

"All correct," Abdallah confirmed. "Only one member of that dynasty survived: Abd al-Rahman I, nicknamed 'The Immigrant.'"

"That's an interesting epithet!" Talha remarked. "They must have called him that because, once the Abbasids took power, all surviving members of the former Umayyad dynasty had to emigrate to other countries?"

"Exactly," Abdallah said with a nod. "Rahman founded his own dynasty and the Emirate of Cordoba in Iberia—Spain, in other words.

And you know that in 822, Abd al-Rahman II became Emir of Cordoba. He launched extensive building projects that led to heavier taxes—and that, in turn, sparked mass uprisings, especially in Muslim al-Andalus. There were also rebels still loyal to the Umayyads, or who were simply anti-Arab in general. I had to put down those revolts with my forces."

"How did Abd al-Rahman II receive you, an envoy of the Abbasid Caliph?" Talha asked.

"Fine. He proved patient and good-natured," Abdallah replied. "He even proposed his beautiful sister, Dana, as my wife, but I politely declined. You know my beloved Mahabbat is waiting for me here. Also, Rahman II aided me in quelling the uprisings and kept me from being captured by insurgents. As a result of our combined victories, two major groups of Spaniards and Arab rebels left the country—fifteen thousand families moved to Egypt, and about eight thousand went to Morocco. But I realized one thing…"

"What is it, brother?" Talha asked curiously.

"That while the enormous expanse of the Arab Caliphate and its many conquered foreign territories indeed bring great benefits—our growing wealth and expanding knowledge about the world and different local cultures—Abd al-Rahman II has shown me that support from the Caliph is valuable. But… he dreams of complete independence from Ma'mun. And let me share a secret with you, Talha: someday, without doubt, that's exactly what will happen."

35

Tashkent, 2023

"We need to keep moving," Sharaf remarked. "But where? Barno, you said you'd take a look at my half of the map. I've seen you studying it."

"Yes, I did," Barno nodded.

"And what conclusions did you come to?"

"You're right that actually finding the treasure without the second part would be difficult—maybe even impossible," Barno replied. "But for now, we can—or rather, we should—at least move forward somehow. I suggest we think carefully together about everything we already know regarding the possible location of the treasure. In other words, we need a standard map of the Abbasid Caliphate."

"You're right," Sharaf agreed, opening the internet on his device and quickly pulling up such a map. "We need to clarify which countries and cities were part of it, right?"

"Absolutely," said Barno. "I'll begin with a bit of history—as a historian and tour guide. The Abbasid, or 'Baghdad,' Caliphate was a feudal theocratic state that existed from 750 to 945, and later from 1194 to 1258, under the rule of the Abbasid dynasty. It included parts of Central Asia, Egypt, Iran, North Africa, and India. It also encompassed lands that are now Arab states in Asia—places like Bahrain, as well as Nejd and Hejaz, which were eventually unified in 1932 to become Saudi Arabia."

"That means the Caliphate spanned a huge area!" Sharaf exclaimed. "So basically, these Abbasid treasures Ma'mun or the Tahirids might have hidden could be in any of those countries or cities, right?"

"Most likely," Barno conceded. "But if we think about it, it's unlikely the most precious valuables would be stashed right under their own noses in Mesopotamia or Khorasan—what's now Iraq and Uzbekistan. What if they were hidden somewhere more remote from the capital? For instance, in my own native Qatar?"

"That's an idea," Sharaf mused. "From what excavations have shown, as far back as the third millennium BCE, Qatar was part of the state of Dilmun, cantered on the island of Bahrain. In the seventh century, Qatar became part of the Abbasid Caliphate and remained under its influence for a long time. It was integrated into the broader administrative and commercial framework of the Caliphate, which was known for its trade routes and strategic position."

"So, possibly Ma'mun's treasure—assuming it really existed, based on your map—could have ended up lost in Bahrain too?" Sharaf suggested.

"Yes, I think so," Barno agreed. "In 827, Caliph Ma'mun dispatched Abdallah ibn Tahir on a campaign against the island of Bahrain. Ma'mun's forces seized the island but couldn't hold on to it. Not long after, the same happened with neighbouring Nejd. Caliph Ma'mun sent his representatives to various provinces of the Caliphate to administer them and collect taxes."

"And what does your 'feminine intuition' tell you?" Sharaf asked. "Where do you think we should head right now?"

"I think we should investigate Saudi Arabia—called Nejd in

Caliph Ma'mun's time," Barno answered, "and see if we can search for the treasure there. Possibly we'll find the second half of your map as well. After that, maybe we fly to Bahrain."

"Sounds perfect," Sharaf agreed enthusiastically. "So, onward to Riyadh and other parts of the old Nejd! I'm buying us plane tickets."

"Let's go!" Barno chimed in support. "And don't forget to bring Tahir's dagger. I'm really curious… where might its scabbard be? Maybe there's a clue in that too…"

* * *

Davron Bakhromov's former friend, Kamil Akbarov, had not gambled out of simple recklessness or weak-willed addiction. He gambled because, as a naturally freedom-loving person, he dreamed of complete independence from his parents—a tyrannical father who insisted on strict traditional ways, and a mother who alternated between coddling him and worrying about him excessively.

He loved freedom in all its forms. So the real threat of prison—now looming closer than ever—frightened him out of his wits.

If I manage to escape this rotten scenario, he silently promised himself, *I'll never sit at a gambling table again!*

When both Bakhromovs put pressure on him, Kamil—being a gentle soul—was unable to resist, and in his fear, he agreed to everything. But once he left the investigator's office, he realized that—despite having signed a "full confession"—he needed to get out of the trap he'd landed in as fast as possible.

He didn't want to confide in his parents or drag them into his problems. But then he remembered that he had an uncle—a lawyer named Najmiddin—with whom he rarely spoke. Kamil called and asked to meet him.

Najmiddin Yuldashev waited for his nephew in a café.

"How's it going?" he asked the young man. "How's my sister? Everything all right with you guys? I spoke to her on the phone the other day and didn't pick up on any serious issues from her voice. But you sounded anxious."

"Mom's fine, thanks," Kamil said. "But, Uncle… honestly, I haven't told her about us meeting. And I'd ask you not to mention anything we talk about to her, okay? She'd just worry."

"All right, it's a deal," Najmiddin replied with a smile. "So out with it—what's going on?"

"It's not… not me," Kamil began, unconvincingly. "It's a friend of mine. He's got a big problem and apparently needs legal advice right away. He can't afford a good attorney, so I was wondering if you'd help. Sorry, but he couldn't come himself… so he sent me!"

"Your friend's in deep trouble with the law, and he invites me over but can't spare twenty minutes to meet me face to face?" the lawyer said in surprise. "So he sent *you* instead—even though, up until today, you've only called me maybe twice a year—on my birthday, or New Year's. And now I get this big honour? My nephew surfaces in need! Look, kid, maybe drop the lies and be upfront? I promise you I won't tell your parents a word about your problem, okay? Don't be scared. Spill it. Because it's *you* who's in trouble, right?"

"Nothing gets past you, Uncle," Kamil admitted, lowering his head. "Yes, you're right. Actually… I could end up in jail."

He explained everything—the charges that threatened him, and what he'd be prosecuted for.

"Signing that 'voluntary confession' wasn't a great move," Yuldashev sighed. "I'm no expert in criminal law or criminal procedure—I'm a notary, remember? But I know this much: you definitely don't want to let yourself get dragged further into the spotlight in front of the victims. I'll personally make sure they receive the money—discreetly—through Dr. Said Mumtazov's attending physician, framing it as a donation from some charity. We're not about to expose you. We can figure out the next steps after that. As for your written confession… not sure. Maybe we can claim you… weren't entirely sane? Then the confession and your signature could be contested in court."

"But then they might stick me in a mental hospital!" Kamil blanched. "How's that any better than jail? What are you on about, Uncle? No, no—I don't want that!!"

"Calm down," his uncle said, cutting off the younger man's hysteria. "I'm only saying we could get a letter. A piece of paper, you follow? I doubt anyone's going to check whether you've been isolated or not. Right now, our priority is to buy you time and keep you out of prison!"

"I see," Kamil said, a bit relieved. "But still, Uncle—please, no such certificates! If word got out, I'd either be ridiculed or never find decent work. I *do* want to, you know, pull myself up and be a respectable man someday."

"That's admirable!" the lawyer responded. "Yes, you're right. I was just brainstorming. Then, my boy, we may need to…"

"Need to do what?" Kamil asked, hopeful.

"Use a cunning trick," Najmiddin explained. "I'll tell you exactly what we'll do. And one more thing—stop being afraid of everyone and everything! It's *they* who ought to be worried that you might blow the whistle on their criminal conspiracy—those Bakhromovs. There's nothing they can put you in jail for. They don't have a shred of real evidence against you on any charge. All they've got is that written confession. And where is it, by the way? Probably in a drawer in that crooked investigator's—Major Bakhromov's—office, right? I'll bet that's the case. But I know someone who works in that precinct…"

36

Sharjah, United Arab Emirates, the same year

Bob Downey was not hiding the stolen Abbasid treasures in his own apartment, nor in his office at the Archaeological Museum, nor at any of his friends' places. He wouldn't have risked leaving them with his ex-wife Hilla, who was just as greedy as he was. The kindly young American woman would have immediately seized the opportunity to profit from them herself and leave her ex-husband empty-handed. And the police, if they ever caught Bob, could search all the places he might frequent. So the adventurer had only one option: find a hiding place for those ancient valuables that no one would ever suspect.

And he found just such a spot—a secret basement room in Fort Al-Hisn, the oldest building in Sharjah, formerly the rulers' residence. Now it's a museum. Bob had once pilfered a key to the basement from a friend who worked as the archive manager in that ancient fortress, just in case. It would never occur to anyone to look for the Abbasid treasures Bob had stolen so recently in what was practically a sacred building for all the locals.

Bob had visited the fort's basement several times to scout it out. And so that he could find the hidden room again after stashing the valuables there, he carefully drew a detailed plan of the fort's basement in his paper notebook.

The morning after his meeting with the treacherous, no-longer-trustworthy dwarf Fernando, Bob began thinking about what to do next. He needed to get rid of this nasty blackmailer—without ending up empty-handed himself.

He had a brilliant idea.

That same day, sneaking into his secret treasure hideaway without anyone noticing, he took just a few of the many gold coins minted with Caliph Ma'mun's name and a small silver bowl—he found it slightly less painful to part with this piece than with some of the others.

Putting them in his backpack, he left the fort completely unnoticed.

Afterward, Bob stealthily boarded Fernando's yacht again, first making sure the mysterious "Spaniard" had gone into town on business.

Then Bob phoned his friend Hajar, an IT specialist, asking to meet. Hajar suggested they meet at his workplace, but out of caution, Bob refused and proposed they meet instead at their favourite tennis club. Hajar arrived at the designated time, and they sat in a corner of the small, almost deserted club café. At Bob's request, the IT pro began searching for any data he could find on "Fernando Gonzalez."

Much to Downey's surprise, it turned out no such person existed. Or, more precisely, there were a couple of people by that name—but one was an eighty-three-year-old living in Argentina, and the other a five-year-old in Mexico.

Fortunately for Bob, during his second covert visit to the

"ghost" blackmailer's yacht, he'd snapped a photo of the dwarf from a picture hanging on the cabin wall—just in case. Now it proved useful. Hajar used a facial recognition program in the Sharjah police's first-level database to track down the "Spaniard."

The man's real name was Amun Muhammad Bekerat, an Egyptian national. With that genuine identity in hand, Hajar hacked both his messaging account and email.

After that, Bob Downey sent, from those hacked accounts, several letters he had prewritten to the appropriate recipients, paying his friend for taking the risk. Then Bob worked up his nerve and called the police, reporting that "Egyptian citizen Amun Muhammad Bekerat, traveling under Spanish documents as Fernando González," would be aboard his yacht *Madjrit* that night at 23:00—and that he had stashed there treasures stolen from the Archaeological Museum, valuables precious to the entire Arab world.

That very night, Amun-Fernando was arrested. The chief evidence of his guilt—besides the gold coins of Caliph Ma'mun and the silver bowl found on his yacht—was a message, allegedly sent by him (though actually part of Bob's ruse), to the museum director. In it, he discreetly offered, behind the government's back, to return all the stolen Abbasid treasures for the price of one million dollars.

The authorities viewed such an offer as the height of audacity and a blatant insult by a foreigner to the country and its priceless heritage.

But once the fake "Fernando" was brought before Investigator Iman, he waved his hands emphatically, denying any involvement in the theft or in sending the letters, shifting the blame onto a certain Bob Downey who worked at the Archaeological Museum.

So far, though, no one had proof of Bob's guilt.

After locating and rigorously questioning Bob, the police let him go—although they did assign a plainclothes officer to tail him for a couple of days. Thus, Bob basically got away scot-free. He now only had to try again to sell the treasures and get a large sum for them.

The next morning, the renowned archaeologist Nazih Abu Jalil was released from custody under a travel ban—at the urgent request of both his attorney and, above all, his friend Saud ibn Mahshud—pending trial. The simultaneous questioning of witnesses and Amun-Fernando yielded nothing: the two men clearly did not know each other at all. The station chief who had ordered Nazih's detention—also the lead investigator on the case, Iman—did not see fit to apologize to the archaeologist; he merely said, "Catch you later." Nazih retorted, "Best to say farewell for good, Officer."

So where are the rest of those Abbasid treasures that Nazih found during his excavation? the disappointed Investigator Iman wondered. *And who really stole them? What a mystery!*

* * *

Tashkent – Manama, Kingdom of Bahrain, the same period

"And now we're flying to Bahrain," Zulfiya announced to Sher, Sanya, and Vanya in a tone that brooked no disagreement.

Sanya, as usual, was prepared to do anything a beautiful woman suggested.

"Whatever you say, boss!" he exclaimed obligingly.

"But why Bahrain?" Vanya asked.

"That's pretty far," Sher added, trying to sound practical.

"Pipe down, 'Captain Obvious,'" Vanya grumbled at Sher. "Still—why?"

"For one thing," Zulfiya began, "Bahrain, along with Qatar, was part of the ninth-century Arab Caliphate. I read an interesting fact online: around the mid-20th century, in the Sakhir Desert—"

"You must mean the Sahara," Sher interrupted, attempting to correct her.

"No, no," the young historian laughed at his naivete. "I mean *Sakhir*! Anyway, in the Sakhir Desert—which, translated from Persian, means 'hills and ridges'—some archaeologists discovered steel scabbards back in the 1950s. One was said to have belonged either to someone among the Abbasids—possibly Caliph Ma'mun himself—or someone very close to him. They concluded that because the scabbard bore an image of Caliph Ma'mun's distinctive turban, with that enormous lemon-like pearl at its crest. I read about it—a splendid orange *melo* pearl."

"So all they found was a scabbard?" Vanya asked. "No dagger?"

"I'm not sure yet," Zulfiya replied. "That's exactly what we need to find out. Maybe no dagger was there—and I don't know if any of the other treasures we're after were found. But it's certainly possible! So I wrote a letter to the Library of the Cultural Centre in Manama, asking them to send me any articles on the subject and, more generally, any materials on ninth-century artifacts and maps."

"You don't just sit around doing nothing, dear Zulfiya," Sanya said admiringly. "You're quite the go-getter! A busy bee…"

"Thank you, Sanya," the historian replied, blushing slightly at his compliments. "Anyway, I just got a reply from the head of the library this morning—inviting us to come in person! They've offered to let us look over, right there on-site, the materials that interest us about ninth-century artifacts and maps. Sher, buy the plane tickets. I've already phoned Kudrat Valiev—he gave the green light for our new expedition."

Sher reluctantly agreed; he would not dare argue with Kudrat himself.

Early the following day, the four travellers arrived in Manama. At the Cultural Centre's Library, the director, Mr. Yakzan Baker, welcomed them warmly.

"I'm so pleased that scholars from Uzbekistan have such genuine interest in my country's history," he said.

After treating his visitors to tea and local sweets, he instructed the library curator to provide these "scholars" with all the resources they needed and said they could use the collection for as long as necessary.

He personally assigned his assistant, Ghiyas, to accompany them on their travels around the country.

Neither Zulfiya nor her companions knew—or even suspected—that the centre's director, Yakzan Baker, had summoned Ghiyas earlier and instructed him:

"Keep a close eye on these people, Ghiyas! If they find anything of value, let me know immediately. Remember: not a single treasure of Bahrain—or of the Arab world as a whole—must leave this country and fall into foreign hands!"

Ghiyas nodded obediently to his boss.

One evening, after several days of searching, Zulfiya arranged a "brainstorming session" in Sher's hotel room. Ghiyas was not with them—he'd gone home to rest.

Each member of the group had to share what they had discovered in the Cultural Centre's library that might be useful.

"I got curious and read about the Kingdom of Bahrain," Sanya began, hoping to impress Zulfiya and, in the process, appear a bit smarter than usual. "In ancient times, it was called Dilmun, and now it's 'Bahrain'—which in Arabic means 'two seas.' It's the only Arab island state, a jewel of the Middle East made up of thirty-three islands, all located in the western part of the Arabian Gulf, just east of the Saudi coast, connected by a causeway."

"And how is that helpful to us?" Sher cut in impatiently. "Sounds like random info."

"Hey, don't interrupt," Sanya snapped at the driver. "Anyway, did you know that oil extraction in this kingdom started back in 1932? Much earlier than in, say, the Emirates! In Dubai, they only discovered oil in 1966 and began extracting and managing it in 1969, which led to Dubai's rapid development. This might be relevant because in the '30s, many Bahrainis tried on their own to find oil—digging around everywhere! Especially in the Sakhir Desert!! That's exactly where ancient treasure could be buried! And that includes our hoard!"

"Well done, Sanya," Zulfiya praised him. "That might be valuable info. I also read an article about a young adventurer from Manama whose name was never revealed, so let's just call him Talib—Arabic for 'seeker.' In those same years, Talib also decided to dig on his own, hoping to find at least a small well and strike it rich to support his family. He had no success with oil—but he did unearth some pottery, mostly jugs, from the Abbasid Caliphate era. One jug even contained an old map with cryptic symbols and the outline of a route to some unknown place! He thought it marked a treasure location, but to his great frustration, he couldn't decipher it."

"Just like us," Sher put in. "We can't decipher our piece of the map either."

"It's not 'ours'—it's our boss Kudrat Valiev's," Sanya corrected him.

"Right, can't argue there," Sher allowed. "Go on, Zulfiya!"

"Talib didn't want to consult just anyone," the historian continued. "He feared outsiders would find out about *his* treasure and seize it, never letting him get near it—let alone profit from it, as the young man had hoped. He did have a son, though, with whom he shared his secret. For many years, the two of them hunted for the treasure, carefully storing that map in their cellar, which apparently had just the right temperature…"

"Yes, I read somewhere that low temperature and low relative humidity are best for preserving ancient documents," Sher said, displaying his general knowledge.

"Indeed," Zulfiya nodded. "They even periodically coated the map with wax so it wouldn't disintegrate from age. But the years passed, and they never found the treasure. Talib died, and his son—unable to decode the map's puzzles—passed it on to a friend of his, a young historian named Hazim, who then lived in Riffa, or Rifa' ash-Sharqi, the second-largest city in Bahrain. If Hazim is still alive, we could try…"

"Find him and talk to him!" Sanya finished her thought excitedly. "Yes?"

"Absolutely," Zulfiya said, smiling. Then she asked, "Has anyone found out anything about the missing dagger's scabbard from the Abbasids?"

"Yes, I have," Vanya spoke up. "The original is kept in the current king's residence. They definitely won't let us in there…"

"Darn it!" Sanya lamented, cutting him off. "I'd have loved to see that scabbard!"

"But by order of the king, they made an exact replica," Vanya continued, "and that's quite accessible—it's on display at the National Museum here. The only difference from the original is the era in which it was made."

"That's excellent news!" Zulfiya exclaimed.

"How does this scabbard help us?" Sher grumbled sceptically. "If it were the whole stash of Abbasid treasure, then sure… but it's just some scabbard from a dagger that probably doesn't exist… Big deal."

"What if there's still something of value about it?" Sanya said hopefully, always siding with Zulfiya's ideas. "A secret or a clue, maybe?"

"Yes! Tomorrow, we'll first visit the museum and carefully examine this so-called 'Ma'mun scabbard'—or whoever it belonged to," Zulfiya decreed. "Then we'll head to Riffa and try to find that historian Hazim. I'm sure Ghiyas will help us."

"Oh dear. I wouldn't trust him completely," Sher warned, more cautious than the rest of his fellow travellers.

"Why?" asked Zulfiya, who was not so adept at reading people. "Everyone here has been so welcoming and friendly! Ghiyas seems like a nice guy."

"All the same!" Sher insisted on his suspicions. "I advise you not to share our treasure-hunting ideas around him. Understood?"

The others in the treasure-hunting group agreed and approved Zulfiya's plans for the coming days. They all headed off to their rooms to rest, anticipating that morning would bring a pleasant, intriguing journey to Riffa.

37

Doha, Qatar, the same period

That evening, hotel owner Sarwan Al-Tawil came home tired, yet in a buoyant mood, and summoned his daughter, Jahiza, to his study.

Jahiza had no idea that her father had recently met with the banker Najib Abbas—and that the primary subject of their conversation had been her. Her father had told her nothing of it thus far.

"Daughter, do you really want to get married that badly?" he began, catching her off guard with the question.

"What makes you think that, Father?" the girl asked, surprised.

"Because, my dear, you practically forced a poor young man to marry you," Sarwan said, momentarily putting on a stern face, as though scolding her. "You compelled him, right? Considering there wasn't even the slightest hint of… rape?"

"He's not exactly poor," his daughter countered, without directly answering her father's question. "His father's got millions. And he—Nizar—is the only heir to all that wealth and their entire family business! Plus, he's not half-witted—he's actually quite a capable young man. So eventually, he'll manage not only to avoid squandering his father's fortune, as many rich brats do, but to preserve and even grow it. So… did someone say anything about marriage?"

She looked at her father hopefully—but it was the hope of a sly fox, having lured her suitor like a partridge into a snug trap, rather than the hope of any innocent lamb.

"Yes, his father… has almost given his consent," Sarwan smiled. "The son obeys him, loves and respects him. Which means he'll do whatever his father tells him."

"Really?…" Jahiza asked, barely hiding her surge of joy. "But that's good news, right, Father? Aren't you happy? Am I not helping you?"

"Me?!" Sarwan echoed in surprise.

"Yes, you said yourself you're having big problems in your business," she said calmly. "So I helped you in any way I could. Are you not… pleased?"

"Well, you're certainly practical! Already thinking several moves ahead, eh?" her father said, standing to gently pat her head. Then, turning serious, he added: "Just be careful, daughter. Don't pull stunts like this again—it's far too risky. You came up with something this time, and it seems to be working. The wealthy heir is being forced to marry you. But in the future—please don't weave such schemes again. Don't play with fire."

Acting as though she agreed, Jahiza said,

"All right, Daddy. So I… can start preparing for the wedding?"

"Indeed you can, my dear," Sarwan smiled. "But it's not just you alone—both our families must prepare. I'll give your mother a quick rundown of the situation tonight—she'll help you with everything."

"Great, Daddy, thank you!" the newly minted bride-to-be said, beaming happily.

"I do have one question, daughter: what about that young man in your class who loves you so much—Sharaf, is it? Didn't you want to marry him?"

"Who's that, Father?" Jahiza replied coolly, as though she had no recollection. "Oh, that pathetic pauper, that loser? What do I need him for? Now I have a truly worthy fiancé!"

* * *

Sharjah, United Arab Emirates, the same year

Investigator Iman interrogated the fake "Fernando" several times and learned from him that he had come into contact with Bob Downey through a shady website. Hearing—as everyone in the country had—about the high-profile theft, he guessed the thief might try to sell the ninth-century treasures through that site, at least initially, during the "get acquainted" stage between seller and buyer.

Thus, Iman realized he absolutely could not dismiss Downey. Meanwhile, the undercover officer assigned to watch Bob reported back that Mr. Downey had been paying frequent visits to Fort Al-Hisn—and not by day, but exclusively at night! That raised the suspicions of both the spy and Investigator Iman.

Iman began tracking new posts by Bob on the darknet, where he had changed his nickname from "Salesman" to "Gold Halif." How did the police catch on? In a hurry and a fluster, Bob had failed to ask his savvy IT friend to mask his IP address. So Bob nearly gave himself away.

Iman told one of his young assistants to temporarily register on that site and message "Gold Halif." Bob, wanting to be as cautious as he had been with the fake Fernando, planned to bring no valuables to the first meeting with the supposed buyer.

Yet the assistant, following Iman's instructions, wrote to "Gold Halif"—that is, Bob—insisting that the entire "merchandise" be brought immediately. He claimed to be a wealthy foreigner, in a rush to fly home for his young son's birthday. Moreover, he said he had brought the full amount: fifty million Sharjah dirhams—nearly fifteen million US dollars! Precisely the figure Bob had been hoping for.

The "buyer" added that he likely wouldn't have another chance to travel anytime soon and also wanted to present his wife with a lavish gift for their tenth wedding anniversary.

In short, the police's well-crafted cover story was so smooth, so tempting to the archaeological museum's Abbasid treasure thief, that the not-so-savvy Bob Downey took the bait.

He was arrested on the spot the next day—caught red-handed. Investigator Iman gathered ample evidence of Bob's guilt and direct involvement in the "heist of the century." This time, Bob couldn't possibly wriggle out of it.

At Iman's request, the director of the Archaeological Museum identified the recovered Abbasid treasures, which had recently been unearthed by Nazih Abu Jalil during his excavations. The valuables were returned to the museum.

* * *

Riyadh, Saudi Arabia, the same period

Barno and Sharaf began their search for the second half of the map and the hidden Abbasid treasure in Riyadh's museums, hoping to uncover records related to the ninth century—during the Abbasid Caliphate.

After checking into a hotel, they visited the Saudi National Museum that very day. It was located in the Al-Murabba district, near King Abdulaziz's palace, the King Abdulaziz Historical Centre, and the Al-Masmak Palace Museum—an archaeological palace of Riyadh.

"You know," said one of the museum guides, "there's someone here in town—a very interesting and truly good man—who might be able to help you! At least, he's been a great help to our museum and its collections. His name is Dagman Yamani. He's a businessman of Lebanese origin, a patron of the arts, and a collector of valuable antique items and artifacts. He's especially fond of anything connected to the Arab Caliphate—including the Abbasid era. I'll give you his phone number. If this busy, respected gentleman is able to spare you some time, you might get the chance to meet and talk."

Sharaf and Barno heartily thanked the kind woman, and Sharaf immediately called Mr. Yamani.

To their surprise, the young Qatari's call was received most cordially.

Yamani invited them to his home that same evening. In typical Uzbek fashion, Barno made sure that she and Sharaf did not arrive empty-handed before such a gracious gentleman and his family. On the way, they bought some thoughtful gifts.

But imagine their astonishment when they arrived and found that Yamani and his wife had laid out such a lavish table—it far surpassed their generous offerings. They were pleased by the warm reception but also felt slightly uneasy. To ensure Barno could follow the conversation, everyone agreed to speak in English.

Noticing the embarrassment of his foreign guests, the attentive host smiled and said:

"Please, make yourselves at home and feel perfectly at ease! I can see you've been taken aback by our hospitality. But first of all, it's our custom to treat any guests this way—especially dear ones. Second, my wife and I took an immediate liking to you. Sadly, we lost our daughter a few years ago, and so we can't help seeing young people her age—or a bit older—as though they were our own children."

Barno and Sharaf offered their sincere condolences to Dagman and his wife.

"And third, my friends," he continued, "I greatly admire your passion for Arab history and culture! I share that passion—I'm deeply drawn to artifacts. What you're doing now is both important and fascinating. So, have you made any progress in your quest for the Abbasid treasure? Please, do eat—try everything, don't be shy!"

Sampling the finest Arabian delicacies and other delicious dishes, Sharaf and Barno exchanged glances in silence. They could hardly reveal all the details of the map and their discovery in Merv—the Tahir ibn Husayn dagger bearing Caliph Ma'mun's portrait—to a stranger right off the bat!

"Ah, I see," the host laughed warmly, with genuine friendliness. "So that's your secret, is it? All right, all right—I'll drop the subject. Then how might I be of help to you? Go ahead, ask any questions you like. And afterward, why don't you stay with us overnight? Please don't argue—here, when guests come from other countries, we usually invite them to stay. That way, we can talk more tonight and in the morning. Who knows if we'll get another chance later?"

"Tell me, Mr. Yamani," Sharaf began, "have you ever heard of Caliph Ma'mun's map, which was drawn on very old fabric? There's a legend that says either the Caliph himself or one of his vassal governors tore the map into two nearly equal parts. Perhaps one person took what you might call the first half, and another took the second. The real value lies in… Well, sorry, I can't elaborate. It's just that we're eager to find out more about it."

"So there's some secret about Caliphs and the kings of Arabia?" Yamani laughed again. "You mean the Abbasid treasure map, yes? The one no one's ever found? And even now, there's no certain information about what exactly the treasure is. But rumours say it's immense—like Ali Baba's gold in the 'Open Sesame' tale."

"How on earth do you…?!" Barno exclaimed in amazement.

"I also know this," the collector went on, smiling playfully. "Among that treasure might be the steel dagger—and scabbard— of Ma'mun's chief general, Tahir. And by the way, he was from Khorasan—so, essentially, your countryman, Barno! Also among the riches is said to be the Caliph's turban with the huge orange 'melo' pearl. That single gem alone would fetch millions at auction. So, my young friends—are you searching for that, perhaps? Good for you!"

"N-no, we're not exactly searching," Sharaf tried to deny, not wanting to reveal the full secret—lest it all be for nothing.

"Well, all right, all right, kids," the host said with an even broader grin, while his wife remained silent throughout the conversation. "I see you're embarrassed. And you both look worn out. My wife has already arranged rooms for you—two guest rooms on the second floor. Make yourselves comfortable. Our housekeeper will bring you a delicious fruit kompot before bedtime."

* * *

That night, in her sleep, Barno seemed to hear the murmur of the sea and felt a slight swaying sensation, but her drowsiness was so overpowering that it didn't truly register. As for Sharaf, he didn't stir at all until morning.

When the pair finally came to their senses, they found themselves bound hand and foot, sitting on cold stones in what appeared to be a cave. Their belongings were nowhere to be seen. They could hear the sound of ocean waves nearby. At first, they thought it must be some cruel or bizarre prank—until they saw... Dagman Yamani standing there with a smile.

"Finally awake, are we?" the businessman said cheerfully. "No, my young friends, this is no joke. I actually dislike humour. You're in a small cave carved into a cliff on the shore of the Red Sea, quite far from civilization. My men brought you here—first by car to the shore, then on my yacht. Didn't you notice anything? My wife's kompot, laced with a potent sleeping drug, was terrific, wasn't it?"

In confusion and alarm, the boy and girl looked around the grotto, then at each other.

"So, let's get to the point," Dagman continued. "For many years, I've been hunting the treasures hidden by Caliph Ma'mun— the Abbasid fortune. Then you two appeared! I've had one half of that map you mentioned, Sharaf, for quite some time now. How could you deceive an elder, hmm? You said you only knew about it second-hand—from hearsay. But from your tone, I realized you definitely had something valuable. I took your map—the other half of mine—from your bag, Sharaf! And now, with or without your help, I can finally find that fabulous treasure!"

"But you're already wealthy, Yamani," Barno pointed out. "Why do you need even more?"

"One can never have too much wealth, my girl!" Yamani beamed. "Don't worry, I won't kill you—I'm a devout man, and such crimes displease me. I'll simply keep you here in this cliff as prisoners. My men will bring you everything you need: mattresses, warm clothing, water, food. But if you dare try to escape, I will become your most merciless enemy. If you behave like obedient, submissive children for a month, I might even allow you to help me search for my treasure. Then, who knows—maybe I'll share part of it with you. A third of a percent. That would be plenty for you, wouldn't it? It's still a lot, believe me! Anyway, I've spent enough time chatting. I must go. Behave yourselves. Now you'll be my eternal hosta—er, guests. You'll soon appreciate how generous and hospitable I am! Didn't you see that last night?"

Barno and Sharaf were utterly stunned. They had expected some difficulties in their travels, but never imagined they'd fall into the clutches of a madman obsessed with the Abbasid hoard—and such a dangerous one at that. They had also never dreamed they'd soon be imprisoned… Both clung to the hope that there was a way out, that they could escape. But then they realized their arms and legs weren't bound by mere rope, but by chains with iron locks.

I do cherish Sharaf as a friend. But why did I ever agree to help him chase these Arab treasures? I still haven't found my father—and now I'm lost to others myself. We should have just stayed home, somewhere safe! Barno thought in despair.

38

Manama, Bahrain, the same period

Sanya effortlessly filched a copy of an Abbasid-era scabbard from the National Museum of Manama. The display case's lock was trivial. While Zulfiya and Sher examined the exhibit—studying the ancient history of the Dilmun state—and Vanya distracted the guard, Sanya quickly picked the lock and made off with a high-quality forgery of the treasure.

"What a strange tip on this scabbard!" Vanya remarked in astonishment. "It looks like a small seal. Look here—there's an embossing in the shape of a crescent."

"Nothing unusual," observed Zulfiya. "Everyone knows that the crescent is one of the principal symbols of Islam. I think it's just a decorative element."

"Then what—a seal? A stamp?" asked Sanya, less knowledgeable than his friend.

"Exactly," Vanya nodded. "It's very tiny. Rulers usually used something like this. But wait… could it be the seal of Caliph Ma'mun himself?! Or of Tahir? Or someone else among the Tahirids? But… why on earth would that seal be here?"

"You sure love asking all sorts of questions," Sanya chided him. "What's it to you?"

Zulfiya, who was firmly opposed to any kind of theft, spoke up.

"It'd be better if you returned this scabbard to its proper place," she pleaded with Sanya. "This could end very badly."

But Sanya didn't return the scabbard; he valued wealth and a secure future far more than he cared about history. So he did everything his own way…

Ghiyas secretly reported the theft of the scabbard to Yakzan Baker, the Director of the Cultural Centre.

"We're not turning them over to our police just yet," Yakzan said. "It's more profitable for us if you continue accompanying these people on their treasure hunts in our country. And if they find something truly valuable, you must inform me immediately. Then we won't let them leave the country with those finds. They'll be detained for a while, and later, of course, we'll deport them all— empty-handed."

The group of treasure-hunting travellers, accompanied by Ghiyas, set off for Riffa.

The venerable historian Hazim Asad was well known to many; his address had been provided by the Ethnographic Museum where he had once worked.

Zulfiya and her companions decided to visit him. Being a solitary man, he was delighted by the unexpected guests.

"Yes, my friends, I once had this map drawn on a piece of ancient fabric," old Hazim began. "A friend gave it to me. But try as I might, I could never decipher its strange symbols. It saddens me deeply that I never found the treasure! I would have lived quite comfortably—like a king…"

"Then please, hand us that map!" Sher demanded eagerly through Ghiyas—who knew English and was translating Hazim's words into Arabic. "Maybe we can decipher its markings somehow?"

"But I don't have it, my friends," the old man replied innocently.

"What do you mean?!" Sanya nearly exploded. "We've come

such a long way only to hear you don't have it? That all this was in vain? Oh, I can't bear it!"

"Hold your wailing," Vanya interjected. "Dear Hazim, where is it? Where did it go? Please, try to recall."

"I remember," said Hazim. "Many years ago, I gave it to my friend—an archaeologist from Qatar—because I had become firmly convinced that there were no such treasures in Bahrain. I couldn't leave my family and beloved work to search in another country. So, my friends, I resigned myself to the fact that I would never live like a sheikh—and it wasn't even worth dreaming about. But truly, my Qatari friend promised me that if he ever found the treasure based on that clearly incomplete map, he would share his riches with me. However, as far as I know, he wasn't successful. At first, he tried to decipher the map and search according to his interpretation of the Abbasid symbols. And he failed. Then he fell gravely ill and handed the map over to his relatives. Soon after, he passed away. But I believe the map remains in Qatar—in Doha."

"Could you possibly give us the contact details of that family?" Zulfiya asked hopefully. "Of course, if you have them. Or at least tell us the name of your friend from Qatar—we'd try to locate the map."

"I might," the old man replied warmly. "But honestly, my inquisitive young friends, I sincerely believe that it's all futile. In order not only to find the treasures of the Arab Caliphs but even to decipher the symbols on the map, you need its continuation—in other words, the second half of the map!"

"The thing is, we actually do have that second half," Sanya suddenly admitted.

All the companions of Kudrat Valiev's young aide—except for Ghiyas, and even his friend Vanya—looked at Sanya in disapproval for having let the secret slip. He had completely forgotten that although the old man wasn't dangerous, Ghiyas—a complete stranger they couldn't fully trust—was with them! Sanya suddenly realized he had made a blunder. But it was too late. Zulfiya noticed that, for a few moments, Ghiyas's eyes had sparked with a glimmer of curiosity—and a hunger for quick enrichment.

"I was just joking!" Sanya tried to cover for himself, patting Ghiyas on the shoulder. But Ghiyas had already understood that the other half of the map did, in fact, belong to this group of "tourists."

"Please note: my late friend from Qatar was named Sahib Yusuf, and his relative—whom he might have entrusted with the second half of your fabric map, as per my notes—was called Karima. That's all. Pardon me—I truly know nothing more."

"That's not a problem at all!" Zulfiya smiled gratefully. "We're flying to Qatar today, and we'll find out everything else ourselves. Right, Sher?"

Sher nodded silently—there was no point in arguing. Though truthfully, he thought they might now fly to Nishapur—the ancient capital of Khorasan and the homeland of the great Omar Khayyam... Well, perhaps they would do that later...

"Now then," Zulfiya continued, "I feel certain that we will eventually find the second half of our map—or at least a true lead to it."

* * *

Saudi Arabia, Red Sea, a Cave in the Rock, the same period

Barno's arms ached from the iron chain and its padlock, yet she strove to remain steadfast and courageous. She didn't even wince; she knew that her friend Sharaf—who was suffering just as much—must not falter out of pity for her. Now more than ever, he needed to be strong, to find a way out and rescue them both.

"Are we really going to die here, Sharaf?" Barno asked when they found themselves alone in a small "room" within the cave.

"Even if Yamani or his aides try to take your life, please—don't be afraid!" Sharaf vowed passionately. "I'd be willing to die if I must, but I will, by any means, save you!"

Had it not been for the danger they were in, Barno might have suspected that his words hinted at tender, special feelings—feelings she, too, secretly harboured for him.

The chamber was sufficiently lit, and Barno gazed at Sharaf with warmth and gratitude, edged with the fear of imminent death.

Then suddenly, an idea struck her, and she immediately shared it aloud:

"Although... Sharaf, if this cunning deceiver truly needs us, perhaps... he won't kill us," she reasoned. Barno squinted occasionally, for Yamani had provided them with a bright spotlight fitted with daylight lamps. "Thank goodness he left us some light. Although it's so glaring—it almost blinds you! I don't want to go blind at this age!"

"I believe you're absolutely right, Barno. If Dagman Yamani truly intended to kill us, he would have done so immediately. Clearly, he isn't entirely confident in his own intellect; he doubts that even with our half of the map, he could locate the Abbasid treasures on his own. After all, the map is filled with symbols and riddles—it can't be plainly read, even by someone fluent in Arabic."

"Then we have no choice but to accept all his terms," Barno continued, sharing her thoughts. "And later, during the excavation, we must make our escape—taking the treasure with us!"

"You do realize, don't you, that with his powerful aides, it won't be easy at all," Sharaf said, shaking his head doubtfully. "By the way, one of those athletic, robust men seems to be standing just behind the heavy cave door—which, I gather, is secured with a strong lock."

"If there's such a lock, then why even have a guard?" Barno wondered aloud. "That Yamani is a strange sort."

"I agree," Sharaf nodded. "But perhaps he really does need us."

"He also mentioned he'd provide us with certain comforts—civilized amenities," Barno added in amazement. "How is it that we're laid out on soft mattresses, duvets, and pillows, and given delicious food, yet we're so securely chained? And how are we supposed to open a door that's locked from the outside? Not to mention disarm a guard?"

"Perhaps Yamani's logic is indeed flawed," Sharaf mused. "But regarding the door and the guard, he's probably just taking extra precautions. As for the locks on our chains—here's what I suspect: his aides will unfasten us for a few seconds, lay us on soft beds for the night, and then chain us to the floor. Look, there are special devices on the ground for that! He intends to let us rest and regain our strength. And for what? Perhaps so he can later force us to dig for treasure…"

"Wow! So… he's been preparing for our 'detention' all along?!" Barno exclaimed in shock. "But how could he have known in advance that he'd meet us? Or about the map?"

"Perhaps he marked this place long ago as a secret dungeon for future use," Sharaf speculated. "And now fate has brought us here. But I'm not about to give up! Barno, we absolutely must get out of here! We'll figure something out—I promise."

"But what?!" Barno sighed in despair. "When I'm as disoriented as I am now, nothing sensible comes to mind. Should we go with him on the excavation when he calls?"

"That's only a last resort," Sharaf replied. "I don't think he'll even bother asking. He'll simply take us along—and that will be that."

"And what are we to do right now?"

"First, I need to see which guard has been assigned to restrain us—and how he plans to do it. I'll try to come up with a clever trick. Please, Barno, trust me! And don't give up too soon. I believe everything will work out for us… And let's not forget the most important thing: Barno, we've finally found it!"

"It?" Barno asked in astonishment, not fully understanding.

"Exactly!" Sharaf exclaimed. "The second half of our treasure map!"

39

Baghdad, Mesopotamia, Abbasid Caliphate, 827 CE

The day proclaimed by the Caliph's heralds had come—a festival day in Baghdad.

Though the assembled crowd in the main square of the capital of the entire Arab Caliphate was not well-versed in such matters, out of fear and respect they thunderously applauded Caliph Ma'mun of the Abbasids.

The Caliph ascended the podium before the vast throng and, with pride swelling within him, proclaimed in a resounding voice:

"My most esteemed subjects! Today is a momentous day in the history of our entire state—and you are its witnesses. Together with you, we hereby inaugurate Bayt al-Hikma—the House of Wisdom! This shall be an Islamic academy for the finest scholars of the East, built upon the ruins of the ancient Persian academy of Gundeshapur. We have resolved that our people must not remain illiterate and unenlightened. Henceforth, we shall become steadfast patrons of all branches of knowledge—especially astronomy."

The crowd once again burst into applause for their Caliph.

"By our most exalted command, and with the aid of our treasury," Caliph Ma'mun continued his address to the people, "measurements of the meridian arc shall be undertaken in the Sinjar Valley. Furthermore, the works of Ptolemy on astronomy have been translated into Arabic. And soon, we plan to establish an astronomical observatory here, so that we may study the celestial sphere in greater depth. With that, my address comes to a close, and I now yield the floor to the venerable Sahl ibn Harun, who has been bestowed the high honour of heading this House of Wisdom."

"Most humbly, I thank you, O Sovereign," said an elderly, grey-bearded scholar as he approached the podium and bowed before the Caliph. Then he turned to the assembled public and declared: "My friends! One of the most important tasks of our academy of knowledge and wisdom will be the translation into Arabic of ancient Greek and Indian works on astronomy, mathematics, medicine, alchemy, and philosophy. Hunayn ibn Ishaq al-Ibadi, a Nestorian proficient in four languages, will be appointed head of the translators at the House of Wisdom. But that is by no means all, my friends. By the will of the ruler of all Arabia, Caliph Ma'mun, the House of Wisdom will also provide religious scholars with a wealth of material for theological debates. First and foremost, these will be texts on philosophy. In fact, outstanding scholars from all corners of the Caliphate—many of them natives of Mesopotamia and Khorasan—shall be gathered here in Baghdad. Moreover, a library, the Khizanat al-Hikma, within our House of Wisdom, will serve as a refuge for itinerant scholars."

The crowd, now beginning to grasp the significance of the event, once again applauded loudly—both for the erudite Sahl and the enlightening Caliph.

Amid the multitude, two great men stood modestly apart. They listened more intently than the rest, for they already knew and understood far more than most. These were the distinguished scholars invited to work in the House of Wisdom and to utilize the library of world science and enlightenment: the astronomer, mathematician, geographer, and historian Abu Abdallah

Muḥammad ibn Musa al-Khwarizmi, and the mathematician-astronomer Abu al-ʿAbbas Aḥmad ibn Muḥammad ibn Kathir al-Farghani…

* * *

Nishapur, Khorasan, Abbasid Caliphate, in Talha's House, 828 CE

"I never knew, Abdallah, that you loved him so deeply… Forgive me—perhaps you still love your brother?" Shamil, the trusted aide of the Caliph, was genuinely surprised. He had arrived on orders to attend the funeral and memorial service of Tahir ibn Husayn's eldest son—the emir Talha. "You're beside yourself, so downcast… You should eat something, at least."

"I can't, *ustadi* Shamil," Abdallah replied quietly, shaking his head.

He was afraid to admit even to his brother Ali that the pain was so great he wanted to cry out loud. Yet Ali understood Abdallah without words, for he too felt the same emotions. The brothers had never wanted to reveal to anyone just how strong and unbreakable the bond of friendship had been among the three of them, fearing someone might try to destroy it. But now, with the sudden death of thirty-year-old Talha, both Abdallah and Ali felt utterly lost.

"Now, Abdallah, you will officially govern Khorasan and Mawara' al-Nahr—here, in Nishapur," Shamil reminded him of Caliph Ma'mun's orders to the youngest of the Tahirids. "It is wise and proper that you've chosen to make Nishapur the capital of your territories. I've heard it is your ancestral homeland. Of course, you were already the emir of these regions, but on paper, the governorships alternated between Ali and Talha, who in practice merely assisted you and followed your orders. Now, however, you must face greater challenges—without Talha's help and support."

Abdallah listened intently to Shamil's words without interruption.

"And Ali will continue to serve as your deputy, right?" Shamil asked. "By the way, the Caliph is very pleased that under your leadership, Ali managed to annex Alexandria to the Caliphate!"

Abdallah nodded silently. Meanwhile, his brother Ali interjected:

"During Talha's time, Islam was introduced into the Sogdian region of Ustrushan, where Zoroastrianism had lasted the longest," he reminded those present of their late brother's achievements, addressing Shamil and everyone else nearby. "Changing the mindset and religion of an entire people is no simple task, yet Talha managed it."

"Yes, yes, I've heard of his accomplishments," the Caliph's aide said with a nod.

Abdallah then looked up at Shamil and asked directly,

"Do you know, *ustadi*, why our beloved brother Talha—whom Ali and I cherished—died?"

"Umm…" Shamil hesitated, unsure whether he should reveal the truth about Talha's death to the Tahirids without the Caliph's consent. Finally, after weighing his thoughts, he resolved to tell Abdallah and Ali what had happened: "You both surely know that Talha was dealing with rebels in Al-Jazira, which is why he was appointed governor of eastern Iran. Under his authority was also Sistan, where local Kharijites were led by Hamza ibn Adarak. The battles between them dragged on for a long time. And yesterday… both Hamza and Talha perished on the battlefield, as true warriors of the Caliphate."

"We are all *ashab al-shurta*—that is, military commanders of the Caliphate and loyal soldiers of our ruler," Ali said humbly, bowing his head.

"And why didn't I see your mother here today?" Shamil inquired curiously. "Did she not come to wash and mourn her deceased son? ... I hope she is well, more or less?"

Ali and Abdallah fell silent once again, sorrowfully. Their mother, Benu, still did not recognize either of them. She remained lost in heavy thoughts and worries about her beloved husband, Tahir, and would hardly be able to comprehend that now even her eldest son was gone. And if she did understand, she might not be able to bear the news. That's why Abdallah and Ali were in no hurry to explain to her who else their family had lost.

* * *

Nishapur, Khorasan, Abbasid Caliphate, in the house of Abdallah, 830 AD

"My dear, our son and I miss you," whispered Mahabbat, Abdallah's wife. "Caliph al-Ma'mun is constantly sending you from one vassal province to another—to suppress peasant uprisings. But all this is extremely dangerous! I do not want to be left a widow in my youth with a small child in my arms."

"Don't speak that way, my wife," grumbled the Emir of Khorasan and Mawara' al-Nahr.

"Of course, your brother Ali and my family will not abandon us, but still, it will be very hard without you," she continued. "I can hardly bear to think of it. And yet, I must. You leave home too often, exposing yourself to danger. Just recently, you returned from Dilmun, over on the Indus River, and from Qatra. Can't you confine yourself solely to the essential duties of your governorship?"

"My dear, my habibti, understand this: that the Caliph entrusts me with these responsibilities is a good sign," Abdallah replied. "First of all, it is an honour for me; it speaks to my status as a statesman, a strong man, and a victorious warrior. In the future, this trust may prove advantageous for us. No, I would never stoop to any treachery or trap. I mean something else: a hope—even if only partial—that our people might one day be free from the might of the Arab Caliphate."

"You know well, my habibi, how dearly your father, Tahir ibn Husayn, paid for that freedom!" exclaimed Mahabbat. "Perhaps you should behave a little more cautiously with Caliph al-Ma'mun?"

"I am already trying to be cautious," Abdallah reassured her. "But I am no coward! One day, our entire land will be completely free from the oppression of foreigners. It is inevitable. I am not thinking only of that, but also of ensuring that my people live in peace and comfort even now."

"I have heard about the laws you enacted regarding the use of water for field irrigation," Mahabbat confided to her husband, "and that you ordered the construction of new aqueducts."

"Yes," said Abdallah proudly. "Now our people can use water more efficiently and secure better harvests on their lands! This means that even ordinary, poor folk will not starve."

"That is all wonderful," his wife approved, "for it attests to your great mercy and democratic spirit toward these impoverished souls. It will make you an even more popular ruler, beloved by all your subjects. But... can we, as members of the upper class, afford to show too many concessions to the peasants? What if, thanks to our generosity and bountiful harvests, they grow strong, rise up, and one day lash out against us?! Such a thing is possible. But it is unacceptable, habibi! Would it not be wiser to keep them in some measure of fear and respect? Especially since our daily sustenance, unfortunately, depends greatly on these unwashed and unrefined plebeians!"

"My dear, I have curbed the excesses of the large landowners—excesses that once reigned unchecked in our provinces towards the peasants. I have reduced their burdens. I am endeavouring to shield both peasants and craftsmen from the cruel treatment inflicted by greedy feudal lords and officials. But all this is not done for the sake of democracy; it is intended to quell peasant revolts and to strengthen the Caliph's central authority! I must, in some measure, fulfil the bequests of my father, Tahir. In a parting letter, he charged me to care conscientiously for my subjects."

"Did he really require that you not keep the peasants as our slaves?"

"No," Abdallah shook his head. "My father never said that. But he believed that unbridled exploitation of the people is counterproductive—it will ruin them and undermine their ability to pay. Exploitation must be measured. He wrote: 'Remember that wealth does not yield profit when it is multiplied and hoarded in the treasury. On the contrary, it grows, it increases when it is spent on the needs of the subjects, in paying them what is due and in relieving them of their burdens. In this way, the prosperity of the masses is achieved. This serves as an ornament for the rulers. It is through this that an era flourishes; through this that glory and power are attained... Moreover, you will thereby have a greater opportunity to collect the land tax due. The land tax you levy will multiply, and your wealth will increase. And with that, you will gain the means to rally an army and satisfy the masses who pour out their gifts.' That was my father's conviction."

"And you can never disobey him?" his wife asked. "Even when he is not present?"

"I cannot. My father was right in many ways. God nourishes us through the hands of the peasants," Abdallah explained. "He welcomes us through their voices and forbids us from oppressing them. Yet, as a ruler, the interests of the large landowners and merchants are far more crucial to me. I demand that they not mistreat the peasants, for without this, no taxes would flow into the state treasury. And the Caliphate very much needs these taxes. Wars—and thus trophies—are dwindling, while the Caliph must continuously dine well, dress elegantly, wear expensive jewellery, and travel…"

40

Doha, Qatar, 2023

Before his wedding, Nizar—the son of the banker Najib Abbas—had wanted to meet and speak with the girl he had "dishonoured" and whom he was now, as a result, compelled to marry. It seemed strange and rather unpleasant to him—an affront to his honour and good name—that he, a well-brought-up and respectable young man from an upright and widely esteemed family, could be capable of such a deed.

"Nizar, my dear," the banker began, addressing his son. "I'm sure you will meet your fiancée, though I would not like to be present at such a meeting at all. Were I to speak with her myself, I'd extract the whole truth from her. I have the feeling that both her insolent father, hotelier Sarwan al-Tawil, and Jahiza herself are lying! But I cannot attend such a meeting with you."

"Understand, Father, we must ask her and find out exactly what happened and how it all transpired." Nizar was trying to clarify his position. "And why did I even go to that nightclub? I was simply in a foul mood that evening. I clashed with a girl I truly like. No, no—of course she did nothing to offend me; she couldn't have! I hadn't mentioned this before, but now I will: she is a young assistant to our chief legal counsel. Her noble name is Ikhtibar. I made a foolish mistake—offering to drive her home after work and suggesting we stop by a café for coffee. But she is so modest that she found the very idea unacceptable. I was overwhelmed by my feelings for her! And so I went and got drunk at the club."

"I see…" the banker murmured, stroking his greying beard. "I guess I can understand you, son."

"And now," Nizar continued with a note of despair, "I, like the ultimate fool, am forced to marry another—a woman I do not love at all! This Jahiza, who has inexplicably landed on my doorstep… And why? For what reason? All right, as I said, in my head-over-heels adoration, I could have offered the fine Ikhtibar a ride in my car and invited her to a café. But could I really have gotten so drunk at the bar as to forget everything? And even raped that innocent creature—this Jahiza?… And in a public place, no less! Father, who am I after this? I am deeply ashamed of myself. How can I wash away this sin? But… the fact is, I remember nothing at all—and I desperately want to clarify every detail of that evening at the club."

"Son, would you allow me—your father—to handle this matter on my own, without your interference or presence?" asked Najib Abbas.

"Well… very well, Father," the young man agreed after a moment's thought. "If that is your wish. It is indeed extremely difficult for me to broach this subject with Jahiza alone."

"Then it's settled," Najib said, smiling at his son.

"Thank you, dear Father," his son replied warmly. "You and Mother understand and support me, as always and in everything…"

* * *

Manama, Kingdom of Bahrain, the same period

"Our guests from Uzbekistan have gone to the airport!" blurted Ghiyas, bursting into the office of Yakzan Baker, the director of the Cultural Centre. "Tickets have already been purchased, and in about an hour, they'll be flying to Doha!"

"You did the right thing by informing me about this," the director said, leaping from his chair. "But why not immediately—as soon as you found out?"

"I called you many times, boss, but you were unreachable," Ghiyas began to justify himself.

"Ah, right!" Yakzan lightly smacked his forehead. "I was at negotiations—and I turned off the sound on my phone, then forgot to turn it back on. Now it doesn't matter. Let's go quickly! We need to get to the airport—urgently! Let's use your car. You drive."

"Yes, boss!" blurted Ghiyas obediently, like a soldier in the army, as he ran.

On the way, Yakzan thought: *What will I tell them? How will I detain them?*

"Actually, they didn't take anything valuable with them," reported Ghiyas on the road. "Only a copy of a scabbard from some old dagger of the Abbasid era. It was stealthily stolen from a museum. But who needs that junk? Its value is mere pennies, even though it recalls the 9th-century Arab Caliphate."

"Fool!" Yakzan became enraged. "They took that scabbard with them—that means it might indeed have some value! Most likely, they know something about it… And why did you drag me from my place if you thought they could be let go in peace?"

"Because they've set their sights on some astonishing antique map that shows the way to the untold treasures of the Arab Caliphs!" Ghiyas exclaimed, nearly colliding with another car in his excitement. "And this map might be somewhere in Qatar. They're just about to fly there."

"Now that is a completely different matter!" Yakzan smiled. "Then you did a good job."

"Thank you, boss," Ghiyas beamed as they pulled up to the airport building.

"We absolutely must find a way to detain them, Ghiyas," ordered Yakzan's assistant. "If they are to fly to Doha, then only with us."

"Yes, of course, boss!" Ghiyas readily agreed, delighted at the prospect—especially since he had never been abroad before. *Well, why not fly somewhere on the boss's dime?*

"Oh, my friends!" exclaimed Yakzan Baker warmly, throwing himself into the midst of a small group of treasure-seeking travellers from Uzbekistan, arms outstretched. "But where are you off to? How can it be? You didn't even say goodbye to us. How inconsiderate… We were looking for you. We wanted to show you more of Bahrain. After all, you haven't seen everything, have you? Besides…"

"Forgive us, Mr. Baker, but we're in a hurry for our flight," replied Zulfiya politely. "You see, we've already checked in and are heading to the departure gate. Truly, we beg your pardon for our haste in not saying goodbye in person. However, we asked Ghiyas to convey our heartfelt regards and gratitude for your hospitality in Manama."

"I wasn't finished speaking, madam," Yakzan said with another broad smile. "I meant to say: besides… you haven't yet had the pleasure of acquainting yourselves with our local police and prison!"

Ghiyas then translated his boss's words for their guests.

"What?!" Sanya erupted. ***"What do you mean?! By what right?!"

"What is the meaning of this?!" Sher also fumed.

Vanya remained silent for the time being.

"What I mean," Yakzan continued, lowering his voice to a near whisper so that only Zulfiya and her companions could hear, "is that for that item you took—well, let's say, unlawfully removed from the National Museum of Manama without my consent or that of its director—you won't merely be prevented from leaving our country; you will be arrested!"

"Why do you say such a thing?" Zulfiya asked, head bowed in guilt as she grasped the hopelessness of their situation. She glanced at Sanya as if to say, *I did warn you!*

"One of you," Yakzan continued, his eyes fixed on Sanya as he identified his role, "is the principal perpetrator of the theft. And the rest of you are his accomplices. After all, you knew of the crime yet did nothing to stop him! Do you understand that I am referring to the replica Abbasid-era scabbard?"

"What do you propose, Mr. Baker?" Vanya asked calmly and coolly, finally joining the conversation. "After all, you… don't intend to imprison us, do you?"

"What a clever and composed fellow you are!" Yakzan exclaimed, looking at Vanya. "You deduced that from my measured tone, didn't you? And from the fact that, if I wished, I could have summoned the police here immediately! Yes, you're right. It's to my advantage to leave you with… partial freedom. On one small condition: you shall share with me any Abbasid treasures you may discover."

"Are you out of your mind?!" Sher snapped again. "We don't have any treasures!"

"But they will surely come into your possession," Yakzan laughed, patting him on the shoulder. "After all, you search so diligently! Which means you will undoubtedly find them. And we shall help each other in this pursuit. I've heard you already possess half of a most intriguing map. By the way, you will allow me a glance at it, won't you? That is, if you don't want to spend a couple of years in confinement. I never claimed I would take everything— though I could have made such a demand, since you're now under my control and dependent on me. But I am a kind and honest man. Therefore, when we find the treasure together, I agree to… fifty percent."

Zulfiya, Sher, Sanya, and Vanya were struck dumb, yet they did their best to maintain their composure. Indeed, Sanya's bag contained the scabbard from the National Museum—and all of them could have been detained at any moment. They could have been imprisoned, or at the very least, deported to Tashkent with a ban on entering any Middle Eastern country in the future. The travellers could not allow such a fate. Thus, they had no choice but to accept all the conditions set by the Director of the Manama Cultural Centre.

Yakzan Baker made a phone call, informed someone of his departure, purchased two tickets to Doha—and flew there with Ghiyas and the group of treasure seekers from Uzbekistan.

* * *

Sharjah, United Arab Emirates, the same period

All charges against the archaeologist Nazih Abu Jalil were dropped. No trial was even required. Now the court awaited the enterprising museum worker Bob Downey.

The judge handed the swindler Downey a rather severe sentence, condemning him to many years behind bars.

"If it had been a simple theft—perhaps he would have received a lighter sentence," explained Saud ibn Mahshud, the head of the Department of Tourism and Antiquities, to his friend Nazih. "But he stole and attempted to illegally sell a major national treasure belonging to the people of Sharjah and all the Emirates! And on top of that, he set you up—an entirely innocent man—in an effort to sully your good name. That's why Bob received a far harsher penalty."

"I still feel sorry for him," said the kind-hearted Nazih, on the verge of tears. "If he is confined in a prison within our emirate, at least I can visit him from time to time and bring him provisions. And who knows? Perhaps, through this forced ordeal, Bob's soul will gradually soften and be cleansed?"

"What an idealist you are, my friend," Saud smiled. "Yet it is heartening that you believe even in such seemingly hopeless people. After all, God is Almighty, and in life, anything can happen. For goodness must always prevail, mustn't it?"

"Right now, you are absolutely correct, dear *ustadi* Saud," Nazih nodded in agreement.

41

Doha, Qatar, the same period

Sarwan's daughter, Jahiza, could not pass up the opportunity she had waited for her entire life: to boast on social media to her friends and acquaintances about her new, enviable status—fiancée of one of Qatar's most eligible bachelors, the son of a renowned banker. On every one of her pages, wherever she could, she posted brief (since there wasn't much to say) yet grandiose and pompous messages accompanied by photographs. No, not with her fiancé— not yet—but rather of herself in various outfits, accessorized with expensive items bought almost daily using money she coaxed from her father, who, without much shame, in turn took it from his future in-law, the banker.

But even all that seemed insufficient.

Though her former "fiancé," Sharaf, now meant absolutely nothing to her, she still felt the need to prove—especially to herself—that her choice regarding her future and a happy family life had been the right one.

Yes, Sharaf had once told her he had set off to distant lands and cities for her sake. Yet Jahiza, ever the realist, didn't believe in mythical ancient treasures, which she viewed as nearly impossible to find and even harder to claim—especially with countless other treasure hunters bound to appear along the way. Furthermore, as a future lawyer, she knew that in almost any country, a private individual who discovered such treasures would, at best, receive only a small percentage of their value—*if* they weren't arrested for unlicensed business dealings in countries where they held no citizenship.

Wasn't Sharaf simply a fool for chasing an invisible "pie in the sky"?

She remembered that she had already turned him down. But was that really her fault? She needed solid, not illusory, guarantees that her chosen one would have inexhaustible financial resources— no matter who he was. However one looked at it, Sharaf had been a hopeless option. There was nothing to regret. And yet… he had been handsome, kind, intelligent. He had loved her deeply and was willing to do anything for her. Could it be that choosing Nizar Abbas was a mistake?

Pondering this, she decided to dial Sharaf's number. But his phone was unreachable. This only frustrated her further and stirred her anger. She wanted to prove to the whole world, to that loser Sharaf, and most importantly to herself, that she was not making a mistake in targeting the banker's family as the prize of her feminine "hunt." She wanted to prove to everyone, once and for all, that she was the smartest and the coolest.

And so she wrote a short message to her traveling, treasure-hunting acquaintance in a messenger app. It read:

"Sharaf, how are you? Why haven't you called in so long? As for me—everything is absolutely perfect! I'll soon be marrying one of the best, richest, and most handsome men in Qatar—and the whole world! That's Nizar, son of the banker Najib Abbas! You may congratulate me. My fiancé and I are the happiest couple on Earth!

I'm not inviting you to the wedding—after all, you're too far away and far too busy looking for artifacts no one needs. But I'm not mad at you. I wish you luck and peace."

Meanwhile, the bank owner, Najib Abbas, had asked his assistants to find the closest friends of his "future daughter-in-law," Jahiza.

It turned out that one of them, Sayyera, had also been at the elite nightclub on the nearly fateful evening for Nizar. She had seen everything Jahiza had done. At first, Sayyera didn't want to betray her friend. But Najib's people promised to help her with a pressing personal issue—and even provided substantial evidence of their sincerity. Only then did Sayyera agree to reveal everything she knew about "that particular" delicate situation involving Jahiza and Nizar.

Just as Mr. Najib Abbas had suspected, every single accusation Jahiza had made against Nizar was a brazen fabrication from beginning to end.

"I personally saw how Jahiza herself slipped something into your young man's drink," Sayyera told the banker's assistants. "Right after that, Nizar immediately got drunk and started acting very strangely—staggering around and shouting all sorts of nonsense. He had probably been drugged with some illegal substance. Almost at once, Jahiza took him by the arm and led him to the restroom. I don't know exactly what happened between them there. I thought maybe she wanted to help him so that later she could somehow... lay claim to him. For example, by telling him he had gotten sick at the club and that she had saved him. I was surprised by his behaviour myself, but my friends quickly pulled me away, and I soon forgot all about it. At the beginning, when my friend poured something into his glass, I didn't intervene because I didn't suspect anything bad at the time. But I'm certain that guy was in such a state later that he simply could not have raped anyone."

The bartender, too—though not immediately, but under a bit of pressure from Mr. Abbas's envoys—admitted that he remembered the evening: a well-dressed young man sitting at the bar with a certain girl had suddenly begun acting completely out of control. But the girl had quickly taken him somewhere toward the exit. The bartender hadn't wanted to make a scene, fearing punishment from his boss for allowing disorder. For the same reason, he hadn't called the police—he was afraid of losing his job.

Having learned all of this, an outraged yet simultaneously relieved and elated Najib Abbas instructed his assistants to inform the hotel owner in Doha, Sarwan al-Tawil—without giving any reasons or details—that there would be no wedding between their children.

* * *

Tashkent, the same period

Said Mumtazov was growing anxious: he hadn't heard from his recently discovered son, Sharaf from Qatar, in many days.

Said knew that Sharaf had gone on a journey in search of some kind of valuables, although his son had not provided any detailed explanation. Despite having given Sharaf his bank card, Dr. Mumtazov didn't know exactly which countries or cities his son planned to visit, nor did he monitor the card's transactions. He didn't want to demean the young man by keeping tabs on him. Still, he fervently hoped Sharaf would return soon. Said dreamed of introducing him to Malika and Sitora. Of course, he realized his wife might not be overjoyed to meet a new, unfamiliar relative—but the meeting needed to happen. Sharaf must not feel unwanted. As of now, Malika was completely unaware that she had a biological brother.

Meanwhile, a friend in the capital's police department passed an extremely important document to lawyer Najmiddin Yuldashev, uncle of young Kamil Akbarov. It was a cleverly and covertly extracted piece of evidence from the investigator's office—a "voluntary confession" made under pressure by Davron Bakhromov's former friend, allegedly admitting to running over Said Mumtazov.

Having obtained this incriminating document that posed a threat to his nephew, Najmiddin promptly destroyed it.

"Now you're practically free," he explained to Kamil. "But that's not all. To keep that insolent police major from stirring up trouble—claiming someone broke into his office and robbed him—and to stop him from trying once again to protect his own son by framing you, dear nephew, or anyone else as a scapegoat, I'm going to take further action myself. You, in the meantime, stay at home and keep your head down. Understood? Good thing it's summer and you don't have classes yet. I'll let you know when it's safe to breathe freely and go wherever you like."

Yuldashev resolved to personally track down the video recording of the accident. He was well aware that Zakir Bakhromov had probably already found and destroyed it—or, more likely, had located and erased all available footage from that stretch of road on that particular evening. But a friend in the police hinted to Najmiddin that they had a skilled IT specialist who likely had a program capable of recovering deleted files.

Taking this specialist along, Najmiddin went to the office of a firm from whose windows one could best see the section of the road where the two cars had collided that day.

"We're from State Security," the lawyer almost spontaneously concocted a "cover story" for the company's system administrator. "We've been entrusted with a crucial, confidential mission: to inspect all computers in this area for possible access to websites that are outlawed by the law. You'll permit us to do that, won't you? It won't take long."

Although the administrator assured these "officials" that they never broke the law, he promptly granted the IT specialist from Najmiddin's team access to the necessary computers. The expert then launched a file-recovery program and easily found the video recordings Kamil's uncle needed. The footage clearly showed Davron Bakhromov, in a white Toyota, hitting Said Mumtazov's Chevrolet on the evening in question.

"Well, now this family of liars and swindlers is in our pocket," Najmiddin beamed into his moustache. "Both the student son and his major-of-police father are going to do time. They'll land right where they belong!"

42

Saudi Arabia, Red Sea, a cave in the cliff, the same period

Late at night, acting on Yamani's orders, a guard arrived, bringing the villain's prisoners bedding and food. In reality, both captives were unable to tell day from night, let alone know the exact hour. Still, from the guard's offerings, they could guess that night was approaching. He set everything down near Sharaf and Barno. Then, he was about to unfasten them from the shackles in the cave walls—Barno first, then Sharaf—and reattach them to chain locks firmly embedded in the ground.

Barno was surprised that only one guard had come, not two or three.

Apparently, Yamani is sure we're so frightened and securely bound that there's no way we can escape! she thought.

Meanwhile, the guard chained Barno to a lock and chain fastened to the ground. The moment he unfastened Sharaf, even for a second, Sharaf—pulling himself together like an athlete and summoning all his strength—quickly and powerfully kicked out with his legs. The guard immediately fell to the ground, striking his head against the edge of the rocky wall.

"Did you kill him, Sharaf?" cried Barno in alarm, reaching out a free hand toward the guard lying there unconscious, blood streaming from his head.

"I hope not," the young man said defensively. "I didn't mean to!"

His hands and feet were now completely free. Approaching the fallen guard, Sharaf first checked his pulse with his right hand.

"Thank God, he's alive," the Qatari sighed in relief.

He took a clean handkerchief from his pocket and pressed it to the man's wound. Then, he placed the pillow the guard had brought under the man's head. Sharaf left the rug and pillow intended for Barno, deciding she would still need them.

"It's a pity we don't have any medicine here," Barno lamented, while Sharaf, taking the guard's keys from his hand, unfastened her from the lock and chain. "Wait... I think I had a small bottle of perfume in my clutch. It has alcohol in it, so at least I could disinfect his wound, like an antiseptic."

"That's a good idea," Sharaf said, still feeling guilty. "But where's your bag?"

"I don't know," Barno admitted. "I only just remembered it. I had it with me at Dagman's place. But I don't know if that man's henchmen brought it here. Maybe we should look for it? If you recall, it's silver in colour."

Sharaf immediately went looking for the clutch. He found it lying not far from where Barno had been held.

Barno was glad it had turned up. Finding the perfume, she poured almost the entire contents of the bottle onto Sharaf's handkerchief and used it to treat the guard's wound.

They then quickly and ravenously ate, for only now—having recovered somewhat from the day's shocks—did they realize just how hungry they were. But they also hurried, knowing that the other brawny guard, waiting at the cave entrance, might come in at any moment upon noticing the wounded guard's delay. And that would mean serious trouble for the two young captives.

Sharaf devised a plan.

"Barno, you rest here for now," he suggested. "I'll take a look around the entire cave, checking its most hidden corners for another exit, if there is one. All right?"

Barno agreed, thinking it a sound idea.

Moving through the dark recesses of the cave for about half an hour, Sharaf discovered that there was no second exit leading outside. But he did find something else—a ledge with a small pool of water. Sharaf guessed that, by some miracle, the pool might be a deep well connected to the sea.

"That might be our only salvation," he thought.

The absence of diving equipment didn't trouble this young but experienced swimmer and diver. He was used to such challenges. His native Persian Gulf had long since taught Sharaf how to dive without oxygen.

He tested the water with his hand. It was icy.

"Even so, I have to inspect this strange well and find a way out of the cave!" he said aloud to himself, firmly resolved to save Barno and himself.

Sharaf jumped into the water of the "well." Despite the pool's small surface area, it turned out to be not just deep, but practically bottomless—because indeed, it opened directly to the sea. All that remained was for him to find a spot where he could surface quickly, safely, and undetected by Yamani's people, who might be somewhere nearby.

A few minutes later, Sharaf emerged above the surface, finally able to catch his breath.

He found the Red Sea water quite agreeable. He'd read somewhere that it was the warmest, saltiest, and clearest sea on the planet.

And how splendid the air of freedom felt! Sharaf could easily swim ashore right now and make his way to a city somehow. But leaving Barno alone in the cave, failing to help her escape, was unthinkable.

He was relieved to see that he hadn't drifted far from the cliffs. At the same time, there were no yachts, boats, or other vessels around—good news, since it meant Yamani's men were unlikely to spot him just yet. But if he swam right up to the cliff where Barno was… how would he know exactly which one housed the cave where she was practically imprisoned?

From articles he'd read on the internet a few days ago, on his way to Saudi Arabia, Sharaf knew this was the country's western region. That meant the beautiful coastal mountain range along the Red Sea must be the Hejaz. He remembered there were quite high peaks here, some reaching 2,500 meters. Saudi Arabia's highest point was Jabal al-Lawz, the "Almond Mountain," in the country's northwest, near the Jordanian border…

But Sharaf had no time to linger on such thoughts—he had to act before the second guard did anything terrible to Barno.

He swam closer to the cliffs. Looking carefully, he finally spotted a metal door with a lock on one of the rock faces. A man stood near that door.

My, what a big, muscular guy, Sharaf thought, silently estimating his own strength and whether it was realistic to knock this giant out, even temporarily.

Climbing ashore, Sharaf felt a wave of relief. Only now did he realize how tired his lungs were from the lack of oxygen, and how pleasant solid ground felt beneath his feet compared to bobbing on even a calm, warm sea.

Then Sharaf saw something that thrilled him: the strong guard—who, now that Sharaf was closer, he could see was armed with a rifle—stretched and did a few quick exercises at his dull post, then grabbed his back in apparent pain. After hesitating for a moment, he suddenly began making his way down from the cliff, disappearing out of sight.

Seems like all that standing on the rocks in one position made his back start hurting, Sharaf guessed. *Maybe he's going to lie down for a while. Even the strong need rest. How lucky can I get! What a stroke of fortune! Maybe there's a camp or at least a tent nearby… Now all that's left is to get up there, break the lock or somehow pry open that entrance door to the cave… and Barno will be free!*

Sharaf began climbing the cliff toward the cave entrance. At last, he reached it and examined the lock, trying to smash it with a suitable rock.

At that moment, he wasn't thinking about the dangers—the giant guard who might return at any second, or the other powerful henchmen of the treacherous Yamani who could appear at any time.

Sharaf was thinking only of Barno—how she was, and how to free her as quickly as possible…

* * *

Doha, Qatar, the same period

To the surprise of Zulfiya, Sher, Sanya, and Vanya—whose freedom of movement was restricted, but who were accompanied by the Bahrainis Yakzan Baker and Ghiyas—they rather quickly discovered information about a now-deceased but once-famous local archaeologist, Sahib Yusuf.

They even found his former home. His daughter, Hawwa, greeted them with warm hospitality. The lady of the house gave them the address of her relative Karima, to whom Hawwa's father had once, for reasons unknown, gifted an ancient map bearing mysterious symbols.

"This strange map has been examined and studied by many people," Hawwa explained. "But as I see it, what's the use of treasures that can't possibly be found? Their location is a complete enigma that, in my opinion, simply cannot be unravelled! Even my scholar father never managed it."

"That's all right; we'll unravel it," Yakzan Baker assured her.

Karima likewise welcomed the unexpected guests warmly and hospitably. Upon learning that most of them were from Uzbekistan, she prepared a generous spread for them.

"Imagine that!" she exclaimed with a radiant smile. "My son Sharaf is actually there in your country right now! By the way, the map you're talking about is with him. I gave it to him in hopes that, if he got lucky, he might unlock its hidden meaning and locate any relics from the Abbasid era. Though, to be honest, I'm not sure it's really possible."

"What did you say about the map and your son?" Sher and Sanya asked in astonishment. "They're in Tashkent?!"

"Yes, yes," Karima nodded. "Didn't you say you were from there yourselves?"

"Uh-huh," Sher confirmed.

"Well, who would've thought!" Zulfiya exclaimed. "So it looks like we… just missed him?"

Yakzan Baker's assistant, Ghiyas, mused to himself,

It would be great if the boss now decides to fly to Uzbekistan as well! I'll get a chance to see that wonderful country, too!

"Well then, friends," Yakzan addressed Zulfiya and her companions, "shall we head to the airport right now? I'm willing to buy you all tickets to Tashkent."

"Maybe we could just fly on our own, without you?" Sanya asked hopefully.

"No, without us—that won't happen!" Yakzan said firmly. "Don't forget: you stole that scabbard from our museum—the one belonging to Caliph al-Ma'mun. Or perhaps it's Tahirid. Either way, it's a crime."

"We can return that scabbard to you—just let us go," Sher offered.

"No, we can't return it!" Sanya objected. "What if we still need it in our search for the treasure? There's some kind of interesting seal on it. And we don't have another set."

"You could've held your tongue for once," Vanya hissed, lightly slapping Sanya on the back of the head.

"Yes, that scabbard really might come in handy," Zulfiya was forced to agree with Sanya. "Though at the moment I'm not sure how."

While the treasure-seeking group stood in line to check in for their flight to Tashkent, Sher stepped aside for a moment to make a phone call.

"Hello! Yes, Uncle Ubay, it's me, Sher," whispered the chauffeur of businessman Kudrat Valiev. "No, we didn't find anything in Bahrain or Qatar. We're heading back home. I'll explain why later. Yes, in person. No, Kudrat doesn't know the details yet either. Just as we agreed—he has no idea. I'll do everything as required. Don't worry. The other part of the treasure map? Yes, yes… We'll find it soon!!"

43

Baghdad, Mesopotamia, Abbasid Caliphate, the Caliph's Palace, 831 AD

"My Lord, your humble servant brings you important news!" announced Sahl ibn Harun, the manager of the House of Wisdom, in a businesslike tone.

"I'm listening, honourable ibn Harun," replied the ruler of Arabia graciously, inviting his visitor to sit.

"You gave the scholars of our astronomical observatory the task of reproducing the appearance of the Earth and compiling the first celestial map," the head of the House of Wisdom reminded him. "Our work has progressed quite successfully. And one of our scholars has put forth a fascinating hypothesis."

"And what is that?" The Caliph only pretended not to be overly interested.

"That in the Great Pyramid of Khufu, in your dominion of Egypt, there exists a secret chamber-cave. And it may contain ancient charts and tables of the earthly and celestial spheres! We would so dearly like to see them with our own eyes, so we can draw our own conclusions… But how might we do this? Perhaps you would consent to sending some of us there on an expedition?"

"Well…" The Caliph paused in thought. "It is possible… Yes, I agree—but on one condition. I myself will personally lead this expedition."

Al-Ma'mun did not share with ibn Harun the fact that he had heard legends of the countless treasures said to be hidden in that mysterious pyramid…

* * *

"Abdallah!" Caliph al-Ma'mun addressed his subject, the governor of Khorasan and Mawara' al-Nahr. He had come to hear the Caliph's latest orders and instructions—commands that the freedom-loving Tahirid had long since come to view more as requests from a partner. "Back in 828, I sent you to wage war against Nasr ibn Shabath, who had seized northern Mesopotamia. In 829, thanks to you, Nasr surrendered and was sent to me. Know this: I value your loyal service! Now I'm thinking of sending you to our province of Egypt to put an end to the uprisings there and drive out the Spanish Muslims who have taken Alexandria."

"You know, O Ruler of Arabia," replied Abdallah, "that I have always been ready to serve you without question and to aid you in all things, despite the past resentments and disagreements held by me and my brothers. But… forgive me! At this moment, I have urgent matters to attend to in Khorasan. Right now is harvest time. That means I must personally monitor all the crops. You yourself know how many peasant revolts sprang up last year at this same time—because of the cruel treatment by merchants toward slaves and hired labourers in the fields. We cannot allow the poor to rebel, and I must ensure order and prosperity in my domains!"

"Yes, I understand you, my son… my friend," Caliph al-Ma'mun agreed. "We have no need for rebellions at present. I sense that I don't have much time left. And I don't want my Arab people, once I depart for that world of eternal bliss and peace, to remember me with malice or speak of me without praise or honour. So you're right: we must not allow the people to rise up against the authorities. And you know… perhaps I will go to Egypt myself! I haven't been there in a long time. I'll personally try to quell the Bashmurian revolts. And besides… there's a certain dream I have. But I might tell you about it later—once I return."

"As you wish, honourable Caliph of Arabia," Abdallah said, inclining his head.

Probably, you simply want to find the pharaohs' treasures in the famous Pyramid of Khufu, thought the sharp-witted young emir of Khorasan and Mawara' al-Nahr as he left Ma'mun's palace. *I've heard you've long dreamed of studying it. But the question is: do such treasures really exist?…*

***

Dibarsis (Al-Giza, or Giza), Misr (Egypt), Abbasid Caliphate, a few months later

Caliph al-Ma'mun's wife, Umm Isa, asked her husband to take her along to Egypt. He agreed. After half a month of preparations, he departed with her and a large force of workers. The Caliph's plans were grand: first, to extinguish the rebellions of the unruly peasants, and then to deal with the Great Pyramid itself.

Al-Ma'mun suppressed the uprisings, killing more than half the Copts in the Nile Delta.

Afterward, he ordered his men to examine the Pyramid of Khufu with the utmost care.

"How are things going with that endeavour, habibi?" Umm Isa asked her husband one day.

"Does it truly interest you, habibti?" al-Ma'mun asked in surprise.

"Certainly!" Umm Isa retorted, slightly indignant. "Otherwise, why would I have come here with you, my dear?"

"Perhaps because you, too, have heard of the treasures hidden in this mighty structure?" al-Ma'mun teased. "And you wanted to be among the first to see them and touch them! You do love gold, do you not?"

Umm Isa remained silent, taken aback by her husband's frankness and his occasionally discomfiting perceptiveness.

"Very well, I'll tell you," al-Ma'mun said with a smile. "On the northern face of the pyramid, at my command, my workers broke through an entrance passage that had been sealed since the time of Roman occupation in Egypt. We spent a long time trying to determine where the true entrance to the structure should be—and my scholars' calculations led us to it. However, it turned out that if we began digging from that main entrance, our work could end up destroying the entire pyramid."

"I heard from one of your officials, habibi, that demolishing the pyramid is part of your plan!" Umm Isa exclaimed. "They say you ordered more than two hundred massive stones removed from this pharaonic tomb, and that your men have created a crater on the northern side. My dear, do you really want to destroy the pyramids as structures of unbelievers? Is that it? Or… for what reason?!"

"So that no one else might be tempted to follow in my footsteps and continue searching within this great ancient tomb!" The Caliph's eyes gleamed greedily. "Because—what if I cannot immediately extract every valuable thing from the pyramid? Or what if some treasures lie beyond the scope of my searches? That is why."

"Aren't you afraid to enter this place of darkness and gloom after nearly three and a half thousand years?" his wife asked timidly, shrinking in fear. "What if the spirits of all those pharaohs and their wives still dwell there?"

"No, I'm not afraid," the Caliph declared confidently. "Those are merely people's inventions. Using a battering ram, fire, and vinegar—which eats away at the stone—my workers have been carving a path into this ancient structure for more than a month. So far, we've uncovered a descending passage and another ascending passage, apparently leading to the pharaohs' tombs. None of my men have encountered any spirits or anything frightening or dangerous. And I was the first to enter the largest gallery of the pyramid and the pharaoh's burial chamber. Unfortunately, only an empty sarcophagus was there…"

"One of your scholars let slip that, at your request, he studied a curious scroll your men found in the pyramid," Umm Isa recalled. "Could you tell me about it? Was there something important in that scroll?"

"Yes," al-Ma'mun admitted without pretence. "Its ancient text was translated for me. It states that within the pyramid there are thirty vaults made of multi-coloured flint, filled with precious stones, abundant wealth, unusual images, lavish stainless weaponry, and golden armour for warriors—treated with a wisely prepared grease so that it never rusts. And there is glass that can be folded yet does not break, along with various mixed potions and healing waters…"

"So our journey here really wasn't in vain, then," Umm Isa said, her excitement rising. "It's not that I need more gold or riches… It's just so intriguing to uncover and learn about something new and unknown—something never before seen!"

"You're right, habibti," al-Ma'mun agreed. "You see, I've already spent a considerable amount of the treasury's funds on this expedition. I want it all to be worth our while! My workers opened a small hole inside the pyramid, where we found some coins—only a small amount so far. But I'm not giving up hope. My men are excavating further, breaking through granite plugs—likely placed there by the ancient Egyptian builders as barriers to guard the royal treasures. I believe that in the end we'll discover even more strange and valuable objects in this ancient and extraordinary tomb of Egypt's old kings. And then what will happen is this: I myself shall safeguard and conceal our treasures in such a way that only the worthy among my descendants will be able to find them…"

"You will show me this place, habibi?" his wife asked hopefully.

44

Baghdad, Iraq, the Abbasid Palace, 2023

"Have you noticed, Haidar, that ever since I fired Garib, the thefts here have suddenly ceased?" Director Basil asked the head of security.

"Yes, *ustadi*," Haidar agreed. "However… I haven't had time to report something else to you…"

"Has something happened again?" Basil grew alert. "Why have you gone silent?"

"Just yesterday, our archivist approached me and informed me that a fragment of an old map has gone missing from the Palace's collection…"

"And which one exactly?" the director asked, tensing.

"To be honest, I didn't fully understand," the guard admitted hesitantly. "It seems it isn't directly related to the Abbasids, but rather to the entire history of Arabia."

"Bring the archivist here at once," Basil ordered. "Immediately!"

"Yes, sir," Haidar nodded. He dashed out of the director's office and hurried down the staircase leading to the semi-basement floors, where the Palace archives and collections were located.

A few minutes later, the keeper of the archives—and simultaneously the head of collections—Alim al-Qayum entered the director's office.

"Tell me, please, esteemed one, why am I learning about the disappearance of one of our collection's items from a security guard, and nearly a day after it happened?" Basil asked Alim sternly. "It would be one thing if an unimportant copy had disappeared—but this is the original of a valuable document, is it not?"

"Yes. Forgive me, Ustadi Basil! I wanted to tell you, but I was afraid," Alim began to explain. "Besides, I was certain I could quickly find that piece of fabric on my own."

"Fabric?!" Basil exclaimed. "So it wasn't a map?"

"It was a map, Ustadi," Alim said, lowering his head. "But it wasn't on paper—it was on cloth, produced in a certain old-fashioned and very specific way. The map dates to roughly the 8th or 9th century. But I'm sure we'll find it—or rather, we'll find whoever stole it."

"I have my own ideas about who it might have been… I'll handle it myself—no need for you to worry about that," Basil concluded.

"So it's possible that it does, in fact, relate to the Abbasid era?"

"Maybe, but that's not certain," Alim replied. "Judging by the dozens of points on the map that coincide with ancient population centres in Arabia, I would hypothesize that it's part of the famous Incense Route map."

"The Incense Route?" Basil repeated. "Ah, yes, I've heard of that. Could you tell me a bit more?"

"Certainly," the archivist responded. "The 'Incense Route,' or 'Frankincense Route,' was one of the oldest trade routes in the world. In antiquity, it connected the southern Arabian Peninsula—what are now Oman and Yemen, and especially the island of Socotra— to the nations of the Mediterranean and Mesopotamia. Precious aromatic substances were transported there: Arabian frankincense from the south, myrrh, and fragrant African spices from places like Zimbabwe and Ethiopia. Myrrh, also called 'smurna,' is an aromatic resin from the bark of certain tropical trees. It's used in medicine and perfumery."

"How wonderful!" Basil exclaimed. "I imagine all modern perfumery likely has its origins in those times, in Arabia… Please, continue."

"The Incense Route was initially overland, by caravan, and later extended to the sea," Alim continued. "Caravans traveling through towns and deserts as early as the tenth century BC sometimes consisted of thousands of camels and stretched for many kilometres. Goods were delivered once or twice a year, and the journey took more than two months.

"Along this route, they also transported gilded resin on camelback. To keep the location of storage sites secret, the slaves' eyes were covered, or a dark net was placed over their heads before reaching the gates of the trading stalls. As a result, only a few people knew the way to these treasures, which at the time were incredibly valuable… Our map may point to one such ancient storehouse! In ancient times, it likely held a great many valuables. But this map isn't complete. There must be a second part of it somewhere in the world. I'd like to find that, too!"

"And this Incense Route no longer exists, correct?" Basil asked.

"Yes, indeed," Alim nodded. "The Incense Route lasted until the fifteenth century. Over time, the incense trade declined. Only a few caravans continued to travel the old roads, mainly transporting essential salt. Even today, however, travellers can admire the heaps of spices and clay ware sold in the markets of Jeddah. Some sections of the ancient Incense Route have been added to UNESCO's list of World Heritage Sites in Asia."

"Thank you, dear sir," Basil said with a smile. "Don't worry. I believe we'll track down whoever pulled off this trick and stole that fragment of our precious map. The thief probably assumed it was a map to the famed Abbasid treasures! I can imagine their disappointment when all they find is… By the way, is there any chance they'll discover something interesting with it now?"

"Unlikely, Ustadi Basil," Alim smiled. "Though occasionally gold was transported along the Incense Route… I think that if someone were to find the second half of this map, they'd discover an ancient cache of Arabian frankincense that's surely long empty by now!"

* * *

Doha, Qatar, the same period

In a fit of anger and fury, forgetting all notions of propriety, modesty, and Muslim humility, hotel owner Sarwan al-Tawil rudely shoved aside the secretary who was trying to stop him and burst into banker Najib Abbas's office like a whirlwind.

"Just what is the meaning of this?!" Sarwan thundered, as though addressing an underling—or worse, an errand boy—certainly not one of the richest and most influential men in the entire country. "How am I supposed to understand this, in-law? Come on, make the effort to explain why you cancelled the wedding!"

"Please sit down, Mr. Tawil," Najib said in a composed tone, as if paying no heed to the man's brazen outburst. He addressed the frightened secretary, who had rushed in right behind the visitor, just as calmly: "It's all right, Zaynab. Now then, Mr. Tawil, what brings you here?"

"I am al-Tawil!" the hotelier corrected him, still boiling over like a kettle.

"Very well, as you wish, Mr. al-Tawil," Najib gently amended. "You must understand—it's the younger generation. Sometimes they come together, sometimes they drift apart…"

"Don't make things up!!" Sarwan shouted again. "Our children haven't had any time to interact privately yet! But you and I had an agreement! That's why my daughter, Jahiza, and her mother are already hard at work planning her wedding to your disreputable son!"

"I'm going to have to stop you there, sir," Najib said, nearly losing his composure under the onslaught of insults. "My son Nizar is a decent young man."

"Then why is it," Sarwan pressed, "that you dare—without fear of public opinion, or scandal over his 'misdeeds'—to put an end to the happiness of our children?! I've been told the wedding won't take place, so what is all this about, hmm?"

"I'm quite certain, Mr. al-Tawil," Najib replied, "that your daughter and my son will find happiness… but only separately. It's become clear they are entirely different, and—"

"Are you making fun of me?" Sarwan hissed, refusing to be placated. "All people are different! That's hardly breaking news. So what? Especially after your Nizar dishonoured my Jahiza…"

"Excuse me! He did not do that!" Najib objected.

"What did you say?"

"My assistants have uncovered every last detail of that delicate situation, Mr. al-Tawil," Najib revealed. "They spoke to many witnesses who described how, on the evening in question at the club, your daughter added a prohibited substance to Nizar's drink. It appears there was never any attempt on his part to assault your daughter. He was in such a wretched state that he couldn't have done anything. And in fact, he's not that kind of person at all."

"What are you talking about?!" the hotelier sneered, pretending not to believe him.

"Yes. I don't know why she did it—why she compromised and set up my boy," Najib continued. "Though I can guess: it was likely so that my son would be forced to propose and marry her. So please, Mr. al-Tawil, don't threaten us with scandal or disgrace! We're perfectly capable of publicizing all your schemes and fraudulent manoeuvres ourselves. You are the 'bride's' father; you can't possibly claim you didn't know what she was up to, correct? Did you and your daughter actually want to end up behind bars? Otherwise, why play such a dangerous game with us? Naturally, by 'dangerous' I'm speaking strictly about your reputation in business, not anything criminal! Of course, all the arrangements we had made regarding my investments in your hotels—I'm cancelling them as well."

Seeing that his and his daughter's entire strategy—this cunning plot—had failed, Sarwan al-Tawil decided on the spot to change tactics abruptly and appeal to Najib's sympathy instead.

"Please understand, dear Mr. Najib," Sarwan began, softening his voice as he probed the banker's mood and attitude after everything he had just done and said. "I love my daughter very much. She's my only child. My joy, my pearl. Of course, I've always spoiled her, allowed her a great deal, and forgiven her many things. But she really is a good girl. So, Mr. Abbas, you and your son—our esteemed Mr. Abbas Junior—please, bear us no ill will. And naturally, we would never dream of tarnishing your honourable names in any way! What I said earlier was in a heat of passion. You see, I believe my daughter is secretly in love with your son… She's modest and shy, and she can't show it to the world. But… You yourself are a father, Mr. Abbas. Please advise me, as the father of my one and precious child—what am I to do? Offer me some wise counsel!"

"You believe your Jahiza has… feelings for my Nizar?" Najib asked in surprise. He had already reached negative conclusions about the girl, but now he began to question them. "Is that so? Well… if that's really the case…"

"It is the case, Mr. Banker!" the hotelier assured him fervently. "I swear it! She can't live without him. And the poor thing is so distraught that you seem to have decided against letting your son marry her. She's become withdrawn, lost weight—she's so upset she can't eat or drink."

"Well, if that's so…" Najib said thoughtfully, "then first of all, I'll speak with Nizar. Then together we'll decide what to do. As it is, I can't promise you anything, al-Tawil…"

"You can just call me Sarwan, Mr. Abbas!" the would-be in-law beamed. "We're practically family, after all!"

"I'm not making any promises," Najib reiterated, "but I'll see what I can do for your daughter."

"I thank you from the bottom of my heart, dear Mr. Abbas! I've always told everyone you're an exceptionally good and wise man!" Sarwan showered him with compliments.

Listening to these flurries of praise, Najib barely suppressed a chuckle: they were far too contrived, disingenuous, and theatrical.

Returning home, Najib recounted his conversation with Sarwan to his son.

"So," Nizar asked again, "the father of this Jahiza says she… loves me?"

"Yes, son," Najib smiled. "You don't believe it? Would you like to find out for yourself?"

"I would. Father, she's never met Bashir, has she?" the younger Abbas asked.

"I'm certain she hasn't," the elder Abbas responded. "She's never been to our house or to any of our bank offices. Why do you ask? Are you hatching a plan?"

"Yes, I've got an idea," Nizar said. "Father, I suggest… staging a little performance for her. Normally, that's not my style, but in this situation, it seems we don't have any other choice. After all, we have the right to know exactly what's going on!"

45

Tashkent, the same period

"How are we supposed to find this Qatari, Sharaf?" Yakzan fumed as they sat down for lunch at the hotel restaurant. "His mother, Karima, gave us his phone number, but we still haven't been able to reach him!"

"Calm down, Mr. Baker," Zulfiya said, cooling his temper. "She gave me the address of one of their relatives—Dr. Mumtazov. More precisely, the address of his workplace. He's an ophthalmologist at a clinic. We'll head there after lunch."

"All right, if that's the case," Yakzan grumbled uncertainly.

Meanwhile, Kudrat Valiev, who had flown in specially from Samarkand after Zulfiya's call, joined the group. To the young woman's surprise, Kudrat not only refrained from dismissing or distancing himself from Yakzan Baker and Ghiyas—nor did he defend his own people from the presence of these insistent foreigners—but it even appeared that he had befriended Yakzan.

Clearly our businessman Kudrat hopes to get something out of this Bahraini, Vanya thought. *He'd better not wind up indebted to him in the end! But oh well, that's his business…*

Sher was seething: any extra people were only getting in the way of finding the treasure.

"So, are we all going to show up at the ophthalmologist's with our great delegation?" he said sarcastically, directing the remark more toward Valiev. "A whole crowd of 'blind folks' at once! That'll terrify people."

"And what do you suggest?" Kudrat countered with another question. "Don't worry, we won't scare them. We all need this, remember? Let me remind you, my friend: you four—along with Zulfiya, Sanya, and Vanya—have flown to numerous cities, and you still haven't found my map! Which means I now have to track down Sharaf myself. You can't do anything without me!"

Both the emotional Sher, as well as Sanya, the more placid Vanya, and even the level-headed Zulfiya were taken aback and offended by their ungrateful boss's unfair words. After all, who but they had travelled so far and uncovered so many clues? Who had actually gotten on the right track regarding the map?

But they all kept silent, saving the confrontation for later. Sher went off to get his car, which was parked outside Valiev's branch office. Sanya, Vanya, and Zulfiya took the passenger seats, while Kudrat himself gave the two Arab guests a lift to Said's place in his foreign-made vehicle.

Said Mumtazov was already back at work, having nearly recovered. At first, he was pleased to learn that his son seemed to be in high demand. But as he listened carefully, he tensed up and regretted letting them into his office in the first place.

"I don't understand: what does Sharaf have to do with some treasures and old maps?" Said said, speaking in English. "I only know one thing: the young man left with his girlfriend for a summer vacation trip through the Arab countries. I gave him some money for it. That's all! I'm certain he knows nothing about any royal riches or Abbasid treasures. Is he an archaeologist, a historian? A treasure hunter? He's just a student—a law student. I think you're looking for your ancient maps in the wrong place!"

"They're in the right place," Yakzan insisted.

"We can't get him on the phone," Kudrat added. "Do you have any other way of getting in touch with him? I should tell you right away—he hasn't been on his messenger either for a while. That's odd for a young man these days; they're usually glued to their phones."

"I haven't been able to reach him for several days myself," Said admitted reluctantly to his new acquaintances. "And I'm worried about him—how he is, where he is, what's going on. So I'm asking you: if you learn anything about my son, please let me know. All right? Here's my card. All my phone numbers are there."

Once they left the clinic, an enraged, flushed-faced Yakzan began shouting at no one in particular, cursing and blaming the whole world for his misfortunes. Ghiyas stayed silent—he was afraid of his boss's wrath.

"So I don't get it," Sher said, stopping short. "We just got back from the Arab countries, right? And now Sharaf is… there?! Does he have our map with him? So it's there too?!"

"First of all, it's not *yours*, but *my* map," Kudrat corrected his employee calmly. "Secondly, yes, apparently he's somewhere on the Persian Gulf. Here's my suggestion: let's go to my main office in the capital. We'll sit down and calmly think this through—where to go next, and how to track down this Sharaf."

They all agreed to do so.

An hour later, sitting in comfortable chairs in the small Tashkent office of the Samarkand businessman, the members of this informal "interest group" began to discuss potential solutions to the problem at hand—and how they might extricate themselves from it.

By then, Yakzan had cooled down a bit. He quietly sipped the beverages offered by their host while snacking on fruit, just like the other guests.

"Maybe we can find Sharaf through the girlfriend he travelled with?" Sher proposed. "Maybe her phone is on. They should be together over there."

"Not a bad idea," Kudrat agreed. Then he turned to Zulfiya, Sanya, and Vanya: "Do any of you know exactly who Sharaf went on this 'journey' with? What did his mother in Qatar tell you? Surely, at some point, he must have mentioned over the phone to her who he'd met here in Tashkent. Or maybe this girl is also from Qatar?"

"No, she's Uzbek," Sanya recalled. "For sure. I think her name is Rano…"

"Barno," Vanya corrected him. "Sharaf's mother doesn't know her surname, and we certainly don't either…"

"Do you all know anything at all?" Valiev snapped at his underlings again. "Who is this Barno? Where does she work?"

"Ah!" Zulfiya exclaimed. "I remember now! Karima mentioned something about tours—apparently, Sharaf's girlfriend was a tour guide around Uzbekistan's ancient cities."

"Right, okay…" responded Yakzan, sounding marginally less annoyed.

"Well, that's at least something," Kudrat said, turning to his new friend. "But on the other hand, there are countless tour offices and travel agencies. How are we going to find this Barno without knowing her last name or even which city she lives in?"

"My uncle has a friend here—Zakir Bakhromov. He's a major in the police," Sher suddenly recalled. "Maybe we could ask him for help finding the girl."

"We're already a veritable army of treasure hunters," Kudrat grumbled. "And now you want to bring even more people into this secret affair? Are you out of your mind? Or is driving a car the only thing you're good at? Then I'll have to share my wealth with your uncle and his major friend, too?! Give me a break!"

"Well, if there's no other way…" Sher tried to justify himself.

Inwardly, he was thinking: *You couldn't even get rid of Yakzan and Ghiyas, now could you? So why is it fine to share treasure with them? Probably because you want them to help you find it in the Arab countries! Then you'll swindle them afterward.*

"What if we ask the cell phone company for help?" Vanya suggested. "We know which operator Sharaf is using, based on his phone code."

"No, the company won't provide that info," Sanya objected. "We've already gone through this. Customer support won't give coordinates of another person's phone."

"And what if Sharaf's phone is in the hands of some thieves or bandits?" Zulfiya added. "Then we're out of luck."

"Why would that be?" asked Yakzan. "Both his parents said the guy's on vacation somewhere. He's probably with that pretty girl, forgetting phone calls and everything else in the world."

"Well… you never know," the woman speculated. "Life can surprise you. Maybe we could send an SMS to his phone, hoping any potential thief might reply in exchange for a reward?"

"Yes! Or promise the criminal a place in paradise for doing the right thing," Kudrat joked. "Whoever turns on his phone and reads that message will immediately melt and hand over Sharaf's coordinates… Fine, I could wire some money for that from my account."

"Don't be hasty, boss," Sher warned. "I doubt that'll work."

"Wait!" Ghiyas exclaimed. "If the guy has an Android phone,

even if it's switched off and far away, maybe we can track it with satellite mapping? Although that would only work if 'Location History' and 'GPS Sharing' were enabled in his map settings… That's unlikely. But there's also Google Find My Device—I heard something about that. I'm just not sure how it works exactly."

"If his phone has an internet connection, that changes everything," Vanya pointed out. "Androids have a device-tracking function through your Google account. That option is always active and runs in the background. If the GPS is also on, then the detection radius might be narrowed down to around 10–15 meters."

"Let's give it a try," Kudrat ordered. "In the end, what have we got to lose? We can always go to the police later."

To everyone's surprise, that final suggestion worked.

Kudrat, Yakzan, and their companions learned Sharaf's exact coordinates, as the young man had indeed left both his internet and GPS enabled on his phone. The not-so-tech-savvy villain Yamani, who had taken Sharaf's phone from him, had no idea that someone might pinpoint the near-exact location of his prisoners.

* * *

Saudi Arabia, Red Sea, the cliffs, the same period

Sharaf was on edge: the lock on the metal door refused to open. At moments like this, it seemed to him that he had only been struggling with it for a few seconds—he didn't realize that, in reality, much more time had passed. Minutes, in fact! And that was plenty of time for another of Yamani's guards, arriving silently to relieve the previous one, to spot the young man.

"Having a tough time with that lock, are you?" the brute

joked. Sharaf barely had time to turn around and see the mocking expression on the newcomer's face before the guard's boxer-like fist knocked him down with a single blow. Sharaf lost consciousness.

He woke up inside the cave. Barno was beside him, in tears from worry and compassion for the young man.

"Thank God you're at least all right!" Sharaf exhaled in relief. "Please calm down. I'm fine. And now we're back together."

"Where were you, Sharaf?" the young woman asked. "I was so worried when I lost sight of you for so long! Did you manage to find a way out?"

"How did you guess?" he replied, still somewhat dazed from the blow.

"Well, the guard dragged you back here from outside, through the door!" Barno explained. "Please, tell me everything that happened to you these past few hours."

Sharaf recounted what he had discovered, both inside the cave and beyond.

They were both so exhausted from the day's events that they didn't notice when they fell asleep.

The next day, Sharaf said to his companion:

"Barno, we need to come up with a new plan to escape!"

"I agree," she nodded. "But nothing comes to mind at the moment."

"Ha! No new plan at all!! You won't manage anything!" someone suddenly bellowed. The door swung open, and like a gust of wind, a figure burst into the cave's "room."

They recognized him right away: it was the treasure-hungry Dagman Yamani.

"I've been thinking about our two halves of the map," he continued, "and I've concluded I can look for the Abbasid treasure in one of the Arabian deserts! And you're going to help me do it. My men will tie your hands and feet again, we'll hop onto my helicopter—much faster that way—and head to the shifting sands in search of the treasure. Don't worry: I've been preparing for this expedition for ages, so I have everything I need. The only thing missing was you—with your half of the map, which is now mine!"

46

Tashkent, the same period

Kamil's uncle, Najmiddin, invited his nephew to *their* café for a private talk—somewhere his parents couldn't overhear the conversation.

"I've obtained not only ironclad incriminating evidence against your Davron," the lawyer said proudly to the student, "but also your 'voluntary confession'!"

Kamil remained silent, wanting to see where his uncle was going with this.

"You're not saying anything? Not even 'thank you'?" the notary asked in surprise.

"Thank you very much, Uncle," the young man responded politely, still not entirely sure everything was fine for him. "So… now I definitely won't go to prison, right?"

"You won't," Najmiddin assured him. "But! Nephew, you know I love my little sister—your mother—and want to spare her any distress. So I've decided not to tear up that damned document just yet. Not until you prove to me, one hundred percent—and not with words but with actions—that you'll never sit down at a gambling table again. Understood?"

"Yes, Uncle," Kamil frowned, uncomfortable with his uncle's pressure. "I won't go back there."

"You have to promise!" Najmiddin pressed on. "And then I'll tear that paper to pieces, and I won't breathe a word of your mistakes to your mother. Deal?"

"All right," Kamil agreed, a bit sullenly. "But I wasn't planning to go back anyway! What do you take me for?"

"Calm down," the lawyer said gently, reining in the young economics student. "I know how you youngsters are. You love to do nothing but have everything—especially more money. And your Davron is essentially the same."

"And what's going to happen to him now?" Kamil asked. "Are you really going to make sure he goes to jail? But… do you have to? Why would you want that? Maybe…"

"I don't get it…" Najmiddin said, surprised. "Are you defending the person who set you up like that? The one whose father nearly had you thrown behind bars?"

"No, I… I'm not defending Davron. It's just… I feel a little sorry for him."

"What did you say?" His uncle was even more taken aback. "And why is that? Have you forgotten how brazenly he blackmailed you? All his nasty tricks and betrayals, which we've talked about more than once? Don't you see—if people like him aren't punished, they'll go on messing up other people's lives, too."

"Davron has… personal problems," Kamil said quietly, a bit afraid of his uncle's righteous anger. "And his father is constantly pressuring him. Plus… he's got some health issues. It seems like… he's going blind or something."

"Really? Out of nowhere?" asked Najmiddin. "Was he staring at some welding?"

"No." Kamil shook his head. "I think it started right after that accident. Maybe Davron hit his head too, though he never admitted it—probably so his father wouldn't take away his car. Though since then he hasn't driven—he gets to the university by taxi or in friends' cars. And recently, in the institute's foyer, he walked right past a girl he really likes, as if he didn't see her. That's odd…"

"Oh, you're such a romantic, nephew!" the uncle laughed. "He probably just had a fight with her. That's all. He's independent, doesn't want to talk to her, acts like he doesn't see her."

"He called her between classes, right in front of me!" Kamil argued. "She was mad at him for not noticing her in the corridor. And that wasn't the only time it happened. He's always squinting. Even in class, he gets confused when reading things off the board or from textbooks. He's probably embarrassed to wear glasses—he's Davron, after all, so proud. He could've used contact lenses, I guess, but for some reason he hasn't thought of that. And I don't want to bring it up. After what happened, we don't even say hello anymore."

"Maybe you're just acting all offended?" the lawyer suggested.

"Yes," the student admitted. "Davron has no idea you almost saved me from prison. Meanwhile, he's the one facing the threat of landing there now…"

"His father, the investigator, has probably discovered the disappearance of that vital document from his desk," Najmiddin objected, "and is now thinking of a way to get his son out of trouble. But don't worry—he won't dare threaten you again or make it public."

"Maybe. But I still feel kind of sorry for Davron," Kamil said.

"I see," Najmiddin sighed. "All right, I'll think about what to do with your poor wretch of a friend."

* * *

Doha, Qatar, the same period

It was evening when the doorbell rang at hotelier Sarwan al-Tawil's house.

His wife Fatima, mother of Jahiza, answered.

"Good evening," said a woman about her own age. "I am a relative of Najib Abbas. I've come to speak with your girl. I know that her wedding has not yet taken place, but I'd like to help you with that matter and offer her some comfort. May I come in?"

"Yes, of course, esteemed lady, please do come in," Fatima replied hospitably.

Entering the living room, the visitor asked that Jahiza be called. Fatima summoned her at once. Jahiza was in low spirits and didn't want to talk to anyone, but her mother persuaded her. The three women sat down for tea and sweets.

"My name is Ustadkhati Risala," the Abbas relative introduced herself to the mother and daughter. "Jahiza, my dear, I've heard from Nizar that before your wedding, the two of you... encountered some difficulties and disagreements."

"What difficulties!" Jahiza burst out, unable to contain her distress and despair. "I was told that this 'crown prince' from the banker's family has refused to marry me. Yes, I know I... well, how should I put it... maybe I pressed him a bit too hard. But the moment I first laid eyes on him, I lost all sleep and peace of mind!

Auntie Risala, I'll be honest and straightforward with you: I love Nizar. It seems like on that cursed night we met at the club, he never really got a proper look at me or remembered me—though I'm the one who saved him from alcohol poisoning!"

Risala tactfully pretended not to know all the details of Jahiza's scheme, though in fact her relative, Najib Abbas, had told her everything.

"You just now said 'crown prince,'" Risala reminded her with a touch of mystery. "But here's the thing: literally yesterday, Mr. Najib Abbas... he flew into a rage at his son for some serious misconduct! Probably something to do with business affairs. And Ustadi Najib made a big decision—to disinherit Nizar, to strip him of his wealthy inheritance!"

"What?!" exclaimed a startled Jahiza. "Oh! Now that's some news..."

"Yes," Risala nodded. "But listen on, Jahiza. We have another relative named Bashir. He's a nice-looking young man, a bit younger than Nizar. Bashir also holds a good position in one of Najib Abbas's banks. You see, both of Bashir's parents recently fell ill with a virus and passed away. He's basically on his own now. He had a very hard time coping with the loss of his closest family members, so Ustadi Najib, who is Bashir's paternal uncle, decided to support him. And since his own son has let him down, he's rewritten the will so that the main share of the inheritance goes to his nephew."

"Must be quite substantial?" Fatima ventured in a conspiratorial whisper.

"Quite," said Risala in the same discreet tone. She turned again to address Jahiza directly. "There's a fair amount of property, plus a controlling stake in the Abbas bank network. So—maybe you shouldn't be so upset that things didn't work out with Nizar. After all, though he's not exactly poor, and he draws a decent salary from his father's bank, there are rumours that the influential banker might fire him altogether any day now. As you can see, Najib has already disinherited him! Meanwhile, Bashir is about to become very wealthy. He has excellent prospects. Think about it. If that option interests you, I can speak with Bashir himself and with his uncle—my cousin—Mr. Najib Abbas, owner of the bank network. Maybe they'll agree that Bashir should take you as his wife… What do you say?"

As Risala spoke, the dullness in Jahiza's eyes faded little by little and was replaced by a growing gleam. By the time the visitor finished, Jahiza seemed much more animated.

"Yes!" the young woman finally burst out. "Of course I'd like you to talk to them about me! I think I'd be willing to marry… what was his name? Bashir!"

"Excellent," Risala replied with a measured smile.

* * *

Tashkent, the same period

Najmiddin tracked down Dr. Said Mumtazov and informed him that if he—an outside party—were to present the police with one-hundred-percent proof from traffic cameras incriminating Davron Bakhramov in the accident that injured Said, the case still might not be opened without Said's official complaint.

"I understand, sir," Dr. Mumtazov replied. "But first I'd like to speak with the person who caused the accident. Then I'll decide what to do."

In turn, Najmiddin promised that, through his nephew—who

was in the same academic year as Davron—he would arrange a so-called "accidental" meeting.

Davron truly was experiencing increasingly severe vision problems. One day, when Davron was alone, Kamil approached him and said:

"Listen, brother, I remember our arrangement. Let's just forget everything—whatever happens, happens. We were friends for two years! Why not go back to hanging out like we used to?"

"Fine," Davron grunted, recognizing Kamil by his voice rather than by sight.

"I realize that you… kind of suffered from that car accident yourself," Kamil began, edging toward the main point.

"Shhh!" Davron hissed, not wanting anyone else to hear. "Why does everyone need to know about it?"

"Yeah, sorry," Kamil whispered. "But you shouldn't blow up about it, all right? You need to see a doctor as soon as possible. I can tell you're not doing well. I know someone really good—why not go see him?"

"Why should I go to some doctor with you?" Davron asked irritably, though he secretly appreciated the concern. "What are you, my mother?"

"No, I'm not your mother—or your father, either," Kamil said with a smile. Davron couldn't see the grin, but he might have guessed it from his tone. "But you do need help, Davronchik, and I have to introduce you to this doctor myself! He doesn't know you, and there's a long waiting list, but I've arranged for him to see you. Where's your car?"

"It's in the shop," the younger Bakhramov mumbled.

"All right, just keep telling everyone that for now," Kamil teased, having figured out his former friend's cover story. "I'll call a taxi."

"What? You mean we have to leave right now?" Davron said, panicking.

"Yes, I told you—I already set up an appointment with him," Kamil explained.

The two arrived at the district clinic near where Kamil lived.

He brought Davron to a familiar ophthalmologist—a colleague and friend of Said Mumtazov. At Kamil's and Najmiddin's request, Dr. Mumtazov also came at the appointed time. Once the district clinic ophthalmologist had completed his examination, he asked Dr. Mumtazov—who had been observing nearby—to step in for further diagnosis and treatment.

Davron had seen pictures on the internet of the doctor he'd hit with his car—the one who had been hospitalized for a long time because of him. Yet Davron didn't recognize him now; his deteriorating eyesight made it impossible. Said realized this but, not wanting to embarrass or alarm the young man with their prior "acquaintance," began the conversation gently:

"Davron, I'm also an ophthalmologist, like my colleague who just saw you. We both arrived at the same conclusion about your vision. You have a retinal detachment in your right eye and traumatic atrophy of the optic nerve in your left—apparently caused by the head and orbital trauma you suffered. This is rather serious, Davron. I recommend that you be admitted to my clinic for surgery. I've personally operated on patients with these exact conditions many times—and all successfully. So talk it over with your parents, and don't be afraid."

"How much? How much does your operation cost?" asked the police major's son. "I... I don't exactly have a lot of money right now..."

"Davron, first of all, you'll likely need at least two operations—

possibly more," Dr. Mumtazov explained. "It depends on several factors, which will become clearer once we examine your eyes more thoroughly. Secondly, for you, it's going to be free."

"Why?" the young man asked nervously. "I… Who are you? Why would it be free for me?"

"I'll explain everything to you," Dr. Mumtazov assured him. "But later, all right? For now, you should go home. I imagine your friend here will see you out. Then I'd suggest you share this information with your parents, and together you can decide the best course of action."

"All right," Davron agreed, still not quite understanding.

"But keep in mind: the sooner we start treatment, the better your chances of at least partially preserving your eyes and your vision," Dr. Mumtazov continued. "Unfortunately, time is now working against you. I'm not saying this to scare you—I just want you to understand how serious it is. The cause was that car accident, correct? Your friend, who brought you here, told me. At first, after it happened, you probably just felt some slight pain or burning in your eyes. But later things got much worse, didn't they?"

"Yeah! But how do you know all this?" Davron couldn't hide his surprise.

"Well, you're not our first patient," Said replied shortly. "Once your health improves, we can have a more detailed talk… about the meaning and value of life."

47

Nishapur, Khorasan, Abbasid Caliphate, at Abdallah's residence, 832 AD

"Brother, I'm continually amazed by your boldness," said Ali, the blood brother and deputy in all affairs of Abdallah, Emir of Khorasan and Mawara' al-Nahr. "I'd even call it audacity. Yes, our father, Tahir ibn Husayn, taught us never to be cowards, never to fear anyone, and to fight bravely for our own rights and those of our subjects. But I think you're being far too reckless!"

"What do you mean?" Abdallah asked, offering his brother some sweets.

"I'm sure you understand," Ali began, "that I'm talking about your independence. You and I are in service to Caliph al-Ma'mun, representing and defending the interests of the Caliphate. You even suppress uprisings in various regions on al-Ma'mun's orders. You hold from him the titles of 'Governor' and 'Emir.'"

"Well, yes," agreed Abdallah. "I know. So what?"

"The problem," Ali said with concern, "is that al-Ma'mun might not be pleased with your excessively open promotion of everything Persian!"

"But he knows we ourselves are Khorasani Persians," Abdallah objected. "Surely we have the right to love our own people and their traditions."

"You're not wrong," Ali continued. "However, the Caliph might catch wind that you've even allowed Persian poets—especially the Shu'ubiyya writers—to praise us by comparing us to the kings and heroes of pre-Islamic Persia! They write about the foundations of the universe in the style of the Zoroastrian *Bundahishn*. And what's more, not in Arabic, but in Farsi! This is despite the fact that we Tahirids have always insisted on our adherence to Arab culture and its expressions. The Caliph could very well interpret this as a sudden conspiracy against him. Aren't you afraid of his wrath?"

"No. Caliph al-Ma'mun doesn't dig that deeply into local matters," Abdallah countered. "He trusts me completely, and everything he knows about our region, he knows from me alone! As for the language—most of our population is Persian-speaking. Arabia is vast, and the Caliph knew that by conquering various peoples, he could only partially influence their worldview. Every nation preserves its traditions for centuries... Remember, we once had a library in Merv that held only Persian-language books! The Caliph knew about it—and permitted it."

"All right, let's suppose so. But still..." Ali persisted. "I'm worried about you, brother—might you end up sharing our father Tahir's unfortunate fate?"

"Don't fret about that," Abdallah said with a smile. "As for the Shu'ubiyya authors... Right now, Shu'ubiyya is an entire movement in the Caliphate! Its proponents advocate equality in Islam between Arabs and other peoples, which is entirely normal. These are people working to revive the Persian literary language and to push back against the dominance of Arabic in literature, particularly in poetry. They're trying to prove that we Persians are in no way inferior to the Arabs in poetry, science, and other fields of progress. And they're right, brother!"

"But is this movement not manifesting itself as an open revolt against the Caliphate's government?" Ali asked.

"No," Abdallah replied. "It's founded on the idea of equality among peoples. And as for preserving and reviving our language—I, for one, fully support it! Especially since it was our culture that laid the foundation for the beginning of the Islamic Golden Age."

"I see," Ali nodded. "Even so… for your daring and fearlessness, you remind me not only of our mighty father Tahir, who was general of the entire Caliphate, but also of the Persian general Abu Muslim!"

"That's too high a compliment, brother," Abdallah said, slightly embarrassed. "I'm not sure I fully deserve it. But… why do you say so?"

"Do you recall the story—one of the lessons our father taught us?" Ali asked. "Abu Muslim was one of the leaders of the uprising against the previous dynasty of caliphs—the Umayyads. He managed to overthrow them."

"Yes, of course," said Abdallah. "But I don't know the details. Will you tell me?"

"Gladly," Ali agreed. "Abu Muslim was originally from the province of Isfahan. Likely a Persian slave—being a 'non-Arab' and not free—he faced significant discrimination under the Umayyads.

"Later, Abu Muslim was sold to Abu Salama, the leader of Abbasid propaganda in Khorasan. They travelled there together. Eventually, he was given as a gift to Ibrahim ibn Muhammad, who freed him and made him an aide, giving him the name 'Abd al-Rahman.' In Khorasan, where the Abbasids had long been stirring up the population against the Umayyads, there was initially some ambivalence about Abu Muslim, given his humble origins. But in just a few short years, he succeeded in uniting Arabs and non-Arabs around him—rallying runaway slaves, Persian peasants, and all others discontent with Umayyad rule."

"Indeed, what an extraordinary man!" Abdallah said in admiration. "How profoundly he affected the history of Persia and all of Arabia!"

"Precisely," Ali concurred. "In the spring of 747, Ibrahim dispatched Abu Muslim as his personal envoy to Khorasan. In May, he arrived in Merv, and by June he had openly risen against Caliph Marwan II, showing remarkable talent as a military commander. In 748, he seized Nishapur and Tus; and in early 750, he crushed the Umayyad dynasty at the Great Zab River. "The Abbasid Caliph al-Saffah, relying on Abu Muslim's help to quell rebellions, rewarded him for his loyal service by allowing him to govern Khorasan—so he became, like you, a governor of that region. He always put the freedom and well-being of our people, the Persians, first. So in a way, Abdallah, you are his successor."

"Thank you for such kind words, brother!" Abdallah said warmly.

"Just be careful, Abdallah," Ali concluded. "When al-Saffah's successor, Caliph al-Mansur, came to power, Abu Muslim's popularity among the people inspired suspicion and envy. In 755, this Persian hero was killed by al-Mansur's guards during an official reception. The news of his death caused unrest and outrage among the people of Khorasan because of al-Mansur's harsh methods… So I'm asking you—take care!"

"I will, brother, I promise," Abdallah said with a smile.

* * *

Marakanda, one of the residences
of the Emir of Khorasan, 833 AD

Abdallah had gone, on Caliph al-Ma'mun's orders, to Egypt and Syria to pacify the populations in those lands who had rebelled against the authority of the Caliphate. Meanwhile, the Caliph himself—now stricken with a serious illness—was resting with his attendants in the local governor's and emir's residence at Marakanda, a city he was fond of.

While at the residence, the Caliph received a visit from a man he deeply respected: a scholar named Sahl ibn Harun, the manager of the House of Wisdom.

"Master, our scholars know how deeply you are interested in astronomy!" Sahl began. "They continue their calculations and discoveries in the observatory you established under the House of Wisdom. Al-Khwarizmi and Al-Farghani have achieved notable successes. Al-Khwarizmi is the author of the book *The Image of the Earth*. He is deeply engaged in determining the true positions of planets and various celestial phenomena; he also compiles astronomical *zij* tables and has accomplished many other feats. As for Al-Farghani—if you recall, he predicted the solar eclipse that occurred last year, in 832! He discovered the presence of spots on the Sun and provided scientific proof that the Earth is spherical. He also determined the dates of the longest and shortest days of the year and has written—or begun planning—several remarkable books on astronomy. Other scholars are working diligently as well. Thus, my Caliph, your creation—the House of Wisdom—and your work of enlightenment will stand as a splendid memorial of you for future generations!"

"Good! I am very pleased to hear it, dear Sahl," replied al-Ma'mun, reclining on a divan. His speech came with difficulty, yet his mind remained sharp. "You speak of 'a memorial' just in time—for soon, all that will remain of me is the memory held by those who come after."

"I sincerely wish our lord a long life and robust health," said Sahl, bowing where he sat. "Memory is a fine thing, but we, your subjects, believe you will continue to delight us with your great deeds for many more years!"

"No, my friend," said al-Ma'mun, shaking his head faintly. "I am dying. And I would entrust a secret to you—one of my most reliable and loyal men…"

"A secret, my lord?" The scholar was astonished. "Forgive me, but are you certain that I, your humble servant, am worthy of such a great confidence?"

"Yes. You are an honest and principled man, a fact I have long confirmed," the Caliph replied. "Otherwise, I would never have entrusted you with such significant state responsibilities—and above all, the House of Wisdom. Now then—near Marakanda, close to Bulungur, there is a settlement called Vedar, whose inhabitants are masterful weavers and tailors. In Khorasan, there is not an emir, vizier, judge, merchant, peasant, or warrior who has not at some point worn the fine, ornate garments made from Vedar's fabrics. Some time ago, I asked one particularly skilled weaving craftsman in Vedar to create a piece of cloth—pure silk such as is used for belts—and on that silk, he was to weave a map. This master was once recommended to me by my friend and military commander, Tahir ibn Husayn."

"Pardon me, my lord," Sahl interjected, "surely this must be one of the star maps you are so fond of? Perhaps one of those discovered in the pyramid in Egypt?"

"You are close to the truth, my friend," said al-Ma'mun, "but not exactly. You, more than most, know that at my request, the Roman and Greco-Egyptian work from Alexandria—Claudius Ptolemy's *Almagest*—was translated into Arabic. It is known as *al-Kitab al-Majisti*."

"Yes, I recall. It's also known as *The Great Mathematical Construction in Astronomy*," Sahl confirmed.

"Exactly," the Caliph continued. "This work consists of thirteen books and includes, among other things: spherical astronomy, a theory of the Sun's apparent motion, a theory of the Moon's motion, the coordinates of the stars, a theory of the planets' apparent movement, and more. I studied it thoroughly myself. It draws upon ancient Egyptian maps and calendars, as well as Hipparchus' first star catalogue—yet it goes far beyond that. Hipparchus' book described 850 celestial bodies, while Ptolemy's includes 1,025 stars and nebulae. And, compared to the surviving fragments of Hipparchus' work, Ptolemy's catalogue is not directly based on them and differs significantly."

"Few rulers in the world can boast such deep knowledge of the sciences as you, my lord," Sahl said, bowing his head again before the Caliph. "Especially in the field of astronomy. But... I gather you are not reminding me of all this by chance."

"You are correct," al-Ma'mun nodded. "In the *Almagest* catalogue, Ptolemy uses various star names that evoke familiar images—for example, Capella as a goat in the constellation Auriga, Regulus in Leo as the king of beasts, Antares in Scorpius with its scorpion symbol, Sirius in Canis Major symbolized by a dog, and so on. I know the scholars at the House of Wisdom are now assigning new Arabic names to stars, but many still derive from that same *Almagest*. Their naming is based on Ptolemy's translated descriptions. The constellation of Giedi—the principal star of Capricorn—means 'little goat' and is depicted accordingly. Thuban, in Draco, is represented as a dragon, while Altair means 'the flying eagle.'"

"How intriguing. I'm eager to see where you're going with this story," Sahl interjected.

"My friend," the Caliph continued, addressing his chief scholar, "over my lifetime, I have amassed a great many jewels and treasures—some of them I took from Khufu's pyramid. Yet I told everyone I found nothing special within it, so that thieves or even members of my own household wouldn't seize my riches. Not my greedy wife Umm Isa—thank goodness she cannot hear us now— nor my son and heir, al-Mu'tasim, nor my other children can be given everything, lest they fight among themselves or, worse still, kill one another in civil wars. I gave them only a small portion for their immediate needs. The majority of my treasures I hid not far from here. But... underground!"

"Underground, my lord?" Sahl asked in surprise.

"Indeed," affirmed the famed Abbasid. "Right after my expedition to al-Giza in Egypt, I ordered my men to dig a deep, long subterranean passage—very similar to what we did in Khufu's pyramid. At the end of this passage lies a large chamber where I stashed my treasure. Alas, I never had the chance to spend it at my own discretion, so I leave it to the descendants who prove worthy of finding it..."

"Oh, my lord! May you live long, and may you yet find a use for it yourself in your great works," Sahl said, his eyes welling with tears.

"I fear it's too late," al-Ma'mun replied. "But as a wise and learned man, you must already suspect I didn't just happen to remind you of the constellations and their star symbols. Interpreting those symbols on my silk map—the one I told you about today—will not be easy. The point is…"

The Caliph paused to catch his breath. Sahl sensed that the ruler of Arabia was struggling to speak.

"Before my talented weaver embroidered the symbols onto the fabric map," al-Ma'mun continued, "I gave him a list of my own creation in which every settlement in my main territories corresponds to the symbol or image of a particular star. But, so as not to confuse those seeking my treasure too greatly, I chose only one well-known constellation—Saptarishi, or what we call the 'Great Dipper.' You, as a scholar, know of it?"

"Of course I do," Sahl replied. "That constellation, with all its stars, is likened to a bear—'the Great Bear.'"

"Precisely," al-Ma'mun continued. "By placing the stars of that constellation in the correct sequence, and locating the geographic point corresponding to its brightest star—that is the road and the door to the subterranean passage. And to keep the secret safe, only two people know these symbols: my weaver and you. I also made the hunt more difficult by tearing the cloth map into two uneven pieces. I gave one half to that honest weaver, whose name I shall not reveal to anyone. The other half I give to you now. Only by combining the two parts, deciphering all the symbols, and performing one more secret procedure can anyone discover the exact coordinates of the entrance to the underground chamber that holds the treasure!"

The Caliph's voice grew fainter. Sahl realized that al-Ma'mun was exhausted. He managed only a few more words:

"That chamber is locked… and the key to the lock… is…"

But Caliph al-Ma'mun could not finish his sentence. A sudden spasm of his incurable illness overtook him—and two days after this conversation, Caliph al-Ma'mun died.

Sahl understood that the countless treasures left behind—wrapped in the secrecy crafted by the ruler's enlightened mind—were intended neither for al-Ma'mun's heirs nor for Sahl himself. There was a greater meaning in this: the mystery was to echo the Caliph's great deeds, wealth, and glory across distant ages and future generations.

***

Vedar, outskirts of Marakanda, Khorasan, Abbasid Caliphate, that same year

"Maruf," said the merchant Gani, addressing the renowned tailor of Vedar in the bazaar. Gani was purchasing a splendid coat of gold-thread-embroidered brocade and a belt made of genuine silk from the best craftsman around. "Many people in Marakanda and Bulungur have heard that not long ago the late Caliph al-Ma'mun himself paid you a visit! They say he lavished you with gifts—a fine new house, several platters of sumptuous dishes from his royal table, and even a whole pouch of pure gold!"

"All right. Suppose he did. So what?" replied the rough-spoken weaver and tailor, without much emotion.

"But then, why did you keep only that house? And only to let all your relatives and some paupers live there? Huh?" Gani pressed on, unable to hide his astonishment. "Instead of enjoying a wealthy life with your wife, you handed out all that gold straight to the beggars in the market! Forgive me, esteemed *ustadi* Maruf, but can we really call someone who does that a normal person? Who just gives away such wealth? And from none other than the Caliph of Arabia?!"

"Well, apparently there are people in this world like that," Maruf noted wryly. "Here you are, merchant—your order is finished. Thank you for your payment. No, I don't need anything extra."

"In that case, maybe you can share the secret? We're all extremely curious: what was it the late Caliph commissioned from you?" Gani persisted, his words flowing without pause. "What did he order—or request—you to make? Maybe he asked you to craft the most expensive robe in the entire Caliphate, inlaid with gemstones? They say he was wearing such a robe on his deathbed. Did you make that?"

"Well… not just me alone," the master replied modestly. "My tailor friends helped as well."

"And people are also saying, *ustadi* Maruf," the merchant went on, "that Caliph al-Ma'mun entrusted you with something important. Some kind of astonishing secret! Will you tell us—your dear acquaintances—what that mystery is? We're not strangers, after all!"

"Excuse me, esteemed Gani, but I'm not sure what you're talking about," Maruf said, turning his head and thinking, *And how does he know this? I haven't told a soul… Perhaps someone in the Caliph's entourage let it slip?* "If that's all, *ustadi* Gani, then I'll be off—I'm tired today, and I still have many orders waiting at home. I need a bit of rest before I get back to work."

"Yes, farewell then. Although let me say this: with the gold the Caliph gave you, *ustadi* Maruf, you could have hired an entire army of assistants," the merchant admonished him. Then, mumbling to himself as Maruf walked away, he added, "Oh, what a man! If I had that kind of money… I'd certainly know what to do with it! But he just tossed it all away—gave it to the poor. Born a pauper, and will forever be a pauper. Eh!"

48

Samarkand, 2023

Captain Ibrahim Salimov of the police had little luck extracting from the detained thug Gosha and his accomplices any information on Fahriyar Tursunov—Barno's father—or where he might be hiding. The criminals claimed they had kidnapped Barno because they were "forced to," in order to locate and threaten her father, using his daughter as leverage. But Fahriyar himself had vanished without a trace.

Even in captivity, Barno often thought about it. She worried about her father, missed him, and fretted over how long he'd been forced to stay in hiding, always on the run. She feared something terrible might have happened to him on top of everything else. He owed a large debt to the gang—no small matter, especially since his business had failed and he had no means to repay the money. Tursunov had kept stalling for a solution, even though Gosha had "put him on the clock" for the debt. But what could be done if there was no money? Sometimes Barno thought, *If only I could find some ancient treasure! I'd sell it immediately to save my father!* Yet Fahriyar didn't even know that his daughter was no longer in Uzbekistan, but in the Arab countries—practically a prisoner—searching for that treasure in the hope of rescuing him…

In the meantime, Captain Salimov was also trying to locate Fahriyar and help his family with the debt. On the advice of a young law student named Sharaf—whom he had occasionally spoken with and messaged before Sharaf left for Arabia—Ibrahim summoned Gosha from the detention centre. He explained to him that it would be easy to prove those "loaned" funds were stolen in the first place. If Gosha continued pressing Tursunov—or his wife or daughter—for repayment, Salimov would officially open an investigation into the origins of that money. Salimov was one hundred percent certain that Gosha would then face additional years in prison for the related crimes.

Finding himself with no better option, Gosha grudgingly relinquished all claims to the money and promised Captain Salimov that if Barno's father turned up, neither he nor his gang would ever again demand repayment as a "debt," let alone with interest. He swore he truly didn't know where Tursunov was now. Ibrahim still didn't fully trust him.

Now all that remained for Ibrahim was "the simple part": actually finding Fahriyar himself. And if the man was alive and well, to let Barno and Ibrahim's young friend Sharaf—both of whom were deeply worried about him—know that he was safe. Since even Fahriyar's wife had no idea of her husband's whereabouts, Captain Salimov issued a republic-wide bulletin to help locate him.

* * *

Tashkent, the same period

The shady millionaire Ubay Rakhimov was seated in one of his ostentatious restaurants, having lunch while he waited for a meeting with his cousin's nephew, Sher. The latter finally arrived.

"Sit down and order something on my tab," Ubay said. "Today I'm feeling generous—despite the fact that you don't respect me."

"What? I do respect you, Uncle!" Sher protested.

"Silence when I'm talking," Ubay snapped, cutting him off. "What did I tell you? That I don't care how much those Abbasid treasures are worth—I must be the first to 'find' them! The glory of that discovery must belong to me! Didn't I make that clear?"

"You made that clear," Sher echoed.

"You're like a parrot," Ubay growled. "No thoughts of your own in that head of yours. Didn't I tell you to give me detailed reports of all your movements and discoveries, hm?"

Sher was too intimidated to speak and merely nodded.

"So—no interesting news for the past several days?!" Ubay glared at him. "Why did you stop calling me? You don't answer my calls or texts. I have to chase you all over the place! What—do you think you're some kind of big shot, that I have nothing better to do than babysit you? Huh?! Who do you think you are? Who pays you? Who puts food on your table?"

"You do, Uncle," Sher murmured, hanging his head in guilt. He suddenly felt like a little boy. He knew how influential and wealthy Ubay was and didn't dare contradict him. "I'm sorry."

"That's better," Ubay said, his tone softening just slightly. "Now, tell me the news."

"Our Samarkand competitor, Kudrat Valiev—the one I officially work for—came to Tashkent and joined our group," Sher began his report. "He was called in by Zulfiya. Two rather unpleasant Bahrainis have forced themselves into our circle as well—the director of a cultural centre and his assistant. For some reason, Kudrat allowed them to stay and even seems to have befriended the director, Yakzan Baker. I suspect Kudrat plans to use these guys in the Arab countries to help find the treasure, then toss them aside like worthless junk once they've served his purpose. Or just send them back home. Kudrat can do that. He's that powerful!"

Ubay shot a displeased look at his cousin's nephew, greatly disliking hearing anyone else praised—especially one of his business rivals. However, he realized he needed to let his incompetent relative finish speaking because this information mattered.

"What about the location of the treasure itself?" Ubay asked.

"We're one hundred percent on the trail of the second half of the treasure map!" Sher boasted. "I already told you, Uncle, that one half is in Zulfiya's possession—well, effectively in Kudrat's hands now. And the other half is almost certainly—about a ninety-five percent chance—with that Qatari fellow named Sharaf."

"So you'll be flying over to Qatar soon, for the second time?" Ubay confirmed.

"No, Uncle," his nephew replied. "Sharaf and his girlfriend are in Saudi Arabia now. We got his exact coordinates—assuming he still has his phone. So tomorrow, we're flying as a group to Riyadh! From there, we'll head to the Red Sea. Somewhere out there— maybe on some excursion or research yacht—that's where Sharaf's located. And the map is there too."

"Well done," Ubay said grudgingly, breaking into a small smile as he parodied his nephew. "An 'excursion' yacht—always the holidaymaker! But that information is actually valuable. Here—take this Visa card for your expenses. You've earned it. But remember: keep in constant contact with me! And the minute you get close to those treasures—immediately, do you hear me, immediately send me all their geo-coordinates! Got it? Then I'll bring along a few journalists, including some from television, and they'll proclaim me the first modern man to discover Caliph al-Ma'mun's legendary hoard! Let the whole world know me first and foremost as a successful collector of luxury and medieval Arabian art! Eh?"

"Yes, Uncle," Sher grumbled, inwardly resenting his uncle's smugness.

"You can go now," Ubay ordered, even though Sher had barely started his meal. "Don't forget to diligently carry out every one of my instructions! Safe travels!"

* * *

The next day, the treasure-hunting group led by Kudrat Valiev arrived in Riyadh. Vanya and Sanya, after studying satellite maps, informed Kudrat and Zulfiya that, judging by Sharaf's phone—if he still had it—his coordinates had changed. Apparently, the young man was no longer near the Red Sea, but in the Rub' al Khali desert.

Kudrat decided they would all rest today after their flight. Tomorrow, they would rent jeeps and head into the desert to find the young man and his girlfriend. But most importantly, they needed to find the second half of the Abbasid treasure map.

***

Saudi Arabia, Rub' al Khali Desert, the same period

Dagman Yamani—no less eager than Ubay or Kudrat to gain fame as a collector and acquire wealth—transported himself and his two captives by helicopter.

"Sharaf," Barno asked the young man softly during the flight, "why didn't you leave me in that cave and just escape to the city? You could have saved yourself! Why did you come back for me and put your life at risk again?"

"Don't you understand?" Sharaf replied quietly, with warmth and tenderness in his voice.

Barno lowered her head in modesty. Despite her captivity and all she had endured, she felt comforted by the possibility that the young man she cared for might also harbour feelings for her. Still, she wasn't completely certain. She reminded herself that when someone is noble by nature, they'd rescue anyone they know—even if they didn't have romantic feelings for them. And Sharaf was indeed a noble person.

In the desert, Yamani's sturdy henchmen were already waiting for them. They had pitched tents in a relatively wind-sheltered spot and set up a cozy lounge area for Yamani himself, fully equipped for his comfortable rest.

"Excuse me," Barno asked one of the big, brawny men, her voice low, "Do you know what happened to that guard who brought us food in the cave?"

"He's getting treatment in the hospital," the strongman replied. "What, was it you who knocked him out?"

Barno didn't want to betray Sharaf, so she merely asked, "Will he… survive? What do the doctors say?"

"He's as strong as an ox, girl!" declared the guard. "Don't worry about him. He's perfectly fine. But you and your friend here, you'd do well not to try anything like that with me, understand? I might not control my strength so kindly!"

Barno breathed a sigh of relief. Later, when she got a moment, she quietly passed this news along to Sharaf. The young man was similarly glad to hear that the guard he'd knocked out was alive and well.

To the mild surprise of Yamani's men, their boss—who was used to flaunting himself everywhere and pretending to be a generous, hospitable "good Muslim"—invited Barno and Sharaf to relax during the daytime in the lounge. A small table there was always set with food, protected from drifting sand by a cloth.

He even assigned each of them their own tent. Of course, Sharaf had to share his tent with one of the goons guarding him, while Barno's tent was locked from the outside at night so she couldn't run away. For basic needs, she had to wait until morning.

But Yamani felt sure the "girl" wouldn't escape alone in the desert anyhow. These precautions were simply "just in case."

After they settled in, the following morning, they had breakfast. In truth, neither Sharaf nor Barno had much appetite, flanked as they were by Yamani and his intimidating henchmen. But Yamani paid no attention; what he cared about was showing the pair both halves of the map, hoping their brains might help him figure it out since he could make little sense of it on his own.

"Why do you assume the treasure lies specifically in this desert?" Barno asked, studying the two halves of the map.

"You don't see that this is clearly desert terrain?" Yamani replied with a question of his own. "I'm no geography expert, but in my opinion, it resembles this one—Rub' al Khali."

"All deserts look similar," Sharaf cut in. "Especially Arabian ones. Especially on old maps. If it were a modern satellite image, we could know for sure. As it stands, this could be An Nafud al Kabir, the Great Nafud, Al-Arakana, Jubbah, Ad-Dahna—any number of places!"

"Oh, you're quite knowledgeable!" Yamani remarked in surprise.

"Yes, our Sharaf is very smart," Barno said, smiling. She felt relieved that neither her hands nor Sharaf's were tied now—though a ring of Yamani's towering guards stood right beside them. "By the way, are you sure it's not the Libyan Desert where the famous pyramids stand? Caliph al-Ma'mun was there, too! Let me tell you, as a historian and tour guide, that according to some accounts, he found pharaohs' treasures there. Besides the usual gold, silver, and copper, it's believed he acquired unique artifacts: ceremonial crowns for both the pharaoh and his queen in pure gold, unbreakable bending glass and mirrors, swords that cut stone, medicinal concoctions, lamps that never go out, an incense stick thousands of years old, and all sorts of other things."

"Really? Is that so?!" Yamani's eyes lit up. "Where'd you learn about that?"

"I've read them in reliable sources," Barno replied. "Among the finds were items made of red gold and precious stones, too. Maybe that's where we need to go? Though… personally, I wouldn't want to. You could handle that yourself. Why do you even need us? We're too weak to dig in the sand—and you have strong helpers. Why don't you let us go, Mr. Yamani? We promise not to tell the police you kidnapped us or file any complaint!"

"How noble you are, yes?" Yamani scoffed, dismissing her

words with a wave.

"Barno, you mentioned something about incense?" Sharaf asked, sounding thoughtful.

"Yes," Barno nodded. "Among the artifacts Caliph al-Ma'mun found in Khufu's Pyramid was a stick of incense. Why?"

"Doesn't it strike you that, first of all, our two maps might not actually be two halves of a single map? That each map might be halves of completely different maps?" Sharaf blurted out.

"That can't be," Yamani said, crestfallen. "I can't have made such a mistake. More likely, you are the one who's wrong, boy."

"Not likely," Sharaf retorted. "Look. The map my mother gave me—passed to her by some Arab archaeologist—has symbols resembling small animal drawings or parts of a human body. It just occurred to me that, in ancient times, people often depicted stars in constellations in a similar manner. Maybe that's the start of a clue to our map? Maybe it's connected to the Caliphate's settlements?"

"That's brilliant, Sharaf!" Barno cried out excitedly at his guess. "I'd been wondering what all these little images and symbols reminded me of! Where had I seen them before?"

"Thank you, Barno," he said, flashing her a quick grin. "And as for your incomplete map, Mr. Yamani—it has completely different markings: pictures of plants and crystals. Maybe you mistook those crystals for gemstones. And I bet you're neither the first nor the only one to have made that mistake. I have a guess about what this map of yours might be. But I'll hold back for now—I need more time to think it through. However, I can say straightaway: not here, but somewhere else, someone else must hold the second part of your map!"

"Fine. I'll also think about what you kids just said," Yamani said with a yawn, suddenly feeling sleepy. "I'll go rest for a bit. You guards—keep both eyes on these two little lovebirds so they don't run away!"

* * *

Tashkent, the same period

Kamil and especially his thorough uncle, Najmiddin, still wanted to see the resourceful, scheming, and entrepreneurial investigator Zakir Bakhromov punished. But... they never got the chance. It turned out that the Republic's Internal Affairs Department's own security division had already taken an interest in the major and begun investigating him. Before long, Bakhromov Sr. was detained for bribery and abuse of office.

Through his connections in the justice system, Najmiddin learned that Zakir faced a significant prison term—exactly what the notary had wanted. Yet he decided not to bring up the story of Davron's accident and forgery in the case against Bakhromov Sr., so as not to "shine a light" on his nephew's name one more time.

The soft-hearted, mild-mannered Kamil was even less inclined to hammer extra nails into the coffin of a major who was already suffering due to life's circumstances. He forgave him—just as he forgave Davron.

Davron Bakhromov himself was being prepared for surgery by Said Mumtazov and his associates at the ophthalmology clinic. They had warned the young man's mother that her son would require nursing care.

"I don't know how to thank you, doctor!" Davron's mother, Madina, wept. "We're going through truly hard times right now. But if you want—or if it's necessary—I can borrow money and pay you for all of my son's operations!"

"No need. That's not necessary," Said reassured her. "I have my own reasons for doing this. One could say I'm interested in the causes of your son's impaired vision… from a professional standpoint. Besides, he urgently needs my help; I can't let the poor fellow go blind. But you'll need plenty of patience. Davron will undergo several major operations. You must realize it'll be a long process."

"Yes, I'm ready for that. Thank you so much!" the woman said again, expressing her gratitude.

"It's all right," Mumtazov replied with a smile.

49

Doha, Qatar, a few days later

Hotel owner Sarwan al-Tawil once again came to the head office of banker Najib Abbas without an invitation. The bank's owner, accustomed to the rudeness and brazenness of the man who had nearly become his in-law, was no longer surprised. He invited Sarwan to sit.

"Ustadi Najib," Sarwan began after an exchange of polite but reserved greetings. Ever since his last visit with the banker—when the status quo had returned to Najib—Sarwan had been doing his utmost to restrain his anger. "I trust you're aware that your relative, Risala, dropped by our home not too long ago…"

"Yes, I heard about that," the elder Abbas answered calmly. "So?"

"She told my wife, Fatima, and our daughter, Jahiza, that you… well, how shall I put it? I'm not even sure."

"Speak plainly, exactly as it is," Najib suggested mockingly. "No need to mince words."

"All right!" Sarwan sighed. It was not at all pleasant for him to be the one bearing responsibility for such a delicate conversation, but he was still desperate not to lose sight of the 'inheritance' that dangled before his eyes.

"I'm listening," Najib said again, maintaining his composure.

"In short, about the fact that you… are deeply hurt by your son, Nizar," Sarwan finally blurted out. "And that you've disinherited him! That after your… forgive me—after you—you won't allow him to become the President of your bank! Is that correct?"

Choosing a crafty and prudent approach, Abbas realized Sarwan was itching to spill all the information anyway. So he didn't answer him directly, instead asking:

"What else did she tell you?"

"She mentioned you have a young relative named Bashir," the hotelier continued. "And that he—this poor orphan who works as some lowly clerk in your bank—will, according to your will, inherit the main portion of your estate, esteemed Mr. Abbas: property and the controlling stake in your network of banks…"

"Suppose so," Najib said evasively, raising an ironic eyebrow. "Are you so very interested in my inheritance, Mr. al-Tawil?"

"No, of course not! How could you think such a thing?" Sarwan tried to defend himself.

"Forgive me," Najib smiled. "It's just that you yourself brought it up right now."

"That's not my point," Sarwan explained as though he were a schoolboy addressing the wise older banker. Still uncertain how to spin things to his benefit, he decided to fib a little. "What I meant was that Risala said your Bashir quite fancies girls like my daughter, Jahiza!"

"Oh? Well, she is a beauty," Najib remarked paternally, paying her a compliment.

"Thank you, esteemed Mr. Abbas," Sarwan beamed with pride for his child. "And our guest also said that Bashir—of course, with your permission and approval as his uncle—would take my daughter, Jahiza, for his wife."

"And what does your daughter, Jahiza, have to say about this?" Najib asked purposefully.

"How so?" Sarwan responded in surprise. "Why, if you yourself propose it, ustadi Najib, naturally she'll fully submit to your paternal will!"

"Except you're her father, not me," Najib reminded him, quietly amused.

"I spoke metaphorically, esteemed sir," Sarwan said, reddening. "Since the wedding of my daughter to your son Nizar collapsed so suddenly—although we'd invested so heavily in it!—maybe you won't let a pure, innocent girl walk around in disgrace, labelled 'defective' and 'abandoned'? Why not marry her off to your nephew?"

"You haven't even seen him once in your life!" Najib burst out into louder laughter. "Never talked to him. How can you possibly know what kind of man he is? Is he worthy of your remarkable daughter? For all you know, he could be some con man or swindler. Or, let's say… quite ugly. And your daughter, after all, is a pretty girl! You think she'd love just anyone? Does it not matter to you whom you marry her to?"

"Oh, come on, Mr. Abbas!" The visitor grew flustered. "How could you think such a thing? No, obviously it matters. It's just that I'm confident any unmarried young man who happens to be your relative, in whom you place your trust, would have to be an excellent husband for any girl!"

"Perhaps," Najib nodded. "But how does your daughter come into it? In what way is she, for instance, better than so many others? Yes, she'll have a little inheritance. But you, as a businessman, must know that large fortunes ally with other large fortunes. I have a very big fortune. And you—well, you do not. That's why you needed my investment, which, as you recall, I ultimately declined."

"But you'll change your mind, Abbas, won't you?" Sarwan started to lose his temper. "You'll revisit that incorrect, reckless, ill-conceived decision?"

Not even the extremely patient Najib had expected such blatant insolence.

"What did you just say?!" he exploded. "'Incorrect'? 'Reckless'? 'Ill-conceived'?! Are you out of your mind, al-Tawil? Who do you think you're calling a fool?"

Najib typically didn't stay angry for more than a minute—he always found ways to calm himself quickly and regain control in any situation with anyone.

"All right, sorry I raised my voice," Najib said, trying to smooth things over. "But you shouldn't have insulted me."

"Never mind, let's forget it," Sarwan responded, with no intention of apologizing himself. "So, what about the investment? Will you give it to me or not? We were just discussing it!"

"I thought we were talking primarily about your daughter," Najib corrected him.

"Well, of course! About her too," Sarwan replied. "Will you let my hotels prosper? In the end, you'd get good dividends yourself, after all! So, what do you say?"

"All right, for now… I'm neither turning you down nor firmly agreeing to it," sighed the weary banker. "I'll think about it further."

Najib had decided to stall for time. In his mind, he'd already concluded he wanted no future dealings with such an unscrupulous and volatile character as Sarwan. But he chose not to tell the hotelier that, in order to avoid further outbursts.

"And about the marriage with my daughter?" Sarwan asked, lacking any tact.

"What do you mean?" Najib replied, pretending not to understand.

"Are you going to marry her off to Niza… I mean, to your relative Bashir?" Sarwan tried to stick all his fingers in his mouth at once, hoping to achieve all his aims in one go.

"No," Najib answered curtly.

"But… how is that possible?" Sarwan said, visibly agitated. "It's true, you never promised. Yet your relative said—"

"She doesn't make those decisions," Najib shook his head. "If she promised you or offered your daughter some assistance, it could only have been her personal wish. But Bashir himself hasn't proposed to your daughter, now has he?"

"But I thought you were the one who sent her to us!" Sarwan groaned.

"No, not I," Najib said slyly. "Why would I? That was… my son's idea."

"Nizar?!" Sarwan couldn't hide his shock. "His idea, Mr. Abbas?… So what, to fool me and my daughter?"

"No one tricked either of you," Najib objected. "I told you plainly some time ago: Nizar and Jahiza won't be getting married."

"But what about Bashir?" pressed Sarwan. "You could marry him to my daughter!"

"He's an adult; he decides for himself whom to marry," Najib explained. ***"And who told you I would actually leave my Nizar with nothing? That's utter nonsense! You shouldn't have believed rumours and gossip. Including those from Risala. Her job was to put you to the test. That's the gist of my... much-beloved son and my only heir's plan! We wanted to see if your daughter truly and sincerely loved Nizar the way she's proclaiming it everywhere—or if it was just another ruse, supported by you, her father, for personal gain. She failed that test spectacularly. The both of us—'the Abbases'—aren't going to ally ourselves with people as greedy as you, nor will we ever do anything to support you. I'm sorry. I won't keep you any longer."

"You won't get away with this scot-free!" Sarwan threatened, rising to his feet, all the while realizing deep down how helpless and insignificant he was compared to the banker's formidable standing, social influence, and sizable fortune.

* * *

Saudi Arabia, Rub' al Khali Desert, the same period

"All right," said Sharaf to Dagman, "let's say you're going to search here in this desert for your so-called 'treasure'..."

"Why 'so-called'?" Dagman objected.

"Because, as I see it, going by your map, it's unlikely you'll find the real Abbasid treasures," the young man explained. "But how do we figure out exactly where they're hidden? At the moment, I don't get it. If we had the second half of this map, that'd be a different story—we might attempt to locate something."

"We should bear another thing in mind," Barno added. "If you haven't noticed, our map is made of silk, while yours is cotton."

"Yes!" the young man agreed with her. "I completely side with Barno: there's no way these two pieces could be two halves of the same map. You need a second piece—also made of cotton, with symbolic images of plants and crystals, not animals or body parts like on our half."

"What if I try looking for the treasure using your half alone?" Dagman insisted. "Understand me, my young friends: with or without you, I must find it!"

"It'd be better without us," Barno said quietly. "We'll manage on our own."

Yamani caught what she said.

"No, you're going to help me!" he pressed on. "You're both bright and good-hearted! Come on, let's eat well again—my men have brought plenty of delicious food from restaurants in the city of Sharurah. Ah… and who's that driving up?"

An unfamiliar jeep halted not far from their camp.

Dagman and his five helpers—three of them, at their master's signal, moving in just in case—shaped their massive bodies into a barrier between the new arrival and both Yamani and his young prisoners. They presumed it could be a tourist, since plenty of people come to the desert in the summertime.

Yamani was less than thrilled by an outsider's appearance, fearing that any strangers might hinder his search for "his" treasure.

A lively, middle-aged Arab hopped out of the vehicle.

"Hello!" he greeted them with a broad, insincere smile for everyone who'd stepped forward. "Oh! No need to greet me with weapons. I'm no enemy. I just want to pitch my tent somewhere around here. First, I'd like a drink, maybe a bite to eat, and a bit of rest. I see you're already set up quite comfortably! Could I, for a fair price, rent one of your tents for a nap? Just a couple of hours! Once I've had a breather, I'll pack up and head on."

"Leave him alone, boys," Yamani ordered his helpers. "He's just some adventurer. And what's got you out here in this heat, ustadi? Pardon, I don't know your name. But sure, come into my lounge. This is all my domain here. My name is Dagman Yamani. I'm Lebanese, from Riyadh, a connoisseur of art."

"I'm Garib," the new desert dweller introduced himself with enthusiasm. "I'm a former tour guide at the Abbasid Palace in Baghdad. But honestly, I'm not into 'adventure' per se, nor am I some typical traveller. Truth is, I'm here looking for ancient storage sites of African and Arabian incense."

"I don't follow," Yamani remarked with a frown, offering the newcomer some tea. "Why would you need that?"

"Come on now," the former tour guide said familiarly, winking at the wealthy man. "We're on the ancient Incense Route, aren't we? In olden times and throughout the Middle Ages, people occasionally transported gold along this route, too. And I figure, not all of it's been found. I even have a map—though it's incomplete."

What a fool—sharing such vital info with me, a total stranger! Yamani thought in surprise.

"Help yourself," he said habitually, resuming his role as a hospitable host. "Whatever God has provided." Then, addressing the Baghdadi, "Honoured Garib, would you let us take a peek at your map—just a glance?" Sharaf asked curiously.

"Sure, go right ahead!" Garib agreed readily, handing Sharaf the piece of map he'd stolen from the Baghdad Palace's collections. "To be honest, I'm worn out trying to make sense of it alone.

Getting nowhere! But please, don't tear it or damage it. See, it's already missing a small corner: some... thief from Tashkent tore it off while I was fighting him. Sorry for such details. It's amazing this map survived at all; it's very old. Made centuries ago. Have you ever seen such unusual fabric maps before? I hadn't, not until this one! Seems to be some ancient technique."

"Looks like they treated it with wax and mutton fat," Barno volunteered her knowledge.

"Yes, that could be," Garib conceded. "What do you see there?"

"Mr. Yamani, where's your map?" Sharaf asked. "Ah, there it is. May I take it?"

Dagman gave it to him for the moment—he had his guards all around anyway, and as a collector, he felt perfectly safe.

"Sure, go ahead."

"Whoa!!" Sharaf exclaimed as soon as he had both cloth maps in his hands. "It seems pretty obvious to any untrained eye that these are actually two pieces of the same map! And it's a map of ancient incense!!"

"Perhaps also other treasures," Barno chimed in. "Believe me as a historian, we shouldn't rule that possibility out entirely."

Dagman's and Garib's eyes both glinted with greed.

"So how do we split the gold and myrrh once we find it?" Yamani asked, already wondering how he'd get rid of this "extra" person and keep his map.

"But!" Barno cautioned, "Keep in mind, treasure hunters, that many centuries have passed since whoever made this map—which you two now share. It's now the twenty-first century! Surely it's all been looted long ago."

"Yes, or buried under layers of sand," Sharaf added, marvelling at how enthusiastic these two little men were about getting even richer from a hypothetical find. "So maybe there's nothing left."

"I'm a lucky guy," Yamani argued. "I'll find something for sure! But how do we search for it? Does the map show precisely where the hoard is?"

"It must be one of the 'storage points' for incense on the Route," Barno theorized. "See, on both halves of your big cloth map, we see different symbols. From what Sharaf guessed, apparently these are incense symbols linked to coordinates throughout Arabia. Let's assume we're in the correct desert. We have no guarantee, but let's try deciphering it! I suspect this map won't contain any excessively convoluted riddles. Did any of you think to bring an ordinary, paper map of the Arabian Caliphate from Ma'mun's era? Or a digital photo, at least?"

"Well, I've got a paper one in my bag," Garib answered. "I'll fetch it. Actually, I wanted to rest and sleep, but once I learned about the second half of my map, I'm wide awake."

"Your map?" Yamani repeated disapprovingly.

"All right, ustadi, your map," Garib said with a falsely humble expression. Deep down, he had no intention of surrendering "his" gold to some outsider glutton.

He went back to the car and retrieved his bag, which did indeed contain a fairly decent modern printed map of the medieval Caliphate.

Sharaf and Barno compared it with the two joined halves of the incense map, woven on cotton cloth. Some of the symbols matched up with actual towns. But in the Rub' al Khali desert, especially on Garib's portion, there were so many symbols that everyone's heads swam. It wasn't easy to make sense of.

"Oh!! I think I've found something!" Barno suddenly exclaimed. "Look: about twenty-five degrees to the east, at a distance of roughly seven kilometres from here, there's a place marked by two identical signs on both halves of the map! I don't see any other such coincidences. Do you?"

"No, none others," Garib agreed, carefully examining both halves.

"That's it!" their "leader," Yamani, confirmed. "No other matches." Then, in a sceptical tone to mislead Garib, he added, "Well, no guarantee. But fine, we'll go see. Garib, you coming with us? Or would you rather rest? Maybe we'll find nothing there anyway, and you did want to nap. This tent is all yours—rest well, you seem worn out."

"Oh no, dear sir," Garib retorted. His eyes gleamed even brighter than before. "Treasure first! I can rest later."

Yamani said nothing, trying to hide his impatience with both the wait for the result and the presence of this pesky "treasure hunter."

He got into his jeep, bringing Sharaf, Barno, and two of his five guards, racing away at top speed toward the spot in the desert Barno had identified. Garib climbed alone into his rented jeep and set off right behind Yamani.

* * *

Samarkand – Tashkent, the same period

Captain Ibrahim Salimov of the police received a call from the capital's hospital. A man matching the description of the missing Fahriyar Tursunov had regained consciousness. However, he still could not remember anything or state his own name.

The next day, Ibrahim went to Tashkent.

After speaking with the attending physician—who was treating the patient's severe head-trauma-induced amnesia—Salimov entered the hospital room of the man who had only recently woken up.

From the photographs Barno had given him, the captain immediately recognized her father. He was delighted that the sweet girl's father had finally been found.

Visiting him in the hospital over the following days, Ibrahim gradually told the patient who he was, what had happened to him before his injury, and that his own daughter had been searching for him.

"And now, Fahriyar-aka," Ibrahim added, "it would be helpful to learn exactly what happened when you left home and never returned."

"Unfortunately, I truly don't recall," Fahriyar admitted. "The doctor says it's likely someone struck me on the head with a heavy object. He also says that, over time, I might remember everything. I don't know. I really hope I do! Unless…"

"Unless what, Fahriyar-aka?" asked Ibrahim.

"Unless it's dangerous for me or my loved ones!" Tursunov concluded. "You say I have a daughter, right? And… do I have anyone else?"

"Yes, your wife," Ibrahim replied. "But what's strange is that I called her on the very first day I came to see you. Are you telling me she still hasn't come to visit? How could that be?"

"Maybe she did," Tursunov said sheepishly. "Maybe I just don't remember. Wait… Not long ago, some woman came by. She brought me some food, watched me closely for a moment, and then left almost immediately. But I didn't recognize her. Could that have been my wife? In which case… why would she leave right away and never come back? And my daughter? Why doesn't she visit her father?"

"Your daughter is a very kind, devoted person," Captain Salimov reassured him. "Had she been in town, she would have come running to see you—more than once! But... as I know, she and her friend have been traveling in the Arab countries for about two weeks. Maybe it's a vacation, maybe business; I don't know the details. Admittedly, recently they..."

Ibrahim paused, realizing he was on the verge of saying too much. Now was hardly the time to unsettle a man who had only just regained consciousness and was still recovering. Later, when he was stronger, Ibrahim could tell him everything.

"No, it's nothing," he said with a smile. "It's all fine. I was just going to say they haven't been in touch as often as one might like. But that makes sense: calls abroad are expensive, and presumably, they don't have reliable internet access on hand. Well, let the young people enjoy themselves on their trip, right?"

"Yes, I agree," Barno's father said, relaxing a bit. "I'm glad she's all right."

"And I hope you'll soon recover, too," Ibrahim added encouragingly, moved by the friendly man's situation but also very eager to find out who had hit him on the head, when, and why—nearly costing him his life.

50

Samarkand, Winter of 2024

Barno and Sharaf were guests at Captain Ibrahim Salimov's home, enjoying tea with him and his family.

As they sat around the table, Ibrahim asked the young people to explain how they had managed to find the Abbasid treasures, which, from what he'd heard, many people had been trying to track down. The pair began, unhurriedly, to recount all their adventures.

They told Ibrahim and his wife about how they had been held captive in Saudi Arabia by the artifact collector Dagman Yamani, who was fixated on finding ninth-century treasures. How Sharaf had tried to free both himself and Barno from a cave in the rocks on the Red Sea coast. Then how Yamani had taken them to the Rub' al Khali desert. How fate had brought them together with Garib, a tour guide from Baghdad and an expert on the Abbasid dynasty. Garib had somehow acquired a second half of the same map Yamani possessed and was also trying to locate treasure with it, though unsuccessfully. That was why he sought help from Yamani and his companions. Apparently, Garib was counting on snatching the treasure for himself and slipping away from Yamani once they found it.

"...But when we arrived at the spot in the desert that Barno had identified on the maps," Sharaf explained, "there was no treasure at all. After digging out the ancient storehouse, we only found a few small crystals of myrrh and an empty box intended for incense—and that was it. It looks like somebody beat us to the hoard and took it all."

"Of course, Yamani flew into a rage," Barno continued. "He forced Garib out rather rudely, while keeping us and his own men back. Garib left immediately, never suspecting that Sharaf and I had a different map—of the real treasure—because Yamani had managed to hide it in the lounge area, away from the Baghdadi guide's prying eyes! After Garib left, Dagman didn't feed us at all, whether day or night—he was too furious and upset. But come morning, he met us in unexpectedly good spirits and generously plied us with various tasty dishes."

"Exactly," Sharaf confirmed. "We were amazed at the sudden change in him and had no idea what caused it. It turned out that while we were sleeping, quite early in the morning, someone in Uzbekistan managed to call my phone—one that Dagman, for some reason, hadn't turned off—and said he was looking for me. Later on, when I saw that man, I was taken aback because we'd never met before. Evidently, Dagman asked him what he wanted with me, but the caller didn't offer any explanation to a stranger. We suspect that Yamani, who has a nose for adventurous quests for ancient valuables, deduced from the man's tone that this individual, too, was somehow tied to ancient maps and the search for Abbasid treasures. So Dagman invited him to come out into the desert, to his camp."

"So then you met this man?" Ibrahim asked.

"Oh, yes!" Barno smiled. "And not only him! To Yamani's shock and our surprise, two vehicles full of people arrived at the desert camp, led by a businessman named Kudrat Valiev—the same one, as we later understood, who had called Dagman."

"Incidentally, that businessman is from here in Samarkand," Sharaf noted.

"Yes," Barno agreed with a nod. "Accompanying him was a pleasant young woman named Zulfiya, a driver and guard named Sher, two Bahrainis—some fellow called Yakzan Baker and his assistant Ghiyas—and two Russian helpers, Vanya and Sanya. Naturally, I was happiest about having another woman there, since for quite a while I'd been forced to associate only with men, unable to talk with anyone about 'girl stuff.' And nearly all these men, aside from Sharaf, were rather rough characters, I must say. As it happened, Zulfiya turned out to be a good person—just an employee of Kudrat's—and a historian, like me. All of that cheered me up somewhat. I hoped these new people might help free Sharaf and me from Yamani's stifling authority. Yes, he wasn't stingy or inhospitable, but at heart, he was still acting like a 'slave owner.' But that wasn't even the most interesting part. The real twist was…"

Barno paused her story briefly, as Ibrahim's wife, Yasmina, took their small children off to bed and served some hot food to the guests. Once everyone had enjoyed the meal and praised the hostess, the conversation about Barno and Sharaf's adventures resumed.

"So, what was the most interesting part, my friends?" asked Ibrahim.

"That Kudrat and his companions had… the second half of our Abbasid treasure map!" Sharaf said excitedly. "We were absolutely amazed and overjoyed—not because we craved riches or further adventures, but because we believed that all these hardships would soon be over. We hoped we'd finally be able to return home to our parents."

"But as for that desert," Barno continued, "given the sections of our map, there was basically nothing left for us to do there. Sharaf and I had deciphered the tricky puzzle of this map—or rather, the beginning of its puzzle. It turned out that all the peculiar symbols on both halves really were the familiar images used by many peoples since ancient times to depict the stars in constellations! When we were all back in Dagman's lounge, studying the genuine map that was supposed to lead inevitably to Caliph al-Ma'mun's treasure, Sharaf and I noticed that both halves of the map showed the image of the most famous constellation in the world!"

"You mean the Big Bear?" guessed Ibrahim.

"Exactly!" Sharaf nodded. "Though in Caliph al-Ma'mun's day, it was often referred to by its most recognizable shape—the 'Big Dipper.'"

"Or more precisely, 'Saptarishi,'" Barno added. "We realized that the stars of that constellation, and thus their symbols and representations in the form of animals or parts of the human body on our map, should precisely correspond to the ninth-century towns of the Caliphate."

"Well, that's something else! You two are very clever!" Ibrahim praised them in admiration.

"Thank you," Sharaf and Barno said, grateful to their older friend.

"So, all that was left was the key task: finding the exact spot where the treasure was hidden," Sharaf said mysteriously. "Or, if we were talking about some passage, then the place where it began."

"We spent quite a while trying to figure it out," Barno went on, "because all the treasure hunters in the desert were already on edge. They'd been waiting so long for the riddle to be solved and to finally see those coveted treasures with their own eyes. Meanwhile, one detail kept bugging me: the near-complete image of the constellation was on both halves of the map—on the part Sharaf's mother gave him, and on the part that Kudrat Valiev brought from Samarkand. Suddenly, I had a flash of insight: what if we didn't join the two halves edge to edge on a flat surface, but instead… overlaid one half on top of the other so that, as far as possible, the constellation drawings lined up? And that's when something astonishing happened: on both halves of the map, a spot lit up that looked remarkably like Alioth—the brightest star of Ursa Major!"

"And when the Samarkand native Kudrat Valiev realized roughly which region on a modern map that spot might correspond to," Sharaf added, "he was as stunned as we were. He said, unable to conceal his amazement, 'That's our Vedar—a settlement near the Bulungur district centre in Samarkand! How could I have been so stupid? Why didn't I think to thoroughly search for the treasure there right away, back when I took the map from the old man who lived in Vedar?! Let's go, now—immediately, we'll fly to Samarkand, then head for Vedar!!'"

"And since Yamani had no intention whatsoever of letting Kudrat and his entire group out of his sight, he quickly bought plane tickets for himself, a couple of his guards, and for us, too," Barno recounted.

"But along the way, I asked him to drop Barno and me off at a hotel in Riyadh," Sharaf explained, "where we'd originally stayed, so that we could pick up our belongings. Naturally, at that time, I didn't breathe a word to Dagman that I had hidden an ancient dagger there…"

"A dagger?" Ibrahim asked in surprise. "You never told me about that."

"Yes, sorry—there was so much to explain, I just didn't get to it," Sharaf apologized. "On the copper blade of that dagger is a stamped image of Caliph al-Ma'mun himself, wearing a turban with a huge pearl the size of a lemon. Anyway, Barno and I picked up our stuff from the hotel, the dagger included, and then we travelled with Yamani to Samarkand, and from there—on to Vedar in pursuit of Kudrat Valiev and his people. How fortunate it was, Ibrahim-aka, that you'd become worried about us for not contacting anyone for so long, and that, using your position as a police captain, you alerted the Samarkand airport security service just in case, giving them our photos."

"Yes!" Barno said happily. "And as soon as we landed, they called you right away, and you freed us from that meddlesome Yamani! After that—well, you more or less know what happened. All of us, with you, along with Kudrat's group and Yamani, went to Vedar— and found an extremely decrepit, almost collapsed little house with stairs leading down somewhere, into a very deep basement. That basement turned out to be a long underground passage heading toward the Ferghana Valley and leading to the storeroom holding the Abbasid treasures. Many centuries ago, labourers of Caliph al-Ma'mun built this underground labyrinth on his orders—an exact copy of the passage they'd made in the subterranean vault of the Egyptian pyramid… This story is actually mentioned in the legendary collection *One Thousand and One Nights* in the 'Tale of al-Ma'mun and the Pyramids!'"

"I was impressed myself," Ibrahim admitted. "Especially by how you, Sharaf and Barno, managed to open the door to that chamber! None of us had the key…"

"Exactly!" Sharaf exclaimed. "At first, we had no clue how. Then I got the idea to pull out my dagger and try opening the door with it, because I noticed it had a seal in the shape of a crescent at the end of the hilt—a symbol of Caliph al-Ma'mun's authority.

When Sanya and Vanya saw me examining that seal, they surprised me: Sanya pulled from his big pants pocket some old—or old-looking—scabbard. It bore the same seal! When I, with Kudrat and Sanya's permission, inserted my dagger into the scabbard—an exact fit for the hilt—something inside the scabbard clicked. Then I pressed the scabbard's seal, now containing Ma'mun's dagger, against the lock on the door. And it… opened!!"

"And what we saw in that chamber," Barno reminded everyone, "even I, being a historian who's read a lot and seen tons of artifacts in pictures, had never seen anything like it before! The entire room was filled with pure gold, countless precious stones, and all sorts of other unique Abbasid treasures!"

"In truth, part of those riches were Egyptian, not Arabian," Sharaf added, "because it's very likely that Caliph al-Ma'mun actually did manage to remove something of value from Khufu's Pyramid, in the tomb of a pharaoh who died a thousand years before his time!"

"Agreed," Barno said. "And the most valuable item in that room was Caliph al-Ma'mun's turban adorned with a splendid orange 'melo' pearl, as big as a lemon! At international auctions, that 'little lemon' would probably sell for hundreds of millions of dollars! Naturally, Kudrat Valiev, and especially Dagman Yamani, were very upset when they found out they wouldn't be getting any of these riches—nearly the whole trove would go to the government and be transferred to the State Treasury of the Republic of Uzbekistan."

"Yes, and we actually sent Ma'mun's turban with that unique orange 'melo' pearl to one of the Caliph's direct descendants—a sheikh from an Arab country friendly to Uzbekistan," Ibrahim explained. "At present, it sparkles in his private collection. As for the other treasures, I suggested that you two, Barno, receive a percentage of their value and make it official, then divide it among all the people who were part of the search. But when I told you that your father no longer needed money to protect himself from the bandits, you insisted on waiving any claim to the treasure money for the sake of charity, which is precisely what we did."

"Remember, Sharaf, how Sher tried to grab that precious turban and run off?" Barno asked her friend. "The thing is, Ibrahim-aka, that Sher had been appointed by Kudrat Valiev as a driver-guard for Zulfiya, Sanya, and Vanya, but it turned out he was actually working for his own uncle, a businessman named Ubay. Once Ubay heard rumours about the Abbasid treasure hunt, he wanted to seize it for himself. But neither Sher nor his uncle—who showed up at the same place—managed to take anything, because by then, the site of that great historical find was already surrounded by the police."

"By the way," Captain Salimov recalled, "it turned out that Grandfather Abbas Salim, from whom Kudrat Valiev deceitfully stole half of the Abbasid treasure map, is some distant relative of mine. And he is also a descendant of the Abbasids themselves…"

"Really?" the young people said happily. "That's wonderful!"

"My young friends," Ibrahim went on, somewhat embarrassed by the question he was about to ask, "I've noticed you two have formed a romantic relationship, so Sharaf, pardon me for asking, especially in front of Barno. But how did your ex-girlfriend in Qatar react to all this?"

"Oh, you mean Jahiza!" Sharaf smiled. "She got it into her head that I'd become extremely wealthy! So she started calling and texting me again. It turns out her weddings—first to the famous Doha banker's son, then to that banker's nephew—fell through. Poor girl, nobody ended up marrying her. But she brought it on herself: a person can't be that devious and greedy! I told her I've fallen in love with another girl—from Uzbekistan. And that, even though her almost-father-in-law, the banker Najib Abbas, had heard about me and offered me a position as a lawyer in his banking network in Qatar once I finish university, I politely declined—so I can stay here with Barno."

"You said his name is Najib Abbas?" Ibrahim asked in surprise.

"Yes!" Sharaf replied.

"Perhaps he's also a descendant of the Abbasids?" the captain suggested.

"It's possible," Sharaf agreed. "Anyway, my girlfriend Barno and I will occasionally visit my mom and stepfather in Qatar during vacations and holidays. But overall, I've decided to settle here in Tashkent for good, where my father, the famous doctor Said Mumtazov, and my sister Malika also live."

"You've already met her?" Ibrahim asked.

"Yes, both Malika and her mother, Sitora. My father introduced us," Sharaf explained. "They're wonderful! I'm really happy to have such lovely relatives. Father had wanted to introduce us earlier, but his accident got in the way. By the way, he told me that out of goodwill, he performed several operations on the guy who hit him—Davron Bakhromov. As for the crash, Dr. Said concluded that Davron likely already had vision problems at the time, compounded by drinking and a lack of responsibility for his actions. But he, Dr. Mumtazov, doesn't blame Davron for anything and won't be filing a police complaint against him. Davron himself sincerely apologized to the doctor and promised never to drink again and never to leave an injured person on the road. And my father promised to keep treating Davron as his patient and, now that Davron's major-of-police father is in prison, to help him with whatever he can."

"That's wonderful," Ibrahim remarked. "I also heard you two flew off to Sharjah not long ago. Why was that? Will you tell me?"

"Of course," Barno nodded. "There's a very fine archaeological museum there, whose consultant is a prominent scholar—historian and archaeologist Nazih Abu Jalil. He got wind of our story about searching for Abbasid treasures—some of which he himself once found in the Emirates."

"He very much wanted to hear the details 'from the horse's mouth,'" Sharaf added. "So Ustadi Nazih invited us to spend a few days with him. Before New Year's, during winter break, we visited my mother and stepfather in Doha, then went on to Sharjah to see Mr. Nazih. He's a wonderful, kind person! He visits a certain Bob Downey in prison—someone who'd once set him up with ancient artifacts—and he takes care of him. We became friends with Ustadi Nazih, talked at length, and exchanged knowledge and impressions about the Abbasid era, the Tahirids, and the Samanids who came after them, who also contributed a great deal to the history of Arab-Uzbek relations."

"Ibrahim-aka… I just have to ask…" Even in the dim light of the evening lamp, it was clear Barno was anxious. "Could you tell me why my stepmother Rasima was jailed? Is it really true that she put out a 'hit' on my father? What exactly happened?"

"Yes, Barno, I'm afraid it's true," Ibrahim responded, frowning as he recalled the grim events. "During the investigation, my colleagues in Tashkent's main police department discovered that Rasima had a lover, Murad, who worked as your father's chief accountant. Murad discreetly transferred all of Fahriyar's funds to offshore accounts, causing Fahriyar's business to collapse. When your father started to suspect what was happening, that pair decided to get rid of him. On top of that, Rasima was still on the hook for your father's debt to the gang, and she had no desire to pay it. She lied to Gosha and his thugs, claiming that Fahriyar did indeed have money but was refusing to hand it over—saying he planned to 'cheat' them. Gosha and his accomplices believed her, got furious, and on the same day your father stopped contacting you, they brutally beat him. Back then, I wondered why Rasima didn't seem worried about your father's disappearance and never filed a police report. Later, it all made sense. Meanwhile, Fahriyar ended up in the hospital, unconscious and in critical condition. He had no ID on him, so for the longest time we couldn't locate him. But thank God, he was eventually found! And I hear he's starting to regain his memory now, yes?"

"Yes, it's improving significantly," Barno replied. "Thank you so much for everything. You took care of my father while Sharaf and I were in Yamani's captivity! I'll never forget your kindness to us… Did they lock Murad up, too?"

"They did, but he got a shorter sentence than your stepmother Rasima," Ibrahim explained. "Seeing as she was the organizer of the attack, which was classified as 'attempted murder.'"

"All right, friends, let's talk no more of sad things, shall we?" Sharaf suggested. "Everything's fine that ends fine! Now we're all happy!"

Barno and Ibrahim agreed.

* * *

Tashkent, Spring of 2024

Feruz-begim, Said Mumtazov, his wife Sitora, their daughter Malika, and son Sharaf with his fiancée Barno all gathered at the home of the elderly man from ancient Vedar—a descendant of the weavers of Abbas Salim and of the Abbasid dynasty.

In front of all their relatives, Sharaf proposed to Barno, and the young woman accepted. Out of respect, they asked the Great-Grandmother Feruz-begim herself to choose the date of their wedding.

It was a touching meeting. Many kind and heartfelt words were spoken there about the good and pious deeds and exploits of past and present generations…

People Remember and Revere History…

In 1935, the International Astronomical Union named a crater on the visible side of the Moon "Caliph al-Ma'mun." His numerous descendants—scattered like stars in the sky—now live not only along the shores of the Persian Gulf and in Central Asia, but have spread all over the globe, just as the descendants of the great Emirs, the Tahirids, and the Samanids once preserved and exalted the ancient Holy Oasis—Khorasan and Mawara' al-Nahr.

www.ingramcontent.com/pod-product-compliance
Lightning Source LLC
Chambersburg PA
CBHW041922160426
42812CB00101B/2505